GLOBAL
SOUTH
ASIA

Padma Kaimal
K. Sivaramakrishnan
Anand A. Yang
SERIES EDITORS

OUTCASTE BOMBAY

City Making and the Politics of the Poor

JUNED SHAIKH

UNIVERSITY OF WASHINGTON PRESS

Seattle

OUTCASTE BOMBAY WAS MADE POSSIBLE IN PART BY A GRANT FROM THE ASSOCIATION FOR ASIAN STUDIES FIRST BOOK SUBVENTION PROGRAM.

Printed and bound in the United States of America

UNIVERSITY OF WASHINGTON PRESS
uwapress.uw.edu

LIBRARY OF CONGRESS CATALOGING-IN-PUBLICATION DATA

Names: Shaikh, Juned, author.
Title: Outcaste Bombay : city making and the politics of the poor / Juned Shaikh.
Description: Seattle : University of Washington Press, 2021. | Series: Global
    South Asia | Includes bibliographical references and index.
Identifiers: LCCN 2020044311 (print) | LCCN 2020044312 (ebook) |
    ISBN 9780295748498 (hardcover) | ISBN 9780295748504 (paperback) |
    ISBN 9780295748511 (ebook)
Subjects: LCSH: Dalits—India—Mumbai. | Mumbai (India)
Classification: LCC DS485.B64 S53 2021 (print) | LCC DS485.B64 (ebook) |
    DDC 305.5/6880954792—dc23
LC record available at https://lccn.loc.gov/2020044311
LC ebook record available at https://lccn.loc.gov/2020044312

The paper used in this publication is acid free and meets the minimum requirements of American National Standard for Information Sciences—Permanence of Paper for Printed Library Materials, ANSI Z39.48-1984.∞

For Madhavi and Sahar
In memory of Dadhi Abba and Rizwan

CONTENTS

ACKNOWLEDGMENTS

This book's journey began at the turn of the twenty-first century. The end of the last millennium, and the beginning of the new one, heralded many transformations in my professional and personal life. It involved multiple journeys: from Pune—the best city in the world, many Punekars believe, and I do too—to Mumbai, and from there to Chicago, Seattle, New Haven, Cincinnati, and Santa Cruz. The passage of time and the journey itself have indebted me to many people. When I landed in Mumbai to work as a journalist and report news on the city, including labor and crime, I understood the need to think historically. This realization of my lack of historical understanding of the city triggered an expedition that took me beyond to make sense of this history. The reader will decide if that journey has borne fruit. What I can say with certainty is that the excursion made me a nonresident Indian and a professional historian.

In Chicago, Dipesh Chakrabarty and Muzaffar Alam created the space for me to savor University of Chicago's intellectual community. Insights from that intellectual formation helped me in Seattle, where the University of Washington remains a generative intellectual community for me. I am eternally grateful to Anand Yang and K. Sivaramakrishnan (who was there all too briefly before he left for Yale) for helping me make Seattle and the UW community home. Priti Ramamurthy, Jordanna Bailkin, Purnima Dhawan, Laurie Sears, Chandan Reddy, Sareeta Amrute, Frank Conlon, Christian Novetzke, Sunila Kale, Craig Jeffrey, Vicente Rafael, Nikhil Pal Singh, and Moon-Ho Jung taught me, through their examples and guidance, how to be scholarly. Frank Conlon bequeathed a tranche of books on Bombay, many of them are cited here. Seattle enabled many friendships: Jameel Ahmad, Sahar Romani, Sandra Gresl, Woonkyung Yeo, Chong Eun Ahn, Shruti Patel, Amir Sheikh, Keith Snodgrass, Jennifer Dubrow, Amy Bhatt, Tapoja Chaudhuri, Sharmistha Ghosh, Leah Koskimaki, Catherine Warner, Hsiao-wen Cheng, Jon Olivera, Scott Brown, Amanda Swain, Rebecca Hughes, and Shiwani Shrivastava provided camaraderie, laughter, food, engaged critique, and intellectual stimulus. Given the importance of Seattle and the University of Washington to my formation, I feel honored that the book is being published by the University of Washington Press. Lorri Hagman and Elizabeth Berg's sage and expert editorial advice has shaped and enhanced the book.

Food, chai, and a shared interest in South Asia marked a memorable year in New Haven and fostered a community: Kasturi Gupta, Rochisha Narayan, Rene Saran, Arupjyoti Saikia, Sumati Sundaram, Aniket Aga, Chitrangada Choudhury, Sahana Ghosh, Kamran Ahsan, Sana Haroon, Tariq Thachil, and Piyali Bhattacharya. The first draft of chapter 2 was written and presented at the Yale South Asia Colloquium in February 2012; I am thankful to all the participants for their suggestions. At Xavier University in Cincinnati, where I spent a lovely year, Rachel Chrastil, Amy Whipple, Kareem Tiro, Randy Browne, and Christine Anderson were very supportive.

The form and content of the book was shaped by University of California at Santa Cruz. The Asia *Plus* writing group in the History Department, with Gail Hershatter, Emily Honig, Alan Christy, Noriko Aso, Minghui Hu, and Jennifer Derr, was a nourishing space not just to try out and develop new ideas but also to think about writing itself. The junior faculty writing group, with Muriam Davis, Thomas Serres, Alma Heckman, and Ben Breen, was another important venue for feedback. Chapters 4 and 5 were presented at the History Department Works in Progress series as a mammoth single chapter. Questions, suggestions, and encouragement from Greg O'Malley, Maya Peterson, Elaine Sullivan, Dana Frank, David Anthony, Terry Burke, and many others sharpened the chapters. Kate Jones, Marc Matera, Matt O'Hara, and Nathaniel Deutsch read various portions of the manuscript and provided engaged feedback. The book has benefited from a variety of intellectual formations on the UCSC campus: I presented drafts of chapters at the Cultural Studies, Department of Anthropology, and the Department of Sociology colloquiums. I am thankful to Vanita Seth, Megan Moodie, and Miriam Greenberg for inviting me to present and to scholars including Anjali Arondekar, Mayanthi Fernando, Bali Sahota, Lisa Rofel, Megan Thomas, Nidhi Mahajan, and many others for their comments and suggestions.

The Bombay workshop convened by Abigail McGowan at the University of Vermont in March 2015, which included Douglas Haynes, Nikhil Rao, Sheetal Chhabria, and Liza Weinstein was not only intellectually stimulating but also supportive and welcoming. Similarly, the book is richer due to the feedback provided by scholars at the South Asia colloquiums at University of Pennsylvania, UCLA, and Stanford University. I would like to thank Ramya Sreenivasan, Lisa Mitchell, Ania Loomba, Akhil Gupta, Purnima Mankekar, Sharika Thiranagama, and Thomas Hansen for their invitation and hospitality. T. B. Hansen read drafts of two chapters and provided incisive critique and suggestions. I have also benefited from conversations with Rupa Viswanath, Arun Kumar, Sumit Guha, Uday Chandra, Usha Iyer, Ajantha Subramanian, Shailaja Paik, Anu Rao, Ram Rawat, Lisa Mitchell, Gyan Prakash, V. Geetha (who read a draft of chapter 2), Carmel Christy, P. G. Jogdand, Namdeo Dhasal, Arjun Dangle, J. V. Pawar, and many others. I am grateful to the anonymous peer reviewers recruited by the University of Washington Press for their insightful and supportive comments. All these people have helped me think through, revise, and reinvent various aspects of the project. They have made it richer; the deficiencies and blind spots are mine alone.

Without the generosity of librarians and archivists in India, England, and the United States, this project would have faltered before taking off. I would like to thank the staff at the Maharashtra State Archives, Mumbai Marathi Granth Sangrahalay, Communist Party of India office at the Bhupesh Gupta Bhavan, Gokhale Institute of Politics and Economics in Pune, Nehru Memorial Library and Museum, as well as staff at Ajoy Bhavan in Delhi, the British Library, University of Washington, and the UCSC library for their help. In Mumbai, Subodh More and Ramesh Shinde provided important materials from their personal collections. To get to these places, I received grants from the American Institute of Indian Studies junior research fellowship, Chester Fritz fellowship at the University of Washington, a writing fellowship from the Simpson Center for the Humanities at the University of Washington, a Hellman Foundation grant, and a Committee on Research grant at UCSC.

Without the munificence and love of family and friends in India, this book would not have been possible. My sister Shaziya and her husband Rizwan's warmth and wit made their home in Mumbai a home away from home. They made landing and living in Mumbai so much easier. Rizwan, unfortunately, passed away before the book appeared in print, but his humor and generosity will forever remain in my memory. My brother Moiz, Prakash uncle and Swati auntie, Darakhshan Khan, Huma and Zameer Sayyed, and Haaris Shaikh and Deepa Kadam shared their homes and their love of Mumbai. I also cherish the friendships of P. K. Chackochen, Murtuza Ghadially, Priya Nair, Monica Bathija, Prashant Shah,

Revathi Venkatesh, Amit Dhorde, Andy Schiffrin, Krishna Pant, and Kavita Char.

In Pune, my father Moinuddin and mother Khairunisa have been always supportive and encouraging of a journey they do not fathom much. My mother may be barely literate, but possibly because of that, she always encouraged me/us to study and read. My brother Aatif completes her brood of four. Aatif and Ashiya, along with Moiz and Naila, make Pune a special place. The next generation of Shaikhs in India, Haaris, Farhan, Rida, and Yaseen, may be growing up in turbulent times, but their good cheer and optimism always provide a corrective to the nonresident Indian's far-removed sense of bleakness. In Hyderabad, the Murtys—Mohan, Gayatri, and grandmother Sarojini—have been steadfastly supportive of my endeavors. In Delhi, my brother-in-law Anand Murty not only opened his home but also enthralled us with his music, cooking, and jokes.

Without Madhavi Murty, my partner, I would have probably remained a journalist. We began our adventure as journalists together, pursued graduate degrees together, and are now colleagues at UCSC. She read my news copy many years ago, and she has read every word of the manuscript, including these acknowledgments. Her insightful suggestions are scattered throughout the book, and her love and comradeship have made this a fulfilling journey. We became parents on my first day at UCSC. Our daughter, Sahar, suffused our lives with joy, made sure that I thought of parenting and the book together, and cheered the completion of every editorial stage. I dedicate this book to Madhavi and Sahar, to my late grandfather, Dadhi Abba, whom I remember almost every day, and to Rizwan.

OUTCASTE BOMBAY

INTRODUCTION

THE INDIAN NOSE MAY BE AN UNUSUAL STARTING POINT FOR A
history of Bombay city. The nose, along with the head, marked social hierarchy in colonial India. In its heyday in the late nineteenth and early twentieth centuries, the width and length of an Indian nose (and the
measurements of the head) provided proof of the group affinity of its bearer
and the precedence he or she commanded in a social hierarchy. In the estimation of the British colonial administrator and commissioner of the
Indian census of 1901, H. H. Risley, these groups were tribes that had transformed into castes over a period of time.[1] Thus the measurements of noses
and heads held the key to a social scientific estimation of castes in India.
The differences among castes, determined by nasal and cephalic indices,
were further cemented by distinctions and similarities in the rituals and
customs of these groups. In this way, caste became a timeless essence and a
building block of Indian society.[2] Indian noses, however, were unruly sig-
nifiers of caste. The structure of social hierarchy based on nasal indices
collapsed under the weight of its own contradictions. As the noted sociologist G. S. Ghurye observed, there was no correspondence between
social hierarchy and nasal indices of people in Bombay province.[3] The
noses of upper-caste Deshastha Brahmins, lower-caste fishermen, middle-
caste Kunbi peasants, and untouchable Mahars had similar measurements. The body thus was an inadequate material referent for caste, and
in Bombay city the nose had to be replaced by another marker. The built
environment and housing enunciated caste difference; they supplemented
the body as material referents for caste in the city. The built environment
and housing are quintessential markers of class, but they are also important sites for living and experiencing caste.

The built environment in Bombay in this period included factories,
docks, railway lines and train stations, roads, schools, parks, places of wor-
ship, the sewage system, water supply, and housing, all of which were
planned and regulated either by city administrators or institutions of the

3

regional and central governments and owned by individuals and companies as private property, or by the city and state as a public good. Housing, a component of the built environment, accommodated residents who lived and worked in the city. As the historian Sheetal Chhabria pithily puts it, housing was an administrative category deployed by the state to demarcate the city, accumulate capital, distinguish and manage populations, and discipline labor.[4] Workers labored in factories and at docks, construction sites, and other places in the city and lived in tenements and slums owned by landlords or state institutions to which they paid rent. Houses, even those in slums, shaped everyday lives, inhabitants' experience of the city, and non–slum dwellers' perception of them. Those who could not afford to pay rent squatted on public lands and sidewalks. Because of the importance of workers' housing and wages for sustaining the working class and the economy built on their labor, state institutions collected data on wages and housing. This data informed studies of the working class in Bombay. Workers in the twentieth century raised the issues of wages—or more particularly, the inadequacy of the money paid to them—and housing (especially after the 1930s). This book builds on these studies and adds another layer of analysis by arguing that caste not only influenced the built form of the city, including provisions for workers' housing, but also underlay its industrial economy. The resulting entanglement of caste and class is evident in the everyday life, experiences, and cultural politics of the urban poor, mostly Dalits (formerly known as the untouchable castes) in the city.

The entanglement of class and caste had the effect of shrouding caste in the cloak of class and, by extension, modernity. It sustained the perception of castelessness in the city.[5] Class is a modern social and political relationship that conveys the dominance of one group over another; it is also a linguistic phenomenon, because experiences of being a class (or any other group) become comprehensible through language. Class is in sync with modern times because in the long march of modernity, the telos, in this schema, is the melting away of older forms of group affinities, such as caste. In Bombay city, with its modern, industrial economy, the gradual withering away of caste was assumed by the votaries of modernity, including the elite trying to forge a nation in late colonial and postcolonial India, Marxists imagining a unified working class, and the leaders of the Dalit social movement, including B. R. Ambedkar. Perhaps Ambedkar's conception of the city, in the 1930s and 1940s, as a space that would enable Dalits to escape casteism in the villages and foster forgetfulness about caste, became retroactive proof of the nonvitality of caste in the city in the late

nineteenth and twentieth centuries.[6] His hopefulness about the future of
caste in the city was in sharp contrast to his appraisal of the Indian village
as "a sink of localism [and a] den of ignorance."[7] Ambedkar's views on the
village were similar to Marx and Engels's considerations on the "idiocy of
rural life" and their vision of the city as an escape from this idiocy.[8] Maybe
this was why the eminent sociologist M. N. Srinivas opined that there was
not enough material to study caste in urban India.[9] The assumption was
that people shed caste on the way to the city or upon arrival there. *Outcaste
Bombay* contends that capitalism and caste shared a symbiotic relationship: they leeched off each other. Industrial capitalism attached itself to
caste and made it a part of its metabolic system[10] to acquire what it lacked
in India in the late nineteenth and early twentieth centuries: the ability to
raise capital to start an industry and to recruit, discipline, and reproduce a
labor force. In the city, access to a job, a wage, and a rented dwelling
depended on a social network in which caste and kinship played a crucial
role. Caste also adapted to the urban context in Bombay by working
through land deeds, private property, tenancy, urban planning, and workers' movements. Caste also animated Marxism and the Marathi translation of Marxist texts and literature. Thus, in the city, caste became
insidious—subtle but robust even as it was insulated in the garb of modernity. The insulation may have obscured it for some people who believed
that enlightened, modern reformers in concert with the various processes
of modern life would make the depredations of some caste practices, like
untouchability, redundant.[11] Instead, caste hid in plain sight in the city. It
shaped the built form and worked through language. Caste was obscured
in the discourse that focused on the built form, such as elite concerns
about slums, sanitation, garbage, filth, and illegal space.[12] The illegality of
slums shrouds caste in our times too.[13] Therefore, apart from the built
environment, language is an important site to study the entanglement of
caste and class. Language here is not just a metaphor for social relationships in which caste plays an important role, but also rules of grammar,
syntax, and translation that shaped communication between individuals
and groups in twentieth-century Bombay.

The time frame of this study is bracketed by two events that accelerated
the process of spatial transformation in Bombay. The city entered the twentieth century reeling from the plague of 1896. The epidemic, attributed to
overcrowding and lack of sanitation in the neighborhoods inhabited by the
urban poor, inaugurated a process of reconfiguring the city. This entailed
urban planning, the history of which since the mid-nineteenth century was

a response to the upsurge of the urban poor in Europe.[14] Planning necessitated the production of knowledge about the city. For instance, the 1901 city census not only categorized humans according to caste and religion but also cataloged the built environment and housing stock of the city. The stated aim of this endeavor was to facilitate the work of an administrative body, the City of Bombay Improvement Trust, created in 1898.[15] Reordering the city also entailed demolition of unsanitary dwellings—designated as slums—and diffusion of the excess population over a wider space and into the suburbs. Suburbanization necessitated land acquisition and urban planning: many laws, institutions, and urban plans were devised over the next eighty years to effect the transformation of the city.[16] One recurring suggestion was to transform the political economy of Bombay in order to disperse its overcrowding. The city's economic backbone in the twentieth century was the cotton textile industry. An important reason for overcrowding was that the laborers for its industries, mostly low-paid, underskilled workers, were housed in slums and tenements. In 1982, the textile industry lurched into an eighteen-month strike. Many mills did not reopen after the strike ended in 1984; their owners sold the mill lands, and the industrial landscape was rapidly transformed into an urbanscape of glitzy shopping malls, luxury apartments, and corporate offices of the service sector. But the demise of the textile mills still did not eliminate slums or overcrowding; the number of slums and the population of the city kept increasing. The entanglement of caste and class is evident in the political, economic, and spatial transformation of the city. Moreover, Dalit cultural politics in the city emerged in the process of the transformation of built form, and the two influenced each other.

CASTE, CLASS, DALITS

What is caste? Caste is an important feature of social hierarchy in South Asia. There are many strands to the caste system; the set of historical relationships constituting caste changed over time.[17] The term "caste," however, is not of South Asian ancestry. It was derived from the Portuguese term *casta*, which indexed the purity of blood and species.[18] The nomenclature was borrowed by the British when they became the preeminent imperial power in India in the eighteenth century and applied to grasp the complex social hierarchies of their colony. *Casta* became *caste*. British administrators used "caste" to allude to the fourfold division of rank (*varna*) and also to the scores of endogamous groups (*jati*) that were slotted into the fourfold hierarchy. This confusion was exacerbated by claims made by *jati* groups to a higher rank in the *varna* hierarchy. The state was called upon to arbitrate these claims and thus played an important role in the working of the caste system.[19] The South Asian states— precolonial, colonial, and postcolonial—played a crucial role in preserving the caste system and worked through it to maintain state power.[20] Like most social hierarchies, caste (both as *varna* and *jati*) entails drawing boundaries between groups and imposing ideologies and practices that justify these borders. In the fourfold system of rank, for instance, the top three ranks were occupied by Brahmins (priests), Kshatriyas (kings, warriors), and Vaishyas (trade and commerce). They were the twice-born (*dwija*) castes and had the right to wear the ceremonial thread. Each rank comprised many *jatis* who, apart from endogamy, also adhered to the principle of commensality of *jati* groups. The Shudras (peasants and artisans) ranked fourth in the hierarchy. The untouchables were outside the *varna* schema and therefore depicted as outcastes, but occupied the lowest rungs of the caste hierarchy.[21] The outcastes included numerous *jatis* too. The touch or sometimes even the shadow of an untouchable was considered polluting. In a hierarchy obsessed with purity, pollution invited stigmatization and exclusion. The exclusion was not only ceremonial but also spatial and took the form of segregation in housing and rituals, as well as restricted use of wells and tanks to draw water for everyday use. In some parts of India, untouchability was marked on the body, and strictures were issued by the local elites to prevent untouchables from wearing clothes, footwear, or ornaments that hindered their perception as outcastes. Clothes on a Dalit body could become a marker of dignified comportment and was resented by higher castes. Thus, in parts of South India, women from the lower castes were prohibited from wearing a blouse under the sari.[22]

Apart from the state, another important arbiter of social stratification was the group that occupied the highest rank in the *varna* hierarchy, the Brahmins. Their expertise and crucial role in rituals, along with their interpretation and transmission of religious and literary texts, gave them a vital position in the hierarchy. Their power was further validated in colonial India when European scholars and colonial administrators recognized their authorship of and felicity with texts that justified caste hierarchy and their preeminent status within it.[23] The valorization of texts composed in Indian antiquity and the recognition of Brahmins as the upholders of sacred traditions undergirded the British assessment of India as a timeless society infused with religious ideas and superstitions. This textually derived view of India's caste system obfuscated the political, economic, material, and legal institutions in which it was embedded in the nineteenth and twentieth centuries. For instance, this perception of caste obscured the labor of lower-caste groups, particularly untouchables, in agrarian settings and underwrote their dispossession from the land on which they labored.[24] Thus, a lower status in the *varna* hierarchy not only imputed an inferior ritual status but also had important political and economic consequences.[25] In late twentieth- and twenty-first-century India too, caste (and gender) have continued to shape access to social welfare programs of the state as well as access to housing.[26]

There were regional variations in the operation of the caste system. The particularities of caste at a specific conjuncture depended on the political, economic, and cultural institutions of the region and the practices of caste there. In western India and the Bombay Presidency, of which Bombay was the premier city, the precolonial state was dominated by the peshwa, the chief minister of the regional Maratha state. Peshwas belonged to a Brahmin caste, while the king, who had mostly become a figurehead during the eighteenth century, claimed Kshatriya status. The peshwas supported and augmented the religious authorities of the Brahmins.[27] With the military defeat of the peshwa by the British East India Company in 1818, the link between the regional state and the patronage of Brahmins snapped, raising the possibility of social transformation. Christian missionaries, for instance, sensed an opportunity for proselytizing lower castes and untouchables in this political vacuum.[28] This did not come to pass; not only did the entrenchment of colonial rule in the nineteenth century not diminish the religious authority of the Brahmins, but it in fact augmented the secular power of some Brahmins through their incorporation into administrative and political institutions. Lower-caste leaders, such as Jyotirao Phule, who were trained in missionary schools in the region, recognized this continuity in the face of political transformation. Phule articulated a critique of the Brahmins for usurping the limited opportunities for social mobility offered by colonial rule. Phule highlighted the dominance of the Brahmins and their denial of educational opportunities to lower castes, which perpetuated their misery and disadvantages.[29] The colonial authorities did not deter the lower-caste critique of Brahmin dominance, and the anti-Brahmin rhetoric resonated in the thriving Marathi-language public sphere in the late nineteenth and twentieth centuries. It coalesced into a powerful non-Brahmin movement that envisioned an alliance of the lower castes, including Dalit castes, which has been called a "cultural revolt" in western India.[30]

Bombay city was an important center for this revolt, which entailed the negation and inversion of Brahminical authority by the lower castes and rejection of the former's preeminence in rituals. Concurrently, the lower-caste rebellion projected a period of tutelage under British colonial rule that would equip them with the social and cultural capital necessary to counter the secular authority of the Brahmins.[31] Bombay city's expansion in the nineteenth century from a trading town into a manufacturing center, with the rise of the cotton textile industry and the inauguration of the Bombay Port Trust and new docks in the second half of the century, was mostly dependent on the labor of lower-caste workers. In fact, between 1864 and 1881, low castes (including Shudras and Dalits)—comprised between 59 and 64 percent of the total population of Bombay city.[32] In the early 1880s, Narayan Meghaji Lokhande, a former textile mill worker, inaugurated two organizations: the Bombay Millhand Association, which mobilized the working class on issues such as the duration of the workday and the length of the workweek; and the Satyashodhak Samaj (Truth Seeker's Society), which marshaled the lower-caste upsurge against the upper castes in the city. The historian Y. D. Phadke has called the workers' movement in the city a sapling of the lower-caste movement.[33] The workers' and lower-caste movements were twinned at their point of germination, and the entanglement continued into the twentieth century, even as some labor leaders sought to disentangle or obfuscate it.

Given the large number of lower-caste residents of Bombay, the amplification of caste affinities in the late nineteenth and twentieth centuries, and the intersection of labor and the non-Brahmin movements in the city, how and why did caste disappear in urban histories of South Asia? Historians of Bombay have studied caste in an urban setting, confirming that middle-class and upper-caste Brahmins embraced and refashioned caste identities in the city.[34] Their caste affinities shaped urban space in the form of caste-based cooperative housing societies in various parts of Bombay. Therefore, any easy assumption about the cosmopolitanism of Bombay must be interrogated, because beyond the myth of the city as a cosmopolitan domain of industrial modernity lies the opportunity to write "the history of the city *as* society"[35] and highlight the historical experiences of religions, classes, castes, and languages in the city. *Outcaste Bombay* extends this line of inquiry and argues that caste was seminal to the production of urban space, and urbanity was central to the making of Dalit cultural politics in the city. Instead of the upper castes, however, the book focuses on Dalits and the urban poor.

The built environment and language were sites for the formation of class and caste identities. Both are shaped by practices of institutions, groups, and individuals and invite the identification of the urban poor with collectives organized along the axes of caste and class. The intersection of caste and class also produced frictions. Caste and class are not sociologically pure or homogenous entities that can be isolated in a controlled experiment. In their everyday practice, they are uneven and jagged, as is evident in the case of Dalits and the urban poor. The complexity of social life and cultural politics cannot be fully grasped by attributing historical causation to caste alone. Class also shaped the contours of ethnic solidarities and could divide groups and even families.[36]

Class is both an analytical category and a social identity. In the hands of one of its foremost exponents, the British social historian E. P. Thompson, class was a heuristic device that could be usefully harnessed to understand social conflict in England of the late eighteenth and early nineteenth centuries, even before the language or discourse of class was available to social groups. In this period, industrial capitalism had not yet become a powerful socioeconomic formation. Sustained experiences of conflict over a period of time facilitated the emergence of class as an identity among workers.[37] Thompson's formulation proved extremely fertile for studies of labor in South Asia, particularly because he had detached class from the existence of a fully formed capitalism.[38] This had a contrasting influence on scholars of labor in South Asia. For instance, in Dipesh Chakrabarty's history of the working class in Calcutta's jute mill, the relevance of capitalism and its attendant category, class, is posed as problematic, and this undergirds his analysis in *Rethinking Working-Class History*. Thus one of his important questions was whether Marxian notions of capitalism and class are universally applicable. In Bombay city, the relevance of capitalism and class was not disputed by scholars. The existence of mass manufacturing, particularly the textile industry, was ample proof of their relevance as analytical and experiential categories. For instance, the historian Rajnarayan Chandavarkar outlines the origins of industrial capitalism and workers' politics in the last century of colonial rule. For him, the strategies of capitalists and the colonial state played an important role in the formation of the working class, along with the connections workers established with "factory proletarians, casual workers, rural migrants, agrarian labour, artisans, 'tribals' and dalits in the formation."[39] One of his most important contributions to scholarship is his disaggregation of the working class to reveal the socioeconomic fragmentation, distinctions, and connections within it. Rather than assume a homogenous working class that eventually attained class consciousness, he urges historians to pay attention to the conjunctures when workers overcame differences and revealed a fiercely held class consciousness.[40] Chakrabarty and Chandavarkar, even if their views on the relevance of class and capitalism did not coincide, together with labor historians such as Nandini Gooptu and Chitra Joshi, facilitated the analysis of the intersection of caste and class.[41]

Let us examine a specific example of this intersection in the life of a Dalit family. In 1903, Ramji Sakpal, who had retired from the British India Army, migrated with his family to Bombay from the town of Satara in western India. Sakpal was a soldier in the Mahar (an untouchable *jati*) regiment, a unit created for Dalit soldiers like him in colonial India. His son was B. R. Ambedkar, who would go on to become a prominent Dalit leader and the chairman of the committee that drafted independent India's constitution. Ambedkar was twelve or thirteen when he moved to the city. One of the reasons his father migrated to Bombay was to educate Ambedkar in the city's educational institutions. The family lived in a tenement in a lodging house (*chawl*) known as Dabak chawl, located in the working-class district of Bombay. Sakpal was entitled to a pension because he had retired from the army, and his older son worked as a security guard in a factory.[42] The family was thus more financially secure than most Dalit families in the city. Class enters our analysis here. Unlike Sakpal's family, living on a pension, many Dalits had migrated to the city in the late nineteenth and twentieth century in the hope of escaping the circuit of dispossession and untouchability in agrarian settings. They found employment in the sanitation department of the city or low-paying jobs in Bombay's textile industry and docks. In other words, migration had made them the urban poor.[43] The urban poor lived in hutments, tenements, and slums, and it was relatively easy to associate class with their dwelling. Sakpal's family considered Dabak chawl respectable or proper (*vyavasthita*), while they deemed the places many other Dalits lived, often from the same Mahar *jati*, filthy.[44] They had borrowed the existing discourse of sanitary and unsanitary housing in early twentieth-century Bombay and used it to highlight class or status distinctions within a caste group. Class in this context was not just an identity formed through political action but also a marker of social hierarchy or status linked to better wages, housing, and social and cultural capital.[45] Thus class and caste were important vectors in this social formation, and the built environment was a material referent for both in the city.

Outcaste Bombay's study of Dalit cultural politics addresses the question of Dalit labor, their experiences (of exploitation and humiliation, for instance) and forms of enunciation, the politics fashioned by Dalits in the twentieth century, and the production of the city itself, in which their neighborhoods, dwellings, and everyday lives became even more precarious. The efflorescence of scholarship on Dalits in the past three decades addresses many of these themes,[46] some of which also informs the new field of Dalit studies.[47] The field's rise has been attributed to the social, political, and intellectual transformations in India during and after the 1980s. This includes the lower-caste upsurge and the rise of new Dalit political formations and activism, including Dalit feminism, in various parts of South Asia and transnationally, along with the entry of many lower-caste and Dalit students to universities. These scholars have posed new research questions and focused attention on caste discrimination in academia. The impetus of Dalit studies has been the rethinking of dominant paradigms—for instance, of Indian anticolonial nationalism, in which Dalit politics was either deemed too particularistic (and therefore not national enough) or in cahoots with British colonialism—and Dalit engagement with the process of modernity itself.[48] Some important examples of challenging and rethinking dominant narratives include the attention to the history of slavery in South India and the effect of the abolition of slavery in the nineteenth century on Dalit castes in Kerala;[49] Dalit labor and the problems of categorization by the state and dominant groups who obscure and appropriate their labor;[50] the important role of violence in maintaining caste hierarchy in the twentieth and twenty-first centuries;[51] the transmutation of Dalits from stigmatized untouchables to a cultural and political minority in the twentieth century who demanded recognition and guarantees from the state, thus producing a paradoxical Dalit subjectivity, and the implication of social science and political theory in the inability to address untouchability and the experiences of Dalits.[52] At the most fundamental level, these scholars linked modernity to the transformation, intensification, and obscuring of untouchability. *Outcaste Bombay* builds on these insights by taking the production of space in the city as the site for the investigation of caste (and class).[53]

Social relationships constituted in space are suffused with power. Caste and class are two important axes for the operation of power; gender is another. Gender intersected with and cut through both caste and class, and there is a rich body of scholarship demonstrating that both caste and class are gendered.[54] For instance, housing was not only a site for warehousing the urban poor, including Dalits, but also a place for reproducing labor.[55] The state, the city, and industrialists were invested in reproducing Dalit labor for the sanitation department and low-wage work in the textile industry and on the docks, and also because they could be deployed as strikebreakers in these places. But women's bodies in the slums and tenements and the process of reproduction itself were stigmatized. For instance, social scientists and reformers studying housing described in lurid detail life in these sites of reproduction, including sex among its occupants and the socio-psychological effects of sex on Dalit children living there. In a nutshell, sex and the reproduction of the urban poor, particularly Dalits, were stigmatized at the point of conception itself. As a result, the labor they offered the city was also devalued. Similarly, in the estimation of some Marxist leaders in the 1920s, women played a supporting role in deterring strikebreakers but did not actively block them. The city's mill owners deployed Dalit and low-caste Muslim men as strikebreakers, setting up a confrontation between women and ethnic groups deployed as scab workers. Moreover, gender is particularly important as an analytical concept for understanding Dalit literature, where not only did sex and slums become an important motif in the 1960s and 1970s, but the field itself was dominated by Dalit men.

ANALYTICAL CONCEPTS

Just as caste and class are materially etched onto the built environment, they are also sedimented in language. Language too predicates social hierarchy and status. In a linguistically plural city such as Bombay, the pecking order included the language of state or administration (English in colonial India), national or regional language, mother tongue, second language, the language of the market or commerce, dialects of various languages, and urban slang. Residents of Bombay in the twentieth century—including Ambedkar, the Marxist intellectuals of the 1920s and 1930s, and the poet Namdeo Dhasal, an icon of Dalit literature and the founder of the Dalit Panther movement in the 1970s—were constantly translating and mistranslating from one language to the other to make sense of their world and help readers find their footing within it.[56]

Language, like the built environment, easily reveals class and frequently masks caste. The eclipsing of caste has the most coherent rationale in the

Marxist discourse of class. Particularly relevant here is the translation of Marxist ideas and pamphlets from English to Marathi in the 1920s, 1930s, and 1940s, in which the city's institutions and Communist intellectuals played a prominent role. In this discourse of radical class (in)equality, caste spoke in stuttered tones. The stuttering indicated the veiled presence of caste when it was lumped together under class. For instance, when Bombay's Marxists translated *The Communist Manifesto* into Marathi in 1931, abstract categories (such as "use value") were rendered in Sanskritized Marathi, while embodied categories (such as "lumpen proletariat") were translated in Bombay's urban argot. In this way, language and translation were implicated in relationships of power.

Translation required translators. The translators had the ability to extract ideas from one historical context, domesticate them, unleash them in another language in a different context, and make them a part of the self in the new context.[57] Indian Marxism was one such endeavor. Early Marxists from Bombay city, such as S. A. Dange, not only translated Marx from English to Marathi but also embraced his vision of a social and political revolution to vanquish capitalism. The city's working class had an important role in this imaginary. Caste haunted class in both the translation of Marxism and its reception by the working class. The scandal of translation, to borrow Dipesh Chakrabarty's phrase,[58] was that the sociological categories aimed at a Marxian transformation of Indian society relegated caste politics to the attic and pushed class struggles to the foreground, so that the leaders of caste movements were dismissed as petit bourgeois intellectuals. Critiques of caste politics did not mean that Dalits shied away from Marx or Indian Marxism or Dalit social movements. Dalits such as Comrade R. B. More in the 1930s organized Marxist reading groups for other Dalits in the city, but he also retained his proximity to Ambedkar and his affinity for Dalit movements.

Language and translation open the possibility of transforming structures of power and are important to the construction of identities. For instance, Dalit identity in postindependence Bombay was created through various processes of translation and articulation in the political, economic, and cultural spheres. Bombay's Marxists and global Marxism informed Dalit identity and cultural politics at particular historical moments. The Marxian notion of a revolution that would end all exploitation was an important motif of Dalit literature and the Dalit Panther movement in the 1960s and 1970s. Dalit literature itself was shaped by translation of the form and content of world literature—Russian realism, African American literature—and was also informed by Marxist writers like Annabhau Sathe. Apart from revolution, the category of the lumpen proletariat, translated as *mavali* by the city's Marxists in the 1920s and 1930s, looms large in Dalit literature. The *mavali*, the criminal, the prostitute, and the vagabond figure prominently in Dalit literature of the 1960s and 70s. Dalit writers dwelled on the lumpen proletariat, critically engaged with it, and exceeded its use by the city's Marxists. The Marxian notions of commodity (shelter/tenement and labor as commodity) and commodification of social relationships within the family were recurring themes too. The description of the process of commodification amplifies the violence undergirding the lives of outcastes in the city. Moreover, Dalit literature's bawdy disregard for the social codes of the elites, its playful use of language, including rural and urban slang, and words borrowed from languages such as Hindi, Urdu, Gujarati, and English were important features of Dalit literature. Some Dalit writers from the 1970s who were also part of the Dalit Panther movement aspired to a revolution within and outside literature that would not just highlight the commodification of Dalit lives but ostensibly end it.

Language and the built environment are not cloistered from each other; in fact they share a dialectical relationship.[59] The making of Dalit identity and Dalit literature cannot be fully grasped without considering the material and social conditions that made it possible. Bombay's built environment and the contestations over it, along with Marathi Marxism and its critiques, played a crucial role in the making of Dalit cultural politics. For instance, housing was an important demand of Dalits in the city from the 1910s and 1920s, and Dalit political leadership in the city emerged in the articulation of these demands. Similarly, the built form of the city was an important material referent for Dalit literature in Marathi. Its urban institutions, including public libraries where English, Marathi, Hindi, and Urdu writers discussed world literature, played a crucial role in making Dalit literature a distinct field. To comprehend Dalit cultural politics, then, it is important to account for processes like urban planning, housing, and Marxism, with which Dalit social movements in the city were in dialogue. In other words, literature and infrastructure were not insulated from each other in twentieth-century Bombay.

SPACE AND TIME TO SPACE-TIME

This opens up the exciting possibility of reimagining the city as a node in which several social, economic, and cultural networks with multiple temporalities and spatial scales—local, regional, national, and transnational—intersected and were entangled at various historical moments. It invites us to move beyond bounded notions of space (city and nation) and time (colonial, postcolonial, and national) and consider the role of groups (Dalits, urban poor, Marxists, and urban planners) in shaping Bombay city. The entwine-ment of spatial scales (city, nation, and global) and processes with different temporalities (Marxism, urban planning, and African American literature) and the entanglement of caste and class does not mean that one nullified the other or could be folded into the other. Caste and class are generally viewed in terms of time. Caste was seen as an inheritance from India's past that found new sustenance in modern times, but the belief was that with a sustained exposure to modernization caste would become moot or at most a footnote in urban life. For instance, the influential Indian Communist M. N. Roy (ca. 1886–1954) believed that with the introduction of modern industries and the production of mechanized commodities, caste was not a "living social factor," and only its economic essence remained relevant.[60] In Roy's formulation, caste and class were in opposite camps and therefore seen as temporal, ana-lytical, and social adversaries. In this dichotomy, caste bore the burden of cultural authenticity and backwardness, and class of universal solidarity befitting modern times.[61]

One important historical process of modern times was capitalism. Cap-italism and class's relevance in understanding historical change in South Asia, particularly the possibilities of their universal reach, has spawned a raging debate in South Asian studies.[62] An important point of contention focuses on the absoluteness of the universalizing processes of capital and class politics in South Asia. The lineage of both capitalism and class poli-tics, particularly working-class politics influenced by Marxism, was the European Enlightenment, which was delivered to South Asia via "the mad and violent agency of imperialism."[63] This taint makes capitalism and Marxism circumspect in the eyes of some scholars. In any case, they argue, the universal thrust of capital and Marxism is thwarted by everyday prac-tices of caste, religion, and ways of being in the modern world.[64] On the other hand, those who emphasize the relevance of capitalism as a category of analysis argue that capitalism and culture (caste and religion) cannot be assumed to be antithetical. As the sociologist Vivek Chibber points out, "Capitalism has spread to every corner of the world despite the enormous diversity of cultures. . . . [C]apital can subsist, even flourish, without hav-ing to revolutionize entire cultures."[65] In other words, processes with different temporalities (class, caste, and capitalism) articulate in practice. This process of joining occurs in space at particular historical moments.

One way to productively harness the debate is to think about *space* and not just *time*. Geographers have done this effectively, highlighting capital's articulation with caste and the existence of multiple temporalities within capital.[66] Capitalism has the "propensity to take what it finds"[67] or "leech"[68] on existing social relationships that help it accumulate more wealth. This phenomenon was not only peculiar to South Asia and caste, but in other global contexts as well, where capitalism worked through existing social formations to accumulate surplus value.[69] In South Asia, the cities that became nodes of accumulation, in which industrial capitalism played an important role, also exhibited the spatial effects of these social relationships. Thus both caste and class were etched into the built form and were evident in slums/*jhopadis*/*bastis* of cities of the region in the twentieth and twenty-first centuries.[70] *Outcaste Bombay* follows in this vein. It posits the production of space—the abstract space of urban planners and the lived space and social relationships of the urban poor and Dalits—as the site in which social, economic, and political processes with different histories intersect, articulate, disarticulate, and entangle at various moments.

Entanglement assumes two or even more strands of ideas, groups, or processes, with different intellectual and political lineages that interact or entwine at particular moments in a given space. One important reason for the entanglement of multiple threads could be the "shared intellectual and political projects"[71] of actors and groups. In Bombay city, Marxists, urban planners, political activists, and writers engaged with ideas from across the world. These groups had different political aspirations, but they shared a rhetoric of modernization and revolution. For them revolution was the desired mode for attaining modernity. Revolution entailed a yearning to overcome the social, political, and spatial constraints of the present (and by extension some inheritances of the past) to create a future detached from these limitations. For these self-professed modernists, revolution was a form they all shared in this historical conjuncture, even as its content was different for each. Thus Marxists in late colonial India aspired to a social and political revolution that would pave the path to socialism, where the state would be first captured and then eventually wither away, if the Marxist line was followed to its conclusion.[72] By contrast, urban planners in the city hankered for a revolution in the spatial organization of the city that would make it more conducive for industrial capital. The state played an important role in this vision. The planners shielded the process of planning itself from the upsurge of the urban poor. For their part, Dalit writers craved a revolution within and outside the field of literature that would invert existing social and cultural hierarchies. To actualize their revolutions, writers, planners, and Marxists disarticulated ideas from various parts of the world and domesticated and rearticulated them in Bombay.

Capitalism and class are important analytical categories with which to examine the two sites for this study: the built environment and language. Caste, an important organizing principle of urban life, cannot be grasped only by studying bodies identifying with particular caste groups but must be sought through revisiting the spatial transformations of the twentieth-century city itself. The urban poor, because of their presumed propensity to overcrowd the city and exaggerate its sanitation woes, were the objects of change and provided the rationale for the spatial transformation of Bombay. A disproportionately large portion of the urban poor were categorized as lower castes by the census reports, many of them as Dalits. All these categories—urban poor, lower castes, and Dalits—were highly unstable and stratified. There were social and political tensions within these groups. At the level of the everyday, the elite of a particular caste group was more likely to maintain contact with the poor in their group through social welfare and patronage than through caste solidarity.[73] The connections explored in the following chapters among caste, class, built environment, and language underline the tensions within these categories and groups.

1 THE HOUSING QUESTION AND CASTE, 1896–1950

BY THE BEGINNING OF THE TWENTIETH CENTURY, PROCLAMA-
tions of a housing problem in Bombay had become commonplace. The
municipal commissioner of Bombay, Arthur Crawford, had acknowledged
it in the 1860s.[1] By 1879, there were thirty cotton mills and several "minor
factories," the Prince's Dock, one of the largest docks in the world when it
was inaugurated in 1880, and several projects of land reclamation and
road, railway, and building construction were under way. Migrant labor
was required for these projects, and the famine of 1877 compelled additional people from surrounding areas to seek refuge in Bombay.[2] The
migrants needed housing. When the colonial government set up the City
of Bombay Improvement Trust after the bubonic plague epidemic of 1896,
it reiterated the need to address the crisis of housing in the city. The plague,
a recurring event in the 1890s and at the beginning of the twentieth
century, had led to an exodus of residents from the city. Plague in the city
coincided with another round of famine in the countryside; the famines of
1897 and 1900 were particularly severe in India.[3] The flight from the city
and deaths due to the epidemic were offset by the "influx of famine stricken
and diseased" migrants.[4] The circulatory movement of people to and from
Bombay city meant that in the 1901 census the population of the city
declined only marginally from the 1891 census and increased rapidly again
between 1901 and 1906.[5] The question for city officials and employers was
how and where to house these people.

Friedrich Engels, in *The Housing Question*, had linked housing to
industrial capitalism of the nineteenth century. In particular, he had
attributed the shortage of housing to the transition to industrial capitalism
and concluded that housing shortages led to overcrowded cities. Two com-
plementary processes contributed to the scarcity: the massive migration of
rural workers to urban industrial areas and the inability of older towns to

accommodate migrants because of a deficit of urban planning.[6] However, overcrowding in Bombay city was caused not by a shortage of houses per se but by the inability of tenants to rent them at affordable rates. Many houses and tenements in the city remained vacant because they were beyond the financial reach of the urban poor. Overcrowding was thus a product of low wages, an abiding feature of industrial capitalism in Bombay. Bombay's economy necessitated a large inflow of people, mostly unskilled, who came from rural areas and other towns in search of employment. Because of their low wages, landlords constructed jerry-built accommodations for them,[7] but renting these was still financially cumbersome for most workers, so they lived in slums or saved on rent money by subleasing part of a tenement from another renter, thus overcrowding tenements and neighborhoods. Thus slums and overcrowded tenements were necessary features of life in the city.

Caste, along with class, shaped Dalit prospects on the housing market. Because caste was an important administrative category, the colonial state heeded demands for housing, along with claims to urban space, made in the name of caste. Class was not absent: there was a discourse on housing the urban poor and the working class in the city, but even in tenements built for the poor, caste was acknowledged and tenements allotted by caste. At the end of the nineteenth century, Bombay's plague epidemic occasioned a new wave of urban planning, along with a discourse of overcrowding and slum reform, and by 1950 the spatial limits of the city expanded to include its northern suburbs, transforming Bombay from the Town and Island of Bombay to Greater Bombay. In this five-decade frame spanning the late colonial and early postcolonial period, most actors we discuss—urban poor including Dalits, bureaucrats and urban planners, capitalists, social reformers and other civil society groups, Dalit political leaders, social scientists, and Communists—looked to the state to solve the housing question. On this question, the state was the arbiter of first and last resort. During this period, Dalit politics changed, too, with a Dalit movement and a new Dalit leadership emerging in the 1920s, which addressed the question of Dalit housing. Contradictions proliferated in the discourses of caste and housing, and the production of urban space and housing became the material referent for caste. Thus, in social scientific inquiries into Dalits in the city, the built environment they inhabited had a perceptibly different material form. Not only was this environment particularly overcrowded and unsanitary, but it was also made of cheap materials, such as tin and palm leaves.

CASTE MATTERS . . . TO COLONIAL ADMINISTRATORS

For the urban poor, caste and class were important experiential, administrative, and political categories that shaped their lives. Class boundaries that delimited elite and nonelite localities, sanitary and unsanitary
spaces, in the city intersected with caste boundaries. Before we delve into
the historical reasons for the importance of caste, let us consider how caste
and class entwined in the history of sanitation in Bombay. Poor migrants
to the city in the late nineteenth century could afford to rent a tenement in
localities deemed overcrowded and unsanitary. These areas were in what is
now central Bombay, but at that time they were located north of the old
city. One important reason for the unsanitary conditions in many parts of
Bombay was that sewage systems did not serve the entire city. As early as
1852, Henry Conybeare, the city superintendent, disparaged the "open
drains . . . and open side gutters by which every street in the native town is
polluted."[8] The government refused to fund a venture to cover the drains
and gutters. In 1858, city administrators and the Bombay provincial government approached the imperial government for three million rupees to
fund a sewage system for the city. The Government of India could not
spare the money because of its exertions in the Indian "mutiny."[9] As a
result, the drainage and sewage system in the city developed selectively: it
was well established in neighborhoods where the city's elites lived and
almost nonexistent in poor neighborhoods.[10] The many reports and proposals for a drainage system in the city after 1858 went nowhere due to geographical, environmental, and economic issues, as well as personnel
disputes. As a result, the municipal commissioner of Bombay, Harry
Acworth, lamented in 1896, the year of the plague, that "the seemingly
dreary tale of reports, and discussions, and commissions led to no imme-
diate end."[11] Sanitation and civic amenities became the mode of creating
elite and nonelite spaces in the city.

The patchwork sanitation system had implications for caste and class
in the city. Because of the dearth of sewage lines in the poorer neighborhoods, night soil (human excreta) from these localities was collected by
Halalkhors or Bhangis.[12] The Bhangis are an untouchable *jati* employed
by city administrations and some neighborhoods in various cities of India
to remove feces from dry latrines and clean cesspools.[13] In Bombay,
Halalkhors brought the night soil from neighborhoods to depots in the
Girgaum, Kamathipura, Sewri, Mazgoan, and Carnac Bunder areas.[14] The
scavengers, along with sweepers, another group of sanitation workers in

the city, belonged mostly to the Bhangi and Mahar castes. The Mahars performed tasks like removing dead carcasses from villages in the Marathi-speaking regions of western India, but by the eighteenth and nineteenth centuries some of them were recruited as soldiers in regional kingdoms and British colonial armies, as well as for work in ammunition factories, and eventually as laborers in railways, docks, hospitals, and sanitation departments in cities. The sweepers (mostly Mahars) in Bombay went on strike twice in July 1889 to demand higher wages, holidays, and protection against exploitation by jobbers. Their employer, the Bombay Municipal Corporation, responded by evicting them from the tenements they rented from the municipality and then deployed scavengers to perform the work of sweeping the city streets.[15] The strikers were forced to return to work, and eventually, the Bombay Legislative Council passed the Municipal Servants Act of 1890, which tightened control over sweepers, scavengers, and other municipal employees. Thus, the colonial state deployed one group of municipal workers—scavengers (Bhangis/Halalkhors)—against another, sweepers who were mostly Mahar, and passed an act that "ensured that the sweeper was more locked into his place than he was previously."[16] The issue of disciplining municipal workers arose again during the plague, when their employer, the municipality, would not let them abandon the city. Housing became an important tool for locking them in place, a strategy that was repeated during a February 1922 strike.[17]

Caste became important to the lives of the urban poor in the late nineteenth and twentieth centuries. Some colonial officials in the middle of the nineteenth century desired to "know" India and insisted that caste and religion were the sociological keys to understanding it. They thus justified collecting more information on Indian castes (and religion) for the governance of their domains. After the 1860s, the colonial state in India undertook the mammoth project of documenting social hierarchies and differences in Indian society. The state generated numerous ethnographies of caste and tribes in the second half of the nineteenth century, starting with the monumental eight-volume *People of India* series, inaugurated in 1866. From the very first census in 1871, they collected information on castes.[18] Colonial officials believed that the representation and classification of Indian society in numbers, maps, and other data would provide them with a lever to govern the country. The census reports and ethnographic surveys entailed drawing boundaries for a neat delineation of Indian society into groups, households, and individuals.[19] This hastened the ethnicization of caste, as administrators deployed caste to demarcate social and spatial boundaries.[20] The state tasked itself with the work of simplifying and maintaining these boundaries.[21] Herbert Risley, the commissioner for the 1901 census, added another layer to the logic of enumerating difference by grounding caste hierarchy in the measurement of heads and noses. By the 1911 census, the association of the body with caste had collapsed under the weight of its own contradictions and was abandoned.

Bombay's administrators and officials deployed caste to make sense of social life in the city in the nineteenth century. For instance, as early as the 1870s, the Bombay health officer's quarterly report tabulated deaths in the city based on the religion and caste of dead persons. Thus, in the fourth quarter of 1879, mortalities among Hindus in the city were 32.67 per thousand, among Muslims 41.41 per thousand, and among Hindu outcastes (i.e., lower-caste Hindus) 57.03 per thousand.[22] In the second quarter of 1896, the figures were Hindus 30.59 per thousand, low-caste Hindus 59.06 per thousand, and Muslims 41.48 per thousand.[23] During the plague epidemics of the late 1890s, the death rate among "low caste Hindus" was "as high as 122 and 143" per thousand.[24] The urban poor were also enumerated in terms of caste. According to the 1881 census, the "Marathas (caste), Musalmans (religion), Native Christians (religion), Kolis (caste), Bhandaris (caste) and Mahars (an untouchable caste)," were the poorest classes in the city, many of them said to "live on starvation diet . . . and a dozen families herd together in houses, only large enough to contain [one family]."[25] For the census officials in the city, class difference and overcrowding were more meaningful when buttressed with a listing of caste and religion. In a city transforming rapidly because of commerce, industry, and migration, caste—the timeless essence of Indian social life—clarified social hierarchy where class on its own was inadequate. Similarly, census officials deployed caste to enunciate the sociological composition of neighborhoods in the city. For instance, the peasant Maratha Kunbis accounted for 47 percent of Dongri's population in 1901, while Mahar Dalits were present in sizable numbers in Upper Colaba, Esplanade, Kamathipura, and Second Nagpada neighborhoods, their numbers having increased considerably between 1881 and 1901.[26] Even overcrowding was attributed to caste. For instance, the Municipal Corporation reported to the Bombay government in 1908 that "the overcrowding in houses is undoubtedly due, in a great measure, to the ignorance and poverty of the people, and the division of them into *communities* and *castes* requiring them *perforce* to congregate in particular localities."[27] The corporation transferred the herding instinct onto the people it said yearned for caste and religious communities. It looked forward to a time when education would inculcate a desire for sanitation among these groups and, coupled with higher wages at some point in the future, dilute the communal bond. The desire to dilute ethnic bonds, which in fact capitalism and the colonial public sphere made stronger, went unrequited largely because of the practices of the colonial government. For colonial administrators, the ethnicization of caste was not just a knowledge project born out of intellectual curiosity but also had "political value" and supported the colonial policy of divide and rule.[28] As we saw with sanitation workers, it also played an important role in disciplining textile workers. In other words, mere classification did not produce or entrench caste; it became amplified and more fractious when entangled with historical processes of colonial administration and capitalism.

The political value of frictions produced by caste and religion had become evident by the end of the nineteenth century. In 1882, India's viceroy, Lord Ripon, had introduced the Local Self-Government Bill, which envisaged the devolution of power to local bodies. This bill, along with the Indian Councils Act of 1892, inaugurated a process of "constitutional reforms," in effect a system of recruiting Indians for imperial ends.[29] These truncated practices of democratization through local self-government attracted many Indian leaders, including Pherozeshah Mehta and Gopal Krishna Gokhale, into city politics and provincial and imperial councils. Pherozeshah Mehta, one of the stalwarts of municipal politics in late nineteenth- and twentieth-century Bombay, was an advocate of the Bombay Municipal Act of 1888, which changed the structure of city governance. The act enabled the creation of the Bombay Municipal Corporation and made the municipal commissioner, who was appointed by the colonial government, accountable to the corporation. The majority of corporation administrators were elected by the city's taxpayers, a tiny electorate. The act also provided for the creation of standing committees to oversee various aspects of governance.[30] Devolution, the government hoped, would contain the politics of Indians within cities and provinces and arrest nationalist critiques of colonial power by embroiling them in the construction of infrastructure.[31] Thus the government encouraged the Indian elite to focus on the built environment in cities and provinces, particularly roads and sanitation. But as we saw with sanitation in Bombay, this was a futile endeavor for city elites because the budget was controlled by colonial officials in Calcutta and London. The strategy of devolution, though, may have dampened the ardor of the national movement led by the Indian National Congress for a few years in the last decade of the nineteenth century.[32]

For their part, the Indian elite viewed the urban poor, including Dalits, through the lens of social reform. They were objects of social service; the goal was to make them subjects of social reform. Elites' service to the poor, and by extension to the Indian nation, was to reform the social practices of the poor, such as their supposed predilection for alcohol consumption, their unsanitary living habits, and their lack of education.[33] The standpoint of the elite reformer was an amalgam of Victorian morality, upper-caste norms of piety, and a fascination with modern scientific theories of collective life.[34] From their vantage point, Dalits and the urban poor were defined by their vices and impure practices. They needed reform. The civilizing mission was fueled by a desire for a robust Hindu community coupled with anxieties about the demographic decline of Hindus. Liberals such as G. K. Gokhale and revivalist organizations such as the Arya Samaj focused their attention on attracting lower-caste converts to Christianity, Islam, and Sikhism back into the Hindu fold. Organizations such as the Servants of India Society, started by Gokhale, and the Depressed Classes Mission, started by Vithhal Ramji Shinde, played an important role in the lives of Bombay's urban poor and Dalit communities in the first half of the twentieth century. They focused on the problems of sanitation and housing and their effects on the health and morals of the poor.

CAPITAL CITY, CAPITAL, AND THE CITY

Capital is an abstract and universal category that acquires texture and concreteness in a local context. In the process of acquiring heft and its discernable form, it becomes meaningful. To operate in a local context, it attaches itself to an existing social hierarchy for easy nourishment. In Bombay, capital sutured itself to caste, making caste part of its "metabolic system."[35] Bombay's merchants who started manufacturing industries in the city in the second half of the nineteenth century imported and adapted the economic form—industrial capitalism—that was well developed in parts of Europe and America. From the early nineteenth century, Indian merchants had found it difficult to raise money in the global market for their high-risk ventures. Instead they raised short-term credit at high interest rates, mostly from caste and kinship networks.[36] The lucrative China trade in opium and cotton was funded through such ventures. The city's merchants from various trading communities—Parsis, Khojas, and Bhatias—made money in the China trade. But by the second half of the nineteenth century, they were slowly sidelined from this trade by rising competition from European firms. Indian merchants diversified their portfolio and started cotton textile industries. Merchants played an important role in the growth of the cotton textile industry not just in Bombay but also globally.[37] In Bombay, the paucity of credit hampered their industrial enterprise. As Chandavarkar notes, "Capital moved more readily into the safer outlets of usury and petty trade, mortgages and property than into industry."[38] In fact, we see the attractions of property and rent from property for Bombay's industrialists after the plague epidemic. Sir Vithaldas Thakersey, a prominent textile mill owner of the Bhatia caste, proposed a plan in the early 1900s to resolve the housing problem for the urban poor. He suggested that capitalists in the city with a charitable outlook form a syndicate and pool their resources to build "sanitary chals [chawls]" for the urban poor. The plan envisaged the Bombay Improvement Trust advancing a loan of an equal amount to the syndicate. After the syndicate had repaid the loan over a period of a few years, the properties or buildings would be transferred to the syndicate.[39] The scheme, which in effect imagined the syndicate as landlords and rentiers in the housing market for the urban poor, was criticized at the time and not implemented.

For the mill owners, the difficulty in raising credit for industries meant that they could not make long-term plans for their mills. Instead, their strategies were geared toward short-term profit. Therefore, growth in Bombay's textile industry was spasmodic. These structural constraints of industrial capitalism had a deep impact on the labor market. For instance, industrial employment in Bombay was volatile, and industrialists hankered for a pliable labor force that would acquiesce to joblessness for a few days followed by intense work over a long workday when there was demand in the market for a commodity. In other words, they wanted a labor force that could be maneuvered nimbly: it would be activated or deactivated quickly and paid low wages.

Migration played an important role in this low-wage economy. Migration of the rural poor was enabled by social and economic changes in the countryside, particularly Bombay province. By the second half of the nineteenth century, peasants in the province produced commodities—either cotton for the global market or grain for towns and cities in the region—in tune with the demands of the market.[40] The peasants were dominated by caste-based networks of bankers, moneylenders, and usurers who controlled the production of commodities.[41] The structure of agrarian property relationships also changed in this period. Capital, in league with the colonial state, advocated a single owner for a unit of property. The property owner was now in a position to buy, sell, raise, and invest capital in his property and generate profit from it. The property owner was also the head of a household. Over a period of time, private property fragmented into smaller and smaller units because of the laws of inheritance.[42] The small holdings pushed many peasants into subsistence farming. The domination of moneylenders meant that some peasants with small holdings grew cash crops, integrating them into the world market economy.[43] In the 1870s and 1880s, political-economic and ecological factors produced a series of famines in the province and impelled the battered small peasants to sell their labor for a wage in the cotton and spinning mills in the city, at least for part of the year.[44] In Bombay province, the household was the unit of production,[45] and the household diversified its streams of income by sending a son or sons to labor in Bombay city in the hope of retaining control over its small rural holdings with the help of their wages. City workers who had rural holdings relied on them during industrial strikes, illnesses, and when women returned to the village for childbirth.[46] Many Dalits were landless peasants, and they formed a sizable number of migrants. For instance, in a survey of the Mahar Dalit castes in the village of Saswad near Pune city in 1912, the agricultural scientist Harold H. Mann found that thirty-seven Mahar men from the village were working in Bombay city.[47]

In the city, access to a job and a rented dwelling depended on a social network in which caste and kinship played a crucial role. For instance, the manager of the Dinshaw Petit Mill confirmed in 1908 that caste was an important consideration in employment at the textile mill.[48] The jobber (*mukadam, maistri*) was a key figure in recruiting workers; jobbers recruited labor from their caste and kinship networks. They also helped them find housing through their network and extended credit in times of distress. This buttressed the jobber's authority over workers, but they were also the channel through which workers conveyed grievances to employers.[49] Many city workers from Bombay province retained rural ties and remitted money, which shaped their relationship with work, housing, and urban politics.

For the urban poor, housing was a commodity they rented from a landlord or a tenant in order to reproduce the family in the city or the village or both. Landlords and rent collectors were important figures in their lives, and their ability to pay the rent was a matter of anxiety. High rents produced anxieties and sometimes led to assaults on rent collectors. The poor devised elaborate strategies to evade paying. Sometimes, tenants absconded without paying rent and then changed their names to rent another tenement, or rented a tenement during the monsoon and abandoned it after the rains. But their political rhetoric focused on higher wages and reduced hours of work rather than affordable housing in the city, at least in the first few decades of the twentieth century. The workers' reaction to housing in the city "served more as a catharsis for their feeling" than the subject of their politics.[50] In other words, they vented their distress over housing conditions by assaulting rent collectors, but their politics was predicated on the assumption that Bombay's capitalists should value their labor more by paying them higher wages.

CASTE AND HOUSING FOR THE URBAN POOR

Housing for the urban poor was a commodity for which they paid rent. The form of the commodity, the house itself, was difficult to define. By their own admission, the census officials of 1901 were flummoxed by "the diversity of structures in different parts of the country" and decided to adopt "whatever definition might seem best suited to local conditions."[51] In Bombay city, the house was defined as "the whole of a building under one undivided roof or under two or more roofs connected inter se by subsidiary roofs."[52] When migrants to the city searched for a dwelling (*ghar, nivara*) in the early 1900s, they, according to the census definition, would be considering a building with an undivided roof, where they might find a tenement to rent or live in as a subtenant. That tenement would consist of one or more rooms. The design of the tenements, whether constructed by private landlords, mill owners, or the state, adapted the design of army barracks. But instead of large halls in the barrack, each tenement had an eight-by-eight or ten-by-ten-foot living area with a common toilet and washing area outside it. The design invited analogies to warehousing of people and imprisonment.[53] If they could not find or afford a tenement, they lived in a hut. The habitation—be it a tenement or a hut—was a place where other commodities, like food and clothing, were consumed, and where the laboring class was sustained and reproduced. But in the eyes of colonial government at the time, the overcrowded localities in Bombay were also incubators of contagious diseases, including the plague, and the solution was to dismantle some of them and build new houses for the poor.[54] The Bombay Improvement Trust was the vehicle for restructuring the urban environment. The Trust was inspired by the City of Glasgow Improvement Trust in its form, including its justification for demolishing housing and buildings in the city in the name of the welfare of its inhabitants.[55] In turn, the Bombay Trust inspired the Rangoon Development Trust later in the twentieth century and was part of the discourse and practices of imperial urbanism in port cities in British Asia, including Singapore and Hong Kong.[56] In its content, the Bombay Improvement Trust acknowledged and worked through caste.

The Trust harnessed the 1901 census for a deeper knowledge of the city. The colonial state had produced knowledge about local conditions in order to administer localities.[57] The city census reports categorized people by caste and religion. In the 1901 census, though, it complemented the work of the Trust. The plague had necessitated "sanitary reformation and improvement" and a need for the "regeneration of the city."[58] The city census report explains:

> The recent constitution of the Bombay Improvement Trust, which requires in its measures dealing with overcrowding in the city the guidance of detailed statistics not hitherto available, and the difficulties experienced by the health department of the municipality in coping with the plague epidemic owing to the want of adequate statistical information concerning the sectional and structural distribution of the population of Bombay, have led to a special elaboration of statistics collected in Bombay Town and Island with a view to meeting the requirement of both bodies. The Census in Bombay has thus placed on record, in accordance with suggestions received from the Trust and the corporation, additional particulars dealing with structural units i.e. the population of the tenement rooms and floors, the description of buildings complete or in course of construction, and the distribution of populations by sections and circles, designed to offer material assistance both to the Trust in their work of reconstructing Bombay, and to the Municipality in arranging for the better sanitation of the Island.[59]

In the 1901 census, the work of enumerating the built environment of the city happened in parallel with counting people by ethnic group.[60] The India census provided an anthropometric key to ascertain caste, and the city census classified houses, tenements, and buildings in the city as it compiled statistics of people living in the houses.[61] The census established overcrowding but also listed "a large number of . . . wholly uninhabited houses" in the city.[62] In some areas of the city, such as Girgaum and Walkeshwar, as many as one-third of the houses were unoccupied, lending heft to the view that the housing question was not about availability of housing but about affordability.[63] The goal of the census was to collect statistics to facilitate the work of the Trust.

On the basis of the 1901 census, the Trust computed that there were 33,402 houses in the city with an average of 23.23 persons living in each house.[64] The census's definition of a house, which remained unchanged for the 1911 census, had important implications for structures that were not a house. One kind of structure that was not a house was a slum. Therefore, an important provision of the City of Bombay Improvement Act of 1898 was the removal of unsanitary slums.[65] The house and the slum now formed a conceptual and discursive dyad; the slum became the "internal other" of the city.[66] A house could be designated a slum if it failed to meet standards of sanitation and overcrowding. The Trust was constituted under the act to target the overcrowded and unsanitary localities of the urban poor, which were deemed breeding grounds for plague and therefore merited demolition. The Trust had a budget and provisions for raising low-interest loans to buy properties in the city.[67] It was also entrusted with the task of acquiring land, both plots deemed unsanitary and overcrowded and vacant lands, from the Bombay government and the Municipal Corporation to build sanitary homes and ease the problem of congestion in the city. Thus the projects of knowing the city, identifying overcrowded localities, listing the number and types of buildings, and enumerating the people in the city cohered in the 1901 census report. The condition of the built environment and the city's housing stock became inextricably linked to the estimation of social life in the city.

Bhalchandra Krishna, a municipal councilor and a member of the Trust, recommended geographical expansion of Bombay to fix the problem of overcrowding. He recommended suburbanization to the north of the city, which the Trust facilitated by acquiring land under a variety of tenures and leasing it for city improvement.[68] Trust schemes facilitated suburbanization in Dadar, Matunga, and Sion at the northern extremities of Bombay city of that time.[69] The spatial solution did not eliminate slums. Krishna complained in 1904 that Bombay's municipal bylaws did not support the Trust's endeavors. According to him, "The Municipal bylaws are permitting the construction of unhealthy houses and the growth of new slums."[70] Slums thus continued to thrive in the interstices of two institutions—the Trust and the Municipal Corporation. Each institution blamed the other for the rise of slums. In places where the Trust demolished slums efficiently, it did not display the same felicity in building houses. The Trust had evicted 14,613 families by March 1909, but had only provided 2,844 rooms in their own chawls. A further 2,220 tenements were built by private developers who had leased land from the Trust.[71] This was inadequate. Thus J. P. Orr, who became chairman of the Trust in 1909, noted the irony of slum clearance in Nagpada, Mandvi Market, and Chandanvadi exacerbating slumlike conditions in adjoining areas.[72] In these parts of the city, overcrowding led to increased demand for housing, which in turn resulted in higher rents. The landlords, attentive to the demands for more housing, subdivided rooms and added new floors to old, unsanitary buildings, aggravating the original problem. By 1909, the Trust was involved in thirty-three schemes, many of which entailed demolishing slums and providing housing for the urban poor in the mill district of central Bombay. Dabak Chawl, where Ambedkar's family lived at the beginning of twentieth century, was built by the Trust.

Caste informed these housing initiatives and the production of urban space. Demands for housing and claims to urban space were heeded by the late colonial state when made in the name of caste. One of the reasons Ambedkar's family lived in tenements with other Dalit families was because the Trust considered caste in allotting rooms in its tenements. In its application to rent a tenement, it elicited information on caste and religion, in addition to monthly pay and rent paid to earlier landlords, and an effort was made to "group particular castes in particular chawls."[73] Caste and class shaped the spatial (re)ordering of the city as well. Nikhil Rao has highlighted the case of land speculators from the Bhatia trading community who bought land from the Trust in Dadar and Matunga, in league with the Trust's push for suburbanization. Some Bhatia landowners started living in these areas. To develop it into a suburb and attract more people from the overcrowded city, the Trust sanctioned the opening of a market near Matunga railway station in 1913. The plans for the market included provisions for stalls selling meat, vegetables, and sundry other commodities. Members of the Bhatia caste, who had formed the Matunga Residents' Association, opposed this. They objected to a "flesh market" near Matunga station since all the people in the vicinity were "vegetarian Hindoos." The association argued that clauses in their deeds required them to sell land only to vegetarians. Eventually, Matunga ended up with a vegetable market, and the meat market was shifted to a suburb farther north in Sion, where there was a Roman Catholic Church—Catholic residents were ostensibly meat eaters. Caste and class, here working through covenants and land deeds, altered urban planning and urban space.[74]

Another example of the relevance of caste in the production of urban space was the case of the Chitrapur Saraswat Brahmans of Bombay city. Saraswat Brahmins used the provisions of the Indian Cooperative Credit Societies Act of 1904 to ameliorate the economic conditions of this high-caste but predominantly middle- and lower middle-class community. The legislation provided for cooperative societies to be organized by members of a "single caste or community."[75] As British official R. W. Ewbank observed, caste was a useful structuring device for cooperatives in Bombay city, "where it is difficult to discover any other nexus which ensures an equal degree of mutual acquaintance among members."[76] In 1906, the Saraswat Brahmans formed the Shamrao Vithal Cooperative Credit Society with the goal of providing low-interest loans to members of the community. Saraswats then formed the Saraswat Cooperative Housing Society in 1915 and acquired land from the Trust in the Gamdevi neighborhood. "The Gamdevi cooperative housing project was a tenant co-partnership. Five buildings were built, each with six tenements of three rooms plus kitchen, bath, veranda."[77] Membership in the society was obtained by an initial payment (four thousand rupees in this case), and the monthly rent for the homes ranged between thirty and thirty-eight rupees per month, which was cheaper than rents for middle-class homes on the open market in the same area. The Saraswat Brahmins deployed the model of a cooperative society to form housing societies in other parts of the city as well in the 1920s and 1930s. Thus caste, along with class, shaped urban space. The Trust was an important institution that acknowledged claims for housing made in the name of caste, particularly by upper-caste and middle- and upper-class groups, but also by Dalits in its tenements. Dalit dwellings were susceptible to being labeled slums.

SLUMS AND THE TRAVAILS OF THE POOR

City administrators attributed slums to the avarice of landlords, lack of civic and sanitary sense among tenants, the attractions of primordial community ties such as caste, poor regulatory mechanisms of civic bodies and an even poorer ethic of implementing extant laws, and the persistence of a low-wage economy. The administrators could not and did not advocate for higher wages, only hoped for it. In their view, slums as a built form posed serious moral and health hazards for slum dwellers. Their solutions to the rise of slums focused on documenting the making of slums and inculcating a healthy dose of social reform—a cultural transformation among landlords and tenants, particularly. It laid out examples of the landlord's greed. For instance, the Trust in its Undria Street scheme documented the process through which the area became a slum. In its estimation, additions were made to existing houses, such as a new floor or bathrooms, by owners with an eye on rents and without regard to principles of ventilation or sanitation. The open spaces between houses disappeared over a period of time. The Trust's solution included acquisition and demolition of these structures, entirely or in part, to create space between the two houses. The fear of acquisition and reduction of the lived space produced anxiety among owners. Remodeling a house to provide a twenty-foot yard at the rear, adequate light, and ventilation would reduce the usable housing area and therefore reduce income for the landlord.

The Trust believed that its one-room concrete structures in Nagpada, which included paved courtyards, drains, open spaces, and internal ventilation, were model one-room housing tenements. But the unaffordable rent—Rs 3.5 to Rs 5.0 per tenement—meant that middle- and lower middle-class tenants inhabited these houses instead of the poor evicted from slums.[78] Needless to say, these norms, even if diligently implemented, could only be applied to buildings constructed by the Trust. They did not solve the problem of slums in the city. In fact, in 1914–15, the city added 45,000 square yards of slums, legally, by adhering to the bylaws of the Bombay City Municipal Act.[79]

The municipality received criticism from other quarters as well. A. E. Mirams, a consulting surveyor to the Government of Bombay, in his evidence to the Indian Industrial Commission in 1917, argued that industrialization in India would thrive if the conditions of workers improved. A flourishing industrialization necessitated "virile and contented workers."[80] Mirams focused on improvement of the built environment, particularly the habitations of the working classes, characterized by "utter wretchedness."[81] He paid particular attention to housing, especially the "celebrated chawls," which were one hundred square feet under the Bombay bylaws.[82] In these places "there is hardly space to move, whole families sleep, breed, cook their food with the aid of pungent cow dung cakes, and perform all the functions of family life. Some of the rooms . . . are often nothing more than holes beneath the sloping roof, in which a man cannot stand upright."[83] Mirams blamed the employers and civic administrators for the condition of workers. The municipality had abandoned the policy of enforcing regulations for light and air in a room, and the employers were unperturbed and inattentive to the conditions of their employees.

Let us pause here to consider three important transitions: one in the management and production of the built form of the city and two in the outlook toward the urban poor. By the end of the 1910s, the tensions between the Trust and the Municipal Corporation, which now had more Indian representatives, had come to a head. The Bombay provincial government responded by creating the Development Directorate, part of the Development Department, in 1920. The Trust had Indian members; the Bombay Development Department (BDD) was entirely an executive body.[84] The BDD's mandate included industrial housing schemes, development of suburbs for residential purposes, reclamation of land, and relocation of industrial areas out of the city. For a few years, it deployed its executive authority bestowed by the provincial government to launch ambitious schemes, but by 1925 its reclamation and industrial housing schemes encountered problems, and the BDD itself was shut down in 1929. Its tenements in Worli attracted few tenants in the first few years because there was no public transport connecting tenements to the mill districts.

The perception of the poor changed too. In the 1910s and 1920s, there was an effusion of statistics on the urban poor, particularly workers in the city. Colonial institutions viewed the poor through the prism of their capacity for labor. They were paid a wage by their employers based on the value of their labor. That wage enabled them to consume commodities, including a dwelling in the city, though it might be in a slum. But since most workers lived in slums, they were unprotected from health and moral hazards associated with it. This posed a problem because it could thwart their industriousness and discipline along with the ability of employers to reproduce the labor at low wages. Therefore, we see an increase in "labor statistics" produced by the Labour Office to offer insights into their living conditions. There were many reports on workers' monthly budgets—their expenditure on housing and food, workers' health, and education. The third change was that these reports differentiated the working class by community, including caste. Ethnic boundaries were important for the labor office. Therefore, Dalits may not be the focus of these reports (unless they were scavengers), but they appear frequently, albeit briefly, as Depressed Classes. Perhaps, in some of the fine social histories of the working class in

Bombay, Dalits are a marginal presence because they appear fleetingly in sources like the *Labour Gazette*.

Since sanitation was defined as a moral defect of the urban poor, the goal was to reform them. The architecture of the tenement aspired to rectify their unsanitary practices. For instance, the BDD tenements did not include a bathing area (*nahni*) inside the room because of fears that it would be used as a urinal. Similarly, the windows of the tenements had cement louvers—slats made of cement—and metal nets covered the slats. The room resembled a cage or a ventilated box.[85] But the objective of the design was to prevent tenants from throwing waste out of the windows, instead training them to discard waste in receptacles provided for the purpose.[86] But these constraints, particularly the lack of a bathing area inside the house, made the BDD tenements unattractive for renters. At least in the first few years after their inauguration in 1920, many tenements were unoccupied. Finally, in 1924 the BDD redesigned the tenements to entice renters. Both new and old chawls included a bathing area in each room, and the windows had shutters instead of cement louvers.[87] Like the Trust tenements, the BDD chawls proved attractive and affordable for the lower middle class rather than the mill workers and urban poor. The urban poor paid between three and five rupees as average rents, while the lowest rent of the BDD chawls in various locations in the city was six, seven, or eight rupees.[88]

Social reformers complemented the impersonal hand of the architect in the sanitary training of the poor, particularly Dalits. They critiqued the BDD in 1921 for spending its resources on reclaiming land, providing it to city elites, and beautifying the city rather than on housing schemes for the poor and the middle classes.[89] But they were also dedicated to changing the social practices of the poor. Reformers from the Servants of India Society and the Social Service League focused on the neighborhoods of the poor in the 1920s and paid "special attention" to tenements in which Dalits lived, endeavoring to organize "lectures on hygiene and sanitation by competent medical men" in these localities.[90]

CASTE, CLASS, SPACE

Dalits too made claims to housing and space in the register of caste, albeit with limited success. At a meeting in December 1923 of the Somavanshi Nirashrit Sudharak Mandali, an association of Mahar Dalits, presided over by a member of the Bombay Legislative Council, J. Addyman, a resolution was passed requesting that the chairman of the Improvement Trust "let two chawls constructed by the Trust at Love Lane Byculla, to members of the depressed classes . . . [along with] two shops for the sale of necessities of life."[91] The Bombay Port Trust similarly had a chawl for Mahar dockworkers in Wadi Bunder, since workers from other castes did not want to live near them.[92] The Somavanshi Mandali's request was probably heeded, because in a few years, Dalits of Love Lane Chawls Scheme 62, Block 2, "wholly occupied by Mahars,"[93] asked the Trust to provide wire gauze for tenements on the ground floor and a compound wall between two buildings. The Trust eventually responded to the request and agreed to defray the expenses (approximately one thousand rupees). But two pleas for concessions in rent for a reading room for Dalit Mahars in the same tenements (Love Lane) did not elicit the same response. The reading room started by the Servants of the Somvanshiya Society desired a nominal rent (one rupee). This was not granted. Another request—by the Bahishkrit Hitkarni Sabha (Society for the Benefit of Outcastes), an organization started by Ambedkar to demand civil and political rights—for a reduction of rent for another reading room in Love Lane chawls was not approved by the Trust, either.[94] But an important aspect of these meetings was the rise of new leadership among Dalits in the city, J. M. Karandikar in the first instance and N. B. Jovle and Nikaljay in the second, who mobilized Dalits in the tenements, passed resolutions, and submitted petitions for the consideration of the Trust. The rise of the new leadership was due to a political upsurge among Dalits in the 1920s that mobilized support on the issue of rights and reforms, like the initiative for schools for Dalit boys and girls.[95]

Dalit leaders petitioned the Trust, but how did administrators view their presence in the tenements? The Trust believed that caste and class accounted for the propensity to overcrowd tenements. For instance, when the Trust debated the ideal size of a tenement—80, 100, or 120 square feet— it suggested that the 120-foot rooms be provided to large families, "which are commonest among Mahars and other low classes."[96] There were 324 Mahar tenants in the Trust chawls in the 1920s. When the Trust considered retrenchment of sweepers on its properties to reduce its annual expenses, the chief officer of the Trust argued that the inhabitants of Mahar chawls "are so filthy that I doubt whether any reduction can be safely made.[97] Stereotypes were deployed to counter austerity measures of the Trust.

Caste and housing were also linked in the Bombay legislature. In the 1920s, Sitaram Keshav Bole, in his submission to the Bombay Government on the industrial housing scheme in the city, outlined the importance of caste to workers' housing. Bole identified with the Bhandari caste, higher in the social hierarchy than Dalit castes, and was a social reformer who opposed untouchability. He was the founder of the Kamgar Hitvardhak Sabha (Society for the Benefit of Workers), the vice president of the Bombay Textile Labor Union, as well as a member of the Bombay Legislative Council. Bole believed the BDD should be more attentive to caste and creed in allotting tenements to workers.[98] He emphasized the role of caste in shaping social and cultural relationships. In the villages, he argued, people lived in separate houses, and each caste resided in a particular neighborhood. For instance, Mahar Dalits lived in Maharwadas, and Mang Dalits lived in Mangwadas. He therefore had reservations about tenement living in the city. He felt that the principle of a separate house for each family with spatial demarcation of castes was not adequately followed in the industrial housing schemes. He lauded the attentiveness of administrators in allotting rooms on the same floor of housing tenements to "tenants whose modes of living approximate or harmonize," meaning people of the same caste.[99] Bole wanted the state to be more receptive to demands in the name of caste. For him the caste system fomented disadvantages like untouchability, but caste was also a resource to contest and transform these practices.[100]

For Bole, caste was the bane and balm of Dalit lives. As a social reformer, he was opposed to the disadvantages of spatial segregation, in particular the lack of access to "public water sources, wells, and *dharmashalas* [rest houses, particularly for pilgrims]."[101] But in the context of housing in Bombay city, he overturned this logic and demanded more housing for Dalits by invoking the norms of social and spatial segregation of castes in villages. Adherence to these spatial arrangements, he felt, would contribute "to the freedom and happiness of life" of the occupants of the BDD chawls. In a nutshell, the Dalits' ability to own or rent the commodity (tenement) became the basis for a free and happy community. In this formulation, the state guaranteed access to housing by providing credit, land, and tenements. B. R. Ambedkar echoed this sentiment. In a speech at Mahad in 1927, he held that the government was the most important and powerful institution: "The manner in which the government thinks makes things happen."[102] Ambedkar's assertions were in line with S. R. Bole's demand for separate Dalit housing. The demand was echoed by the *Report of the Depressed Classes and Aboriginal Tribes Committee of the Bombay Presidency*, published in 1930, which Ambedkar coauthored. The report argued that Dalits had problems finding accommodation in the city, and therefore the state should give them land and access to credit for buying private property, allowing them to construct their own homes and become home-owners.[103] Making demands did not mean they were always heeded by the state. Nevertheless, the clustering of Dalit homes in tenements and slums became the basis of social scientific investigations of the city.

SOCIAL SCIENCE, CASTE, AND THE BUILT ENVIRONMENT

Social scientific studies of Dalits in Bombay in the 1920s and 1930s fore-grounded the segregation and relevance of caste to the spatial arrange-ment of the city. In these studies, the material referent for caste was the built environment. Scholars based these studies on government reports and valued the importance of observation and experience of the localities of the urban poor. In these studies, Dalit houses were deemed more unsan-itary, precarious, and flimsy, echoing the observation of the social reform-ers. In fact, social scientists relied on social workers to collect evidence for them.[104] The social scientists and reformers were part of a similar intellec-tual and discursive formation in this moment. The intellectual lineage of social science in Bombay has been traced to social reform.[105] In these stud-ies, the pollution associated with Dalit castes was transferred to the built environment, particularly slums. And in a complimentary move, the unsanitary environment made caste more meaningful in the city. For instance, in economist A. R. Burnett-Hurst's study of labor and housing in Bombay city, he comments that Dalits "have filthy habits and live in squalor. . . . [T]hey eat fish, meats, the carcasses of cows, buffaloes, sheep, and goats . . . also food left by other people . . . [and] drink strong liquor."[106] Burnett-Hurst's intention was to capture the chaos and messiness of working-class tenements, particularly those built and managed by private landlords. He disdained landlords. For him, there was nothing redeeming about the built environment of the urban poor:

> Approaches to the chawls abound with dirt and filth. Kutchra or
> household refuse, and even excreta are thrown from the windows of the
> upper floors onto the streets and into the compounds. The refuse cast on
> the streets is generally cleared away, but that thrown into the compound
> generally accumulates, as it seems to be nobody's business to remove it.
> The compound and the approaches to the chawls are generally "kutcha"
> [unpaved] and in the monsoon they soon become quagmires with pools

of water. Long after the cessation of rain the pools of water remain,
become stagnant and form excellent breeding-grounds for the malaria
carrying mosquito.[107]

In this cheerless estimation of housing for the urban poor, Dalit housing was a particular and separate category. It also had a different aesthetic.
According to him, Dalits had difficulty obtaining housing in the city, "as
no other community will live near them. When they cannot find room in
the chawls set apart for them, they live in sheds or huts." These habitations
had a different materiality; they were built using cheaper materials. The
sheds had roofs and walls made from flattened kerosene tins. There were
no windows: "Holes in the rusty tin walls and roof provide the interior
with light and air. The floor is only about 3 inches from the ground." The
roofs of some sheds or huts were made of dry leaves of date or coconut
palms, and the occupants shared the space with domestic animals like
cows, calves, goats, and hens. The area around these structures was "generally defecated [sic]."[108] Burnett-Hurst's solutions to the problems were
social reform and social welfare initiatives in which the city's industrialists, the colonial government, and social reformers played a crucial role.

Slums irked the 1931 census officials too. After the release of the city
census report, the problems of overcrowding and unsanitary habitations of
the urban poor, more than three decades after the institution of the Trust,
vexed city officials and mill owners. R. P. Masani, a former municipal
commissioner, blamed the government, the Municipal Corporation, and
the city's residents for these problems. He yearned for an institute of social
research—a "sociological laboratory for the continuous investigation of
the social problems of the city"—that would paint a "realistic picture" of
the conditions of the urban poor.[109] The Tata Institute of Social Sciences
had not been created yet. But the newly instituted Sociology Department
of the University of Bombay was attentive to the conditions of the urban
poor and the Dalit caste. G. S. Ghurye, a faculty member there, in his 1932
classic *Caste and Race in India*, had dismissed the relevance of Risley's
anthropometric elucidation of caste difference. G. R. Pradhan was his first
student and the first to be awarded a PhD in sociology in India. He published a book in 1938 titled *Untouchable Workers of Bombay City*.

Pradhan's thesis harkened back to the discourse of social reform and
the formation of a strong Hindu community at the turn of the century. The
historical context, though, had changed. In 1936, Dalit Mahars in Bombay
had passed a resolution for conversion from Hinduism to other religions to

escape the depredations of untouchability. Pradhan made an economic argument against it. He held that conversion to Christianity, Sikhism, or Islam will not "change the economic conditions of these people."[110] Instead, he believed that a reformed Hinduism would accommodate Dalits. Pradhan placed tremendous faith in the social reformers who would dilute the "caste spirit" and help assimilate Dalits into the Hindu society. The process of assimilation required the "concrete knowledge of life conditions."[111] Pradhan tasked himself with the work of providing this data and the "right solution," ostensibly to the question of assimilation. Housing and the built environment were important sites for collection of evidence and became the basis for his prescriptions for reforms. In fact, he contended that Dalit housing was the most important issue because of its effects on health and efficiency.[112] His evidence, which included photographs of these sites, provided a rationale for segregation and documented the work to be done by Dalits and reformers to further assimilation.[113] Pradhan was transfixed and repulsed by what he saw. He drew his readers' attention to the filth in the alleyway: the "rubbish" composed of a mixture of solid and liquid waste, "heaps of rotting garbage and pools of sewage."[114] The Dalit home, the site of reproduction, held further horrors for him. The overcrowding in these homes affected the health and morale of the people living there: "On account of insufficient space the natural sex function of the married couples takes place with the full consciousness of other inmates in the same room. It is not strange, therefore, that boys and girls of tender age exhibit sex tendencies earlier."[115] The psychosocial effects of cramped housing resulted in "young girls of the classes [being] easily attracted" to prostitution.[116] Pradhan neatly synchronized the built environment, caste, class, and the morality of people living there. This node of Dalit life needed amelioration and would lead to assimilation into the Hindu fold. Housing was the most tangible problem in the node because it was making Dalits "sick . . . tired, dull and cheerless."[117]

Pradhan's account of life in the tenements does not capture the rich texture of life there. For instance, his dull and cheerless people nonetheless fell in love. In 1943, a young Dalit woman named Yashoda Pandurang Jadhav from the BDD tenements in Naigaum eloped with a young Dalit man named Vaman Gopal Mudbadkar, much to the chagrin of a caste association, the Mahar Jati Panchayat Samiti. Yashoda's father, Pandurang Jadhav, had committed to her engagement to another man, Jayram Khaire. Three days before the engagement, Yashoda and Vaman eloped and married with the consent of Vaman's father, Gopal Mudbadkar. The caste association was displeased, because breaking a promise of engagement was against its rules. The angered association fined Yashoda, Vaman, and Gopal, whom they identified as the culprits in the case. They were asked to pay a fine of twenty-five, ten, and ten rupees, respectively, with Yashoda's fine the largest. The three refused to pay the fines and were ostracized by the association. Love, romance, and the drama of elopement and ostracism were obscured by Pradhan's optic of the cheerlessness and depredation of Dalit lives.[118] There are many other stories of political mobilization, reading, and playing or listening to music from the 1930s and 1940s that could illustrate the dissonance between Pradhan's social scientific inquiry and the rich texture of Dalit lives in the city.

Pradhan's policy recommendations, though, were in line with the dominant discourse of the time and were thus influential. In Pradhan's vision of social reform, the Bombay provincial government, the Bombay municipality, private individuals, and civic associations played important roles in addressing the housing problem. He recommended that the government and the municipality offer plots of land free to individuals and associations. They would then build housing colonies, with a cap on rent for Dalits. At the same time, they would ensure "modern methods of sewage disposal . . . adequate and suitable sanitary arrangements and water supplies" and train people in the use of these facilities.[119] In this way, the conditions that invited revulsion could be set right through the mechanism of private property and rent control, facilitating the assimilation of Dalits into the Hindu fold.

RENT CONTROL, PRIVATE PROPERTY, AND DALIT HOUSING

A government inquiry committee recommended the need to control rents in the city in 1939 and provided a rationale for imposing limits on the free-market law of supply and demand. It declared housing a public service and encouraged the construction of more tenements for the urban poor.[120] The Bombay Rents, Hotel, Lodging House Rates Control Act was passed in 1947. But rent control, imposed by the Bombay government since 1918, then lapsing in 1928, had many unintended consequences. Landlords blamed rent control for their failure to repair tenements, in effect producing more slums. Pradhan's other policy recommendations for cooperative housing societies and private property resonated with the Dalit movement. By the end of the 1930s, a cooperative housing society for Dalits of the Mahar caste had been built in Khar, now a suburb of Bombay. The idea of a housing society was mooted by stalwarts of the Dalit movement in the city, Sambhaji Gaikwad, Govindrao Adrekar, and C. N. Mohite.[121] They suggested Ambedkar ask the Bombay municipal commissioner to allot land for Dalit housing. The Koknasth Mahar Co-operative Housing Society was established, and by 1940 three houses had been built there. Thus suburbanization or the northward expansion of the city resonated with the Dalit movement.

B. R. Ambedkar believed that rent from property would finance the Dalit social movement in the city and other regions of India. In the late 1930s and early 1940s he petitioned the colonial government, the Indian elite, and the Dalits themselves for land grants and funds for the acquisition of property. In his view, small donations from Dalits would complement bigger grants from wealthy donors. In a letter to the viceroy and secretary of state of India, he laid out his vision for a Dalit social center. The center would consist of a hall to hold meetings, which could also be leased out for functions, a printing press to "vent grievances" of the Dalits, a library and reading room, and spaces for trade unions of Dalit workers.[122] The activities of the center would be funded by renting the hall and buildings constructed on the lands of the center. At the time of writing the letter, Ambedkar informed the viceroy that he had leased a plot of land in Dadar. The land measured 1,100 square yards, but he sought the government's help in acquiring an adjoining plot measuring 1,200 square yards. He proposed to create a trust for the management of the center. The Bombay Scheduled Caste Improvement Trust was inaugurated in July 1944 on a plot measuring approximately 2,300 square yards.[123]

While Ambedkar illustrated the importance of rent to finance the Dalit social movement, the movement itself demanded lower rents or rent-free Dalit housing in the city. G. M. Jadhav, known as Madke Buva, asked the Bombay government in his speech at the third conference of the All India Scheduled Castes Federation in 1945 for lower rents, separate housing, and higher wages for Dalits.[124] Interestingly, Madke Buva turned the association of Dalits with filthy housing on its head. He invoked it to illustrate the need for increased wages and low rents. He demanded that the Bombay government allot the BDD chawls in Worli, Shivdi, Naigaum, and DeLisle Road to Dalits because the tenements and huts in which they lived were extremely filthy (*atyanta galicha*).[125] He challenged, "If the Bombay government takes it to heart, they could effortlessly build separate and cheap housing for the untouchables."[126] Separate housing for Dalits in the 1940s—a demand we also saw in the 1920s—was a social and spatial arrangement that fascinated Ambedkar and was perhaps influenced by the idea of a national community that was circulating at the time.[127] Ambedkar, of course, did not demand a separate nation but instead articulated a notion of Dalit villages in which Dalit minorities from various villages could be aggregated to conjure majorities in a new village.[128] A majority in a separate Dalit village would negate the debilitating effects of marginalized lives in spaces dominated by caste Hindus. This utopian vision of social engineering required British governmental support, which was not forthcoming during the Second World War.

Instead the Dalit social movements petitioned the state, laid out demands, and agitated for concessions. Madke Buva demanded an increase in the minimum wage for Dalit municipal workers. Their wages, he said, should be increased from twenty-five to fifty rupees and then progressively augmented to seventy-five. He also demanded separate electorates for Dalits in the Bombay Municipal Corporation.[129] He believed that reintroducing separate electorates, an agreement with the British government that Dalits had surrendered after the Poona Pact of 1932, would help the Ambedkar-led Scheduled Castes Federation win seats in the corporation. In 1946, another important Dalit leader from the city, P. T. Borale, who represented municipal workers on the Government of India committee on labor, argued for rent-free housing for municipal workers, citing their "special nature of work" and the "great difficulties" they faced in housing in the city.[130]

DREAMWORLDS FOR THE URBAN POOR

We get clues about what this housing might look like from the visions of influential men. These men invoked the urban poor, not Dalits particularly. In their view, the congested lives of the urban poor would be transformed into a dreamworld of uncluttered living. In the famous Bombay Plan proposed by leading industrialists from Bombay, housing for the poor was an important consideration. In this plan, the house, imagined in abstraction and at a remove from the housing practices of the urban poor, was at the center of the imagined social life of postindependence India. According to the plan, such a house would measure at least five hundred square feet at the rate of "100 square feet of house per person" and enable the person to inhale "3,000 cubic feet of fresh air per hour." The Bombay Plan envisaged a massive rebuilding of existing houses according to the criteria listed above and estimated an expenditure of approximately

1,400 crores in this endeavor (1 crore = 10 million rupees). According to the plan, housing for the poor should meet "certain standards" of ventilation, lighting, waste disposal, and water supply, but some of these standards might be modified to suit local conditions.[131]

Like the Bombay Plan, which envisaged a house with "certain standards," the Housing Panel of the Greater Bombay Scheme published its report in 1946, on the cusp of India's independence. That panel identified the "over-crowded" one-room tenements as the "drawback from which the city suffers."[132] The other problem involved the squalid slums of Bombay.[133] The conditions in one-room tenements and slums, the report maintained, had a direct bearing on mortality, crime, and delinquency.[134] Therefore, better housing would "create happiness . . . and provide good medium and atmosphere of healthy growth for the rising generation."[135] The panel's solution for the slums was eradication; it recommended an "attack on the worst slums,"[136] compulsory acquisition of land, and provision of alternate housing for those dispossessed from localities such as Nagapada, Chakla, and Kamathipura.[137] Their imagined habitation for the urban poor was a tenement that had "two living rooms, kitchenette . . . a built in cupboard, a raised platform . . . pegs for hanging clothes and minimum of three electric lights."[138] Moreover, the house would have 250 square feet for four persons or sixty square feet per person, a toilet inside the house, a fair-sized verandah, a common washing place, and a roofed terrace for sleeping in the summer.[139] These utopic visions, not uncommon for a nation about to become independent, if fructified would have transformed the habitations of the urban poor into homes. As the eminent Bombay architect Claude Batley said, "Only one percent of houses in Bombay can be called homes." According to him, the "Brahmin clerks' houses in Old Parel village were . . . delightful little homes with their verandahs and balconies, their richly carved teakwood brackets, their over-hanging upper stories, and their roofs covered by the wonderfully effective and cool double country-tiles."[140] In his view, because slum dwellers did not feel affection for the places where they lived, their living quarters by definition could not be considered homes and therefore warranted demolition.

Like social reformers, social scientists, industrialists, and city administrators, the city's Communists had participated since the late 1930s in the discourse of "filthy conditions, unsanitary dwellings, perennial housing shortage and rack-renting."[141] They lamented the steep rise in rent for the dwellings of the urban poor since World War I and cited the housing conditions of toilers in the Soviet Union, which were better than any capitalist country.[142] The Russian Revolution had "swept away slums. . . . [T]heir place has been taken by well built and bright workers' districts, and in many cases the working class districts . . . are better than central districts."[143] The Communists in the city, following the Soviet example, wanted the Bombay government and the Municipal Corporation to ensure cheap housing for the working class. In 1947, the Communist-led All India Trade Union Congress requested that the Government of India set up a National Working Class Housing Board to establish standards and policies for suitable housing, prepare standard plans and general housing schemes, and ensure building materials, in sufficient quantity, at reasonable rates.

Thus Bombay's booming industrial and commercial economy in the late nineteenth and twentieth centuries necessitated the warehousing of the urban poor in tenements and slums. British colonial administrators as well as private landlords strengthened caste in the city by deploying it as a basis for housing the urban poor. Moreover, city administrators allotted land for cooperative housing societies by upholding caste as the vector for the formation of such societies. Upper-caste cooperative housing societies sprouted up in the first half of the twentieth century. The localities in which the urban poor, particularly Dalits, lived, as a result of the policies of the administrators, landlords, and rentiers appeared perceptibly filthy to city officials, as well as to social reformers and social scientists. In this way, housing and the built environment became the material referent for caste in the city. The emerging Dalit social movement worked within the paradigm of colonial administration, demanding more tenements for Dalits and land and credit for setting up cooperative housing societies. These demands were not very successful since most Dalits in the city continued to live in slums and tenements. By the 1930s, working-class movements that had initially focused on higher wages and not directly on housing demanded better housing for Indian workers, similar to the purported housing for Soviet workers under Communism.

2 MARXISM, LANGUAGE, AND SOCIAL HIERARCHY, 1920-1950

IN THE 1920S AND 1930S, BOLSHEVISM EXERCISED THE MINDS OF the British colonial government in India. The British branded it an aggressive ideology that sought to dominate Asia. Bolshevism, they believed, aspired to strike at the most vulnerable point of the British Empire: India. To arrest the rising tide of Bolshevism, the colonial state designed a surveillance apparatus that scrutinized the personal correspondence of Communist leaders, sought to prevent the publication and transmission of Marxist texts, and arrested trade union leaders in cities such as Bombay and Calcutta. After they landed in jail for being Communist, many read Marx, often for the first time, and became Marxists. The peculiar journey from Communism back to Marxism was not uncommon.[1] One of the foremost Indian Marxists, M. N. Roy, confessed that he wrote his book *India in Transition* having read nothing of Marx. The book, it must be mentioned, enabled his entry into the highest ranks of the third Communist International and was hailed by Lenin as the first Marxist interpretation of Indian history.[2]

Roy was not the only Indian Communist with limited or no engagement with Marxism in this period.[3] In Bombay city, Shripad Amrit Dange had a similar trajectory. Dange was a young radical nationalist who started engaging with socialism in 1920-21. He, along with a group of young student radicals from the city,[4] participated in the M. K. Gandhi-led Non-Cooperation Movement but over a period of time became disenchanted with it. He published a pamphlet in 1921 titled *Gandhi vs Lenin*, where he laid out his critique of Gandhi. In this text, he cited Karl Marx only once, to explain capitalism's treatment of labor and its reshaping of their lives and their workday.[5] In fact, the novelist Leo Tolstoy, the Italian nationalist

Giuseppe Mazzini, the Indian nationalist leader Lokmanya Bal Gangad-har Tilak, and the British philosopher Bertrand Russell were cited more often than Marx. One important reason for Dange's limited engagement with Marxism and Bolshevism was the paucity of this literature in Bombay. As Dange said, "There is not much literature . . . on the Russian Revolution and the Bolsheviks because our government takes great care to guard the gates of India against the entry of authentic literature on the subject. What has been allowed to enter is written by men, who hate the Bolsheviks and are of imperialistic tendencies. In such a situation it is difficult to write with confidence on the subject."[6] By his own admission, he read *The Communist Manifesto* after the publication of *Gandhi vs Lenin*, in the library of Ranchoddas Lotwala, a wealthy benefactor in Bombay city.[7] At this point in his life (1921), Dange was not convinced of the viability of Bolshevism or Gandhism in "practical life." In his view, Gandhism suffered from "unwarranted faith in the goodness of human nature," while Bolshevism "ignores human interests and sentiments."[8] He was enchanted instead with another political figure: Bal Gangadhar Tilak, the Indian nationalist from Bombay province whom he implicitly posits as a synthesis of Gandhi and Lenin. Tilak was the genius who spoke "boldly" and "vigorously" against "tyranny," who destroyed the pessimism of Indians "and made them hopeful about the future, in struggle, while serving humanity."[9]

Dange upheld the power of religion, a lineage he traces from Tilak to Gandhi, and preferred Gandhi's ideas of nonviolence and noncooperation, which he said were part of India's heritage, over violence, which he believed would attend the transformation to Communism. Communism, he said, "was fraught with coercion and violence."[10] Dange's views at this time contrasted with M. N. Roy. Roy had reservations about bourgeois democratic liberation movements in general and the leadership of the Indian National Congress, of which Gandhi was an important leader, in particular.[11] He had condemned the Gandhi-led "non-cooperation, Khilafat programme," the spinning wheel and all other activities of the movement in India."[12] Roy, nevertheless, claimed Dange as his local agent in India in a speech to the Fourth Congress of the Third International in 1922, even though Dange publicly repudiated Roy's views on the Indian national movement. The colonial state's intelligence agencies believed this disavowal to be a farce. They declared that Dange's critique of Roy was "superficial. Qui s'excuse, s'accuse." They also believed that Roy was overstating the case for an organized Communist presence in India.[13] As far as Dange was concerned, at that moment, Bolshevism, Communism, and Marxism seemed more foreign than intimate to him because they were not part of India's past. For the foreign—Marxism—to fulfill its promise, it needed to be translated, transmitted, and domesticated or vernacularized to help in the appraisal of India's past, present, and future.

Intellectuals and activists (mostly male) undertook the enterprise of transmitting, translating, and domesticating Marxism in Bombay's spaces and institutions. Marxism trickled into their world of anticolonial nationalism, industrial capitalism, and workers' politics. The social history of Marxism and socialism in the city evolved in the context of the cultural practices of Marxists and the urban poor. The idea of socialism that dribbled into Bombay at this time (early 1920s) was not the Marxian idea of a socialist state that would eventually wither away. Instead, the socialism in circulation at this time could be traced to the German Social Democrats, American socialists, and Russian social democrats, particularly the Mensheviks. The Soviet leader V. I. Lenin accused them of misreading Marx and accommodating the national bourgeoisie.[14] What were Bombay's socialists reading, thinking, and writing, alongside socialist texts? Caste was important in the process of translation and domestication, as was the engagement with Marxism of the Dalits and the urban poor, including the working class. Two translations are of concern here. First, the colonial states' translation of the cultural and political activities of Bombay's Communists with the help of Indian translators and spies provide an account of Marxists in the city. Second, translation implies the process of appropriating, reading (or not reading and misreading) Marxism and reshaping it to reflect Indian society. Indian Marxists read the literature that dribbled past the British censors as if it contained the essence of a universal critique of capital. It promised to illuminate the workings of Indian capitalism and imagine a revolutionary transformation of society that would alter the lives of the urban and rural poor. Revolution, Indian Marxists believed, would bring about an inversion in the relations of power. Indian revolution would herald the communal ownership of the means and instruments of production.[15] Therefore, Marxists translated the promise of revolution into vernacular languages such as Marathi (most important here), Gujarati, Bengali, Urdu, and Hindi, where a broader audience could decode and gain a Marxian sociohistorical understanding of India's past and present.

To translate some Marxian categories, such as oppression, Indian Marxists deployed caste terms like "Dalit" to emphasize the experience and embodiment of oppression. Similarly, to domesticate Marxism, Dange posited the existence of a commune in India's antiquity where there was no caste. But caste also posed a problem for Indian Marxists: Would a political revolution upend the social relationship in which caste was an important feature of social hierarchy in South Asia? Indian Marxists had to address this question. They hoped that capitalism would desiccate caste to such an extent that their work would be to aggregate workers, devoid of caste affinities, into a working class. But instead, capital in Bombay city attached itself to caste like a parasite, and instead of shriveling, caste was working and reproducing itself through caste. Not only did caste play an important role in the recruitment of labor, but caste differences were activated to sever political solidarities among workers. For instance, Dalit workers were hired as strikebreakers by the city's textile mills during the strike of 1929.[16] As a result, the city's Communists were faced with the caste question; alas, capitalism had not obliterated it. It created a wedge between their political theory and social practice. In political theory, Marxists invoked caste as an object of negation. Here, caste identity was seen as temporally out of sync with class solidarity. The theory laid great store on the capitalist transformation of social relationships and the resultant weakening of caste. As M. N. Roy said, "Caste was the basis of socioeconomic organized production" and exploitation. Therefore, with the introduction of modern industries and the production of mechanized commodities, caste was no longer a "living social factor," and only its economic essence remained relevant.[17] Its economic quintessence could be encapsulated within class. Therefore, caste was class. Similarly, the influential British Communist R. Palme Dutt said, "The crippling institution of caste will only be overcome . . . by the advance of modern industry and political democracy, as new social ties and common interest replace the old bonds."[18] On the contrary, the injection of modernity had ensured that caste adapted itself to industrialization and the everyday practices of workers and unions. For instance, in the 1920s, Dalit workers had to drink water from separate pitchers in the textile mills. Moreover, they were not hired in the weaving department of mills because weaving necessitated the use of saliva to join broken threads, and the spittle of an "untouchable" was deemed polluting.[19] The Communist union did not address this practice initially and only did so reluctantly.[20] The folding of caste within class also faced another hurdle: the colonial state in the 1920s and 1930s continued to recognize caste as an important administrative and political category. For instance, Dalits demanded political representation and housing on the basis of caste.[21] This created a paradox: modern industry and political democracy, which in Dutt's formulation would eliminate caste, instead strengthened it.

Socialists and Marxists invoked caste in translating and transmitting political texts and mobilizing workers for the Indian revolution. In the first instance, the structure of language defeated them: the translation of Marxism from English to Marathi necessitated the use of terms denoting caste. "Dalit," for instance, was used for the oppressed proto-middle class of feudal Europe in the Marathi translation of *The Communist Manifesto*. Another important practice of translation was the politics of rendering abstract and embodied categories of Marxism. Thus abstract categories such as "use value" (*upyukta vastu*), "exchange value" (*vikriya mola*), or "mode of production" (*utpadanpaddhati*) were translated in Sanskrit (the "language of the Gods," to borrow Pollock's evocative phrase) or Sanskritized Marathi, but embodied categories such as "lumpen proletariat" (*mavali*) were translated into a lower-register, urban slang in this case. Other embodied categories, such as "worker" (*kamgara/kamkari*) and "capitalists" (*bhandvaldara*), do not have Sanskrit roots. The linguistic hierarchy in translating abstract and embodied categories suggests that Indian Marxists were enmeshed in social hierarchies that their political theory aspired to transform. Practice staggered behind theory. Here, caste informed the categories of translation. Moreover, the political and social revolution struggled to address caste. Bombay's Marxists regarded the anti-Brahmin and Dalit movements of the time as assertions of caste identity by an emerging middle class within these groups and rebuked them. For their part, Dalit and anti-Brahmin leaders demurred in their support of Indian Marxists based on the inability of their theory and practice to account for the vitality of caste in everyday life. An anonymous article in the weekly *Samata* (Equality), started by B. R. Ambedkar, noted, "Communism could uproot the mammoth tree of Tsarism in Russia, but Brahminism will survive its onslaught. The tree of Brahminism will remain with its roots intact [in India]." The article further chided Indian Communists for their disembodied conceptual apparatus: "They have little knowledge of the strength of Brahminism. Their heads are in Russia while their bodies live in India."[22]

The people from Bombay city in this chapter include Communist intellectuals like Shripad A. Dange and Dr. Gangadhar Adhikari.[23] Adhikari earned his doctorate in chemistry from Friedrich Wilhelm University (now Humboldt University) and was a member of the Communist Party of Germany before he returned to India in 1928 and became an influential

Communist leader.[24] Dange, after his early reservations about Bolshevism, established himself as a Communist leader and ideologue in the 1920s, for which he was jailed in 1924. I also discuss leaders such as Arjun Alwe, G. R. Kasle, and R. B. More, who—apart from being Communists—were involved in other important social movements of the time, particularly the movement against upper castes and the anti-Brahmin movement in the city, in the case of Alwe and Kasle, and the Ambedkar-led Dalit movement in the case of R. B. More.

THE COMMUNIST UNIVERSE AND ITS READING LIST

Communist literature trickled into the city. We get a sense of the reading lists of Communists from the colonial government's list of what they deemed "Bolshevik" literature seized in Bombay. The government's surveillance apparatus kept a watch on the mail of seventeen people, at various post offices in the city, and "held-up . . . considerable number of packets containing communist literature" from foreign countries.[25] In 1922, much of the literature intercepted by the Criminal Investigation Department (CID) was from post offices in the city: the General Post Office of Bombay, the Sea Post Office at Ballard Pier, and the Kalbadevi, Mandvi, and Umerkhadi suboffices. The CID was particularly attentive to mail from Germany and reported that "envelopes with names of commercial firms in Germany" were used to transmit Communist literature.[26] In addition to post offices, vessels arriving at the Bombay port were searched by custom officials with the intention of "preventing the importation of Communist arms, ammunition and literature into India." They also surveilled passengers and goods entering the city from the Portuguese colonial ports of Goa and Daman near Bombay city.[27]

The literature seized by the CID in 1922 included writings by and from Socialist intellectuals and organizations in Germany, the United States, and Britain, but not much from the Soviet Union. For instance, the list of seized Bolshevik literature includes many writings of M. N. Roy, who was in Germany at this time. These included copies of his *India in Transition, India's Problem and Its Solution, What Do We Want, Roy's Programme for the Indian National Congress*, and copies of the newspaper *Vanguard* edited by him. "Roy" was clearly an important keyword for searching and seizing Bolshevik literature. The list also included many pamphlets and speeches by the American Socialist Daniel De Leon (1852–1914). These included De Leon's 1896 speech delivered in Boston, "Reform or Revolution," a lecture delivered in Newark, New Jersey, in 1904 titled "The Burning Question of Trade Unionism," and pamphlets like *Socialism vs Anarchism, Women's Suffrage, Principles of Industrial Unionism, Who Pays the Taxes*, and his translation from the German of Karl Kautsky's *The Capitalist Class* and *The Working Class*. The confiscated literature also included the British Communist J. T. Walton Newbold's *Marx and Modern Capitalism*, Jack Nichol's *Revolutions and the Intelligentsia*, T. J. Holmes's *Socialism: Aim, Methods, and Tactics as Applied to Twentieth Century*,[28] and Friedrich Engels's *Historical Materialism* and *The Development of Socialism from Utopia to Science*. The last pamphlet was probably a version of Engels's *Socialism, Utopian and Scientific*. Many of these pamphlets aspired to introduce readers to the ideas and practices of socialism that were in circulation in western Europe and America in the first two decades of the twentieth century. The list did not include any writings of Karl Marx. In fact, the Russian Revolution of 1917 and its effects on Marxian textual scholarship are barely visible in the list of Bolshevik literature confiscated by the colonial intelligence department in 1922.[29]

Despite the comprehensive apparatus for arresting Bolshevism in the post offices and ports of Bombay, Marxist literature seeped into the city. One node of transmission was a Bombay businessman: the merchant and landlord Ranchhoddas Lotwala. Lotwala was also the managing director of Hindustan Ltd., which published a daily, *Hindustan*. He was attracted to Dange's ideas after the publication of *Gandhi vs Lenin* and founded the Ranchhoddas Lotwala Trust for the propagation of socialism in India.[30] According to Dange, leftist radicalism would have been delayed in India by two decades but for Lotwala.[31] Lotwala set aside profits from the rent of a four-story building in the Girgaum Road area of the city for this purpose. Thus rent from private property funded the initial propagation of socialism in the city.[32] Lotwala had started collecting literature on Marxism and Leninism on his trips to Europe. Dange read *The Communist Manifesto* for the first time in his library.[33] On a trip to England, Lotwala interacted with labor leaders in England and acquired Marxist literature, which he brought to India, publishing some of it through his Hindustan Press.[34] *The Communist Manifesto* was published for the first time in India by his press in 1922. The other pamphlets published by the press included Friedrich Engels's *Wage, Labour and Capital*, a pamphlet published by the British Socialist Party, Lucien Deslinières's *The Coming of Socialism*, Paul Lafargue's *The Religion of Capital*, Rajani Palme Dutt's *Communism*, and Karl Kautsky's *The Working Class*.[35] Lotwala also bought the Marathi-language daily *Indu Prakash*,[36] which Dange had joined as a journalist in 1921. Dange oversaw the publication of a series of articles on Lenin by Vaman Sathe between November 1921 and March 1922. By August 1922, Dange had left *Indu Prakash* and started an English-language weekly, *The Socialist*. The issues of *The Socialist* advertised the pamphlets published by Lotwala's press, and its editorial office in the Thakurdwar locality of Bombay was advertised as the place to purchase the pamphlets.[37] The weekly not only provided a venue for the propagation of socialism but also cultivated a circle of socialist revolutionaries such as S. V. Ghate, S. V. Deshpande, S. S. Mirajkar, and V. H Joshi, who became founding members of the Communist Party of India a few years later in 1925.

The early Communist universe in Bombay was sustained not just by the generosity of a Bombay merchant (Lotwala) and the city's Communists; it also included people like Babu Karim, a lascar on the ship SS *Tarantia*. Karim had minimal education, having studied only until the fourth grade in Urdu and Marathi. He had arrived in the city as an eleven-year-old in search of employment in 1912 or 1913. He worked as a hotel boy in several hotels until 1920, when he joined Anchor Line, a Scottish shipping company, as a coal man and started his life as a seaman. His work as a seaman compelled him to acquire functional knowledge of English, and he began to speak and eventually read it. Karim became a Communist in the United Kingdom. He attended several labor meetings on his visits there and became a regular reader of the Communist newspaper *Daily Worker*. He visited workers' book stalls in Glasgow, Liverpool, and Manchester, collecting Communist literature, which he brought to India to distribute to his friends. When Karim was eventually arrested in Bombay in October 1934, the custom authorities recovered "communist literature" from him, and "more literature belonging to him was found in the possession of another lascar working on the same boat."[38] Upon his arrest, he stated that he had "no sufficient knowledge of English. I can read a little but I cannot understand the meaning properly."[39] To decode the message of socialism, Babu Karim relied upon his "educated friends" in Bombay.

The transmission of socialism was the goal of early Communists in the city. The ambition was to familiarize readers with its principles, goals, and visions. The socialist imaginary was transmitted to India in the English language; its early readership was thus limited to those with the ability to comprehend English. These readers of socialist messages, transmitted from Euro-America, appropriated them to shed light on the Indian social conditions of the time. In the early 1920s, English was a lingua franca of socialism because it created a channel of communication between its readerships in India, albeit limited, and socialists in Euro-America, including the Communist International. One particular embodiment of the transmission of messages across this channel was the People's Publicity Service, which was set up in March 1923 by Dange, K. N. Joglekar, and T. V. Parvate in Bombay to broadcast "authentic news about the life, doings and movements of emancipation of the Indian people"[40] to newspapers outside India and provide news from foreign countries to the Indian press. Dange and Joglekar also formed the publishing house Labour Press in June 1923. These endeavors were short lived, but they bolstered Bombay's role as the crucial node in the channel for transmitting the dreams of a future socialist state where "no parasite" would fatten on the fruits of their labor.[41] The translation of these messages into the regional vernacular, Marathi in the case of Bombay's Communists, ensued a little later.

The messages were decoded by Bombay's Communists in the context of the M. K. Gandhi–led noncooperation movement. His discourse of *swaraj* (self-rule) and practice of *satyagraha* (resolute embrace of truth) dominated Indian politics. Bombay's Communists made global socialism meaningful to themselves and other readers in this context. In this scenario, the "parasites" "fattened" on the labor of peasants and workers were the colonial state and the Indian elite. In the words of S. A. Dange, "The cause of our misery lies in two things: the foreign domination and the indigenous vulture, the class that preys upon the wealth of the nation and the bread of the toiler. We shall have neither of them."[42] To be meaningful, socialism had to capture the relationships of power in Indian society. But more importantly, it had to convey the message to those who would overturn these relationships of power, the "real people," some of whom Gandhi had mobilized, but many of whom were still "apathetic" to *swaraj*. The "real people of India shall own the land, capital, and instruments of production. Then alone will the people fight for *swaraj* and win it, quite a different sort of *swaraj* from the bourgeois Raj."[43] The "real people" comprised "the peasants, the workers, the untouchables" and all those struggling to cobble together two meals a day and a bare existence. The early Bombay socialists aimed to organize an All India Socialist Party under the umbrella of the Congress Party, remain a minority within the party, and transform it as a vehicle for class politics. "We must be untiring and persisting in this until we finally succeed in swamping the Congress."[44]

THE BHAGAVAD GITA AND MARXISM

Socialists had to grapple with caste. The process of engaging with caste itself would ensure the domestication of "foreign" ideology. Once that process was inaugurated, Marx and the Bhagavad Gita, a Hindu religious text, were in concert in their philosophy of history. Dange attempted this ambitious task in the third issue of *The Socialist*, where history and mythology combined to evoke an age when people did not know want or misery and where "everyone was happy and even death dared not enter the precincts of man's kingdom at an ungracious time!"[45] He located this age in India's antiquity, during the Aryan age of India's past. He posited a commune at this time, in which "people could produce what they wanted without being slaves to another. . . . Everyone worked for all and all worked for everyone, acknowledging no master but the wisdom and love of each other. They had no *State* and no *Government*."[46] In Dange's view, the paradisiacal Aryan commune experienced turbulence after it grew in size and migrations brought it in contact with other groups. The contact with others and the ensuing competition forced the commune to arrive at a mutually agreed division of labor to "preserve the commune in unadulterated form."[47] In this way, two classes were born: those who did productive work for the commune—peasants, traders, and artisans—and another class composed of "defenders of faith and country." Over a period of time, the arrangement became permanently embedded and produced a mental attitude in which division of work was justified as natural. The unproductive classes— the defenders of faith and country—felt superior to the artisans and peasants and wanted to make the division of work in the commune permanent. In order to cultivate an attitude of superiority among the unproductive classes and by extension foster a sense of inferiority among other groups, they invoked God and religion, and castes were born. According to Dange, in "the days when the Commune decreed castes to be unchangeable . . . the Paradise of the Commune was lost."[48] For Dange, castes came into existence to satisfy the economic needs of a society (the Aryan commune) whose rulers thought it was the best arrangement at the time.[49] He attributed his self-confessed economic determinism to Marx. He referred to Marx, but in actuality he was quoting Friedrich Engels from the 1888 preface to the English edition of *The Communist Manifesto*. "In every historical epoch the prevailing mode of economic production and exchange and the social organization necessarily flowing from it form the basis upon which it is built up, and from which alone can be explained the political and intellectual history of that epoch."[50] He equated Marxist economic determinism with the teachings of the Bhagavad Gita. He said:

> The Geeta itself lends indirectly its support to the Marxian explanation of history, to the theory of economic determinism; when the Geeta records the Testimony of the Lord Krishna that He had created the four divisions on the basis of *guna* and *karma* he means nothing else than this that the divisions were an economic necessity of production distribution and so on, that the castes had come into existence neither from sin or merit, neither from Moksha nor Hell but simply to satisfy the economic needs of society in a form, which the rulers of society thought best at the time.[51]

Based on the concurrence of Marx and the Bhagavad Gita on the validity of economic determinism and the existence of an idyllic commune in Indian antiquity, Dange domesticated socialism almost concurrently with the attempt to propagate it in India. Dange's utopian rendition of the Aryan past had already come under attack by lower-caste movements in the late nineteenth century. These movements had developed a counternarrative on the Aryan invasion and subsequent usurpations of their land.[52] Dange had paid no heed to them.

DOMESTICATION AND VERNACULAR ENTANGLEMENTS

By 1924, the Bombay Communists were discussing the importance of starting vernacular newspapers, the need to make these publications self-sufficient, and the possibility of reducing the influence of the English-language press.[53] The decision to move beyond English entangled socialism in the longer history of tension between Sanskrit and Marathi. The vernacularization of socialism entwined it with the history of another vernacularization, in which Marathi had displaced Sanskrit as the dominant language of elites in the region. Historically, the corpus of writings in Sanskrit was circumscribed to "ritual, philosophy, theology, and poetry,"[54] and its use was restricted primarily to a ritual community, the Brahmins. With the start of the common era, however, Sanskrit became a cosmopolitan language, its use extending beyond rituals to a "new sociology" and a political language of selfhood.[55] Even as it became cosmopolitan, it was never quotidian; its use was limited to elites in various regions of South, Southeast, and Central Asia. A vernacular literature emerged, or rather was crafted by regional elites in different parts of India toward the end of the first millennium and the beginning of the second millennium CE, as a vehicle for self-expression.[56] The Marathi vernacular found its most famous literary expression in the thirteenth-century text Dnyaneshwari (attributed to a saint named Dnyaneshwar). Marathi incorporated many Sanskrit words into the language.[57]

In this entwinement of English, socialism, Sanskrit, Hindu mythology, and Marathi, the role of Marxist translators became important. The entanglement condensed multiple temporalities and spatial scales into the history of Marathi Marxism. For instance, spatially, transnational socialism had to address Indian nationalism and caste. The translators domesticating Marxism aimed to mobilize Bombay's industrial workers for an Indian revolution. Thus the global world of Communism was telescoped into the local world of Bombay Communists. An important expression of this contraction of the spatial scale was the political party Dange and his associates called the Indian Communist Party, Bombay, even before the formation of the Communist Party of India in 1925 or the Workers' and Peasants' Party of Bombay in 1927.[58] The translators took it upon themselves to localize the cosmos of socialism. They appropriated and adapted it into Marathi via the mediation of Sanskrit. These entanglements had a bearing on the practices of translating socialism into Marathi.

Translation assumed bilingualism and the ability of the translators to subordinate the structure of one language to the other.[59] In the case of western India and the Marathi language in particular, the production of bilingual intellectuals proficient in English and Marathi dated back to the early nineteenth century and bore the imprint of the colonial education policy designed to create a class of collaborators in India. An effect of this policy was that bilingual intellectuals entertained hegemonic aspirations over other Marathi readers who could not speak or read English in the public sphere.[60] Most, though not all, of these intellectuals were men from the upper castes. A crucial feature of the Marathi-speaking public sphere was a virulent discourse against the lower castes in the late nineteenth and early twentieth centuries. An important reason for the harshness of the discourse was to counter a scathing critique of the hegemony of upper-caste intellectuals by lower-caste radicals.[61] One of the defining texts of this anti-lower-caste discourse was Vishnushastri Chiplunkar's rebuke of Jyotirao Phule, an icon of the lower-caste movement in the region. Lower-caste polemicists too countered these assertions in the public sphere. Chiplunkar was particularly critical of Phule's willingness to negotiate with British colonial administrators and his enthusiastic views on the education offered in missionary schools. Nationalism became the rhetorical weapon for challenging low-caste assertions of identity. Communist intellectuals waded into this imbroglio, mimicking the anti-lower-caste rhetoric in tone and content. Thus, for instance, Dange, in an editorial in *The Socialist* titled "The Brahmin and Non-Brahmin War," invoked the imagery of Brahmins under siege and maintained that "a regular fascist terror has been executed on isolated individual Brahmins." He accused the leaders of the non-Brahmin party of being "unpatriotic and narrow-visioned" because of their support for British colonialism and their unwillingness "to accept the comradeship of class."[62] He blamed caste politics in general and anti-Brahmin politics in particular for stymying a politics that would overcome the particularity of caste and embrace the universality of class. The translation of socialism into Marathi became entangled with the particularities of this history: socialism encountered caste and in the voice of the socialist upbraided non-Brahmins for letting loose a reign of terror on Brahmins. One reason for the censure of the non-Brahmin movement was its positing of an alternate universalism, in which all the oppressed castes (not class) who were imbued with a low social status by the Brahmins allied to form a community of the oppressed. Phule had called it a *shudra-ati-shudra* alliance.[63] These tensions also percolated in the translation of Marxist pamphlets.

THE WORKING-CLASS PUBLIC SPHERE

During World War I and for a few years afterward, Bombay's economy had boomed, bringing "unprecedented" profits to the mill owners.[64] In this period, the workers had mobilized to demand higher wages and discovered the benefits of industrywide strikes, as opposed to strikes in one mill or one department. By the mid-1920s, however, the markets slumped, and mill owners introduced "rationalization schemes" and cut wages. The workers mobilized to defend their earlier gains. This was the context for the translation of Communist texts into Marathi: to introduce and popularize socialism among workers and create the conditions for "stable" trade unions in the city. The leaders supported the translation of Communist literature into Marathi. One votary of translation was Shapurji Saklatvala. He hoped that the British Communist Rajni Palme Dutt's *Modern India*, published in Bombay by Sunshine Publishing House in 1926, would be translated into Marathi and other important vernacular languages.[65] He hailed the book as the "forerunner of new political literature on British imperialism and on the genuine economic and social rights to freedom of India's peasants and workers."[66]

Saklatvala's propagation of the rights of workers and peasants paralleled the emergence of workers' and peasants' parties in various parts of India after 1926. These parties were not an avatar of the Community Party of India, nor were they front organizations, which were more palatable to colonial authorities. They were in fact the institutional expression of a united front of "the working class, peasants, and the petty bourgeois."[67] The Workers' and Peasants' Party (WPP) of Bombay was formed in February 1927 and included many left-wing radicals and Communists.[68] They, much like the All India Socialist Party, aspired to work inside the Congress Party as its left wing and aimed to "establish swaraj [complete national independence] wherein the means of production, distribution, and exchange are publicly owned and socially controlled."[69] The WPP founded the Marathi weekly *Kranti* (Revolution) for the city's working class. The weekly translated and published reviews of *Modern India. Kranti* suspended publication in 1927, after a few editions, but resumed publishing during the 1928–29 mill strikes. It became the main source of printed news for workers, providing them with news on the strikes in various mills, the mood of the workers, and the decisions of strike committees.[70] It reminded workers that their agitation was for "getting workmen on the ladder of happiness. The workmen cannot be happy unless and until capitalism is killed . . . but every workman understands that capitalism cannot go away by murder . . . and therefore a workman is never out for a murder."[71] By the second half of 1920s, then, the translation of socialism into the Marathi vernacular had begun, and *Kranti* had familiarized workers with the discourse of anticapitalism and class struggle.

Workers' strikes, the printing press, unionization, and the propagation of socialism in the 1920s created a working-class public sphere in the city. The workers comprised laborers in Bombay's textile industry and docks, as well as sanitation and railway workers. Apart from organizing themselves in various trade unions, they were also part of neighborhood associations. The workers had various terms and tenures of employment—some had regular employment, while others found irregular work, often recruited daily at the gates of a factory. Not all workers had similar experiences in the labor market, and they were not socially homogenous. For instance, there was a class hierarchy based on the different modes of employment. The segmentation of workers by class intersected with caste, religious, and gender differences. In fact, these differences were the basis of recruitment into the labor market, and as Rajnarayan Chandavarkar has pointed out, industrialization further intensified the sectionalism of the workforce.[72] The workers overcame differences such as caste at historical moments like industrial action or strikes, but when the moment passed the differences resurfaced.

The neighborhood was an important site for the propagation of socialism. By 1927, the Communists, working through the Workers' and Peasants' Party, had made inroads into some existing unions in the city, including the Girni Kamgar Mahamandal (Grand Organization of Textile Workers).[73] Through the unions, they established relationships with mill workers, communicated their vision of socialism, and popularized class analysis. The Communist foray into unionization drew strength from the rationalization schemes introduced by mill owners in 1927 and 1928. For instance, in August 1927, the Sassoon group of mills asked its weavers to manage three looms instead of two for a 20 percent wage rise. The weavers walked out in protest, fearing impending job redundancies.[74] Communist leaders such as K. N. Joglekar started attending and addressing workers' meetings. Over the next few months similar schemes were introduced in more mills (and other departments of the mills, such as the spinning and winding departments) and workers went on strike. By April 1928, there were disputes over wages and rationalization schemes in fifty-two mills, and a joint strike committee of eighty-five members, including many Communists, was set up to coordinate the activity of strikers.[75] In May 1928, Communists on the strike committee formed their own union—the Girni Kamgar Union (GKU; Textile Workers Union).

Communists such as Dange, R. S. Nimbkar, and Mirajkar mobilized workers in working-class neighborhoods. They rallied workers in the city's public spaces, streets, and economic and cultural institutions. The media played an important role in shaping and articulating workers' experiences. In these spaces, Communists propagated their ideas orally as well as in print. Intelligence officials and spies assiduously recorded the oral dissemination of socialism and justified the incarceration of Communists, who devised strategies and assumed aliases to escape surveillance. These were the spaces of the soaring rhetoric of Communist leaders, particularly during strikes, where war metaphors were used to describe the confrontation between workers and Communism on the one hand and capitalism and the colonial state on the other. The rhetoric of revolution envisaged the overturning of the political order—the defeat of capitalism and the colonial state. The translation of Marxism became meaningful in this context.

It was in the public sphere that Communist intellectuals and workers became "we," entwined in the common objective of a workers' revolution that some of them held would necessitate armed violence. Leaders from the Communist universe came to Bombay with messages of socialism, narrated here in the form of stories,[76] and exhorted Bombay's workers to form trade unions. For instance, Benjamin Francis Bradley, an engineer who was a member of the Communist Party of Great Britain, arrived in the city in September 1927, as an agent of the Crab Patent Underdrain Tile Company, with two hundred British pounds for Indian Communists.[77] He addressed the city's workers at public meetings and exhorted them to unionize and celebrate May Day. At the Tramway Men's Union meeting on April 2, 1928, he spoke of the benefits of joining the union and lauded trade unionism as the only weapon to fight capitalism. At the GIP Railway Workmen's Union he advocated the principle of one union for one industry and upbraided leaders of Indian unions for their ignorance of the principles of trade unionism. "They were always keen on applications, petitions and round table conferences, but the lot of labourers could not be improved by such methods, because the capitalists were very well organized and could always benefit at the cost of disorganized workers."[78] He conveyed similar messages to the Bombay municipal workers and the Bombay Dockworkers Union, Mazgaon Branch, in May 1928. During these meetings Bradley narrated stories of labor, its unionization, and its strikes in Great Britain. The experiences of foreign workers were made comprehensible to Bombay's workers through the medium of and the telecommunicative powers of socialism and translation. According to Bradley, unionization would force capitalists to address workers' grievances, such as low wages, and if they went unheeded he recommended strikes. He was appointed treasurer of the Joint Strike Committee during the general strike in the textile mills in 1928. During the strike, he addressed workers in their neighborhoods. At a meeting in Nagu Sayaji Wadi in May 1928, he pointed out that the existing leadership of the national movement demanded self-rule (*swaraj*) but did not address workers' grievances. He also donated forty pounds to revive *Kranti*, which had been dormant for a few months.

Translation played a crucial role in Bradley's interactions with workers. His speeches were delivered in English and translated into a local language by an Indian Communist. For instance, on August 2, 1928, he addressed the striking mill workers in an open area opposite Dinshaw Petit mills in the Kalachowki locality. He spoke in English and called mill owners and the colonial government devils (*saitan*). K. N. Joglekar translated his speech into Marathi. In September 1928, he addressed two meetings at the Delisle Road Cement Chawls and encouraged workers to inculcate a spirit of revolt against capitalism among their children. He also informed them about a plot for revolution in England and spurred the city's workers to "make all necessary preparation to keep the capitalist under your thumb."[79] In the public sphere stories of the dramatic inversion of the power relations between capitalist and workers, brought about by workers themselves, found sustenance and traction. These stories of revolution helped Bombay's workers imagine new ways of being in the world and at the same time captured their experiences of hunger, poverty, and exploitation. Bradley was arrested for conspiracy to commit treason against the colonial state and dispatched to Meerut to stand trial in 1929.

To be meaningful, the stories of revolutions in distant lands needed to address the particularities of Bombay workers. When another Communist, S. H. Jhabwala, addressed mill workers at Nagu Sayaji Wadi in 1928, he translated the promise of revolution: "We want Soviet Government like Russia. The income of the Russian worker increased six-fold. Instead of one room, they now get four rooms to live. In American the workers go in motor cars and work only for six hours. In India they ask us to work for 10 hours. Less work makes men wise. We have not made any progress because we work hard. If we have a labour government the hours of work will be less and each and every man will get sufficient food to eat."[80] The veracity of the story of Russian workers living in four-room homes is beside the point. The important point was that a revolution and a government along the lines of a Soviet government would address the problems of poor housing, long workdays, lack of food, and low wages. To achieve this, the workers needed to join trade unions and go on strike. Some insisted, as Joglekar did, that workers go to their villages and encourage agricultural workers to join the strike. The movement of workers from the city to the villages had the additional benefit of sustaining them on their rural holdings at a time when no wages were forthcoming owing to the strike.

The Communist leaders decoded the revolution for their public. For a laborer listening to the soaring rhetoric of their leaders, revolution may have meant many things. It entailed unionizing, striking, challenging the strikebreakers, confronting the police boldly (as Dange stated) and fighting back if they were beaten by the police, throwing shoes at a judge (as Kasle did), or exhorting workers to slap journalists and newspaper vendors for their critical coverage of the strike (R. S. Nimbkar advised them to assault the staff of *Times of India*.[81] These practices were based on the belief that they were morally upright while their opponents—capitalists and the colonial state—were morally compromised since they were the "devil." In these speeches, language, particularly vernacular language, became a weapon with which to publicly abuse authorities with names such as "ass," "fat ass" (*lath gadhav*), "fool" or "corrupt" (*haramkhor*), "knave," and *dacoits*.[82] Revolution meant confrontation with and reversal of authority, either through a secret plot hatched by workers (like Bradley said of workers in England) or other extraconstitutional means. The inversion of authority entailed not just an imposition of power over capitalists but also disciplining potential strikebreakers: the *mavali*, as the Marathi *Communist Manifesto* would call them, and Hindustani-speaking North Indian migrant workers identified as *bhaiyyas*.[83]

Revolution necessitated clear boundaries between the revolutionaries and their class enemies. Those demarcations sometimes overlapped with ethnic and caste boundaries like the North Indian *bhaiyya* or the Marwari capitalist. In this revolution, women had a supporting role. As S. S. Mirajkar noted, women should picket textile mills armed with brooms and help in beating *bhaiyyas* and *mavalis* for breaking picket lines.[84] By contrast, Arjun Alwe addressed a meeting near Morarji Goculdas in September 1928, thanking women for attending in large numbers but warning them against participating in scuffles with mill managers or strikebreakers. He added, "It is not a happy thing that women should take part in any struggle so long as men are alive in Maharashtra and in India. The males only should surround the mill and keep a close watch on the persons coming out of it."[85] The meanings of revolution and the making of a socialist state were thus paved with a jagged path of meanings, significations, and social hierarchies. Despite the rhetoric of revolution and violence, the strike itself was largely nonviolent.[86] It ended in October 1928 with the workers getting some concessions from the mill owners.

INCARCERATION AND TRANSLATION

In March 1929, thirteen Communist leaders from the city (of thirty-one across India) were arrested and charged under Section 121-A of the Indian Penal Code for conspiracy to commit treason against the colonial state. They were incarcerated in the North Indian town of Meerut from March 1929 to 1933. Jail was a fecund site for turning self-identified Communists and socialists into Marxists. Some of the work of translating

Marxism was accomplished in Meerut jail, where the Communists closely engaged with Marx and Engels. One of the incarcerated, the Bombay labor leader S. V. Ghate, called it the "University of Marxism-Leninism."[87] It was relatively difficult to obtain Marxist literature in Bombay city because of the surveillance apparatus of the state, but in prison inmates were granted access to Marxist texts after they contended that these texts were crucial to their defense. *The Communist Manifesto* was translated here. Internment in Meerut did not make the city's Communists irrelevant to Bombay's public sphere. The prisoners used their trial as theater to propagate their ideas. S. A. Dange was expelled from the Communist Party of India while in jail for participating in "factional activities" in Bombay city.[88] The imprisonment of its foremost leaders brought about a change in the Communist leadership in Bombay. B. T. Ranadive, S. V. Deshpande, and Suhasini Nambiar took control of the activities of the Textile Workers' Union, which had been at the forefront of the 1928 strike, and in April 1929 called for another strike, which lasted until October. By January 1929, the union officially boasted 54,000 members, with over 100,000 members unofficially, but by 1930 the membership had declined to 800.[89] It was riven by factional disputes. Deshpande and Ranadive led one faction each, and another was affiliated with Roy, who had returned to India after his expulsion from the Comintern in September 1929 and was arrested in Bombay in 1931.[90] These factions left a mark on the city's public sphere too: Deshpande's faction started the Kamgar Vangmay Prasarak Mandal (Society for the Propagation of Literature of the Working Class)[91] and Ranadive's group started the Marksist Vangmay Pracharak Mandal (Society for the Transmission of Marxist Literature).[92] Roy's group inaugurated Shramjivi Sahitya Mala (Workers' Literature Series) and counted S. A. Dange's wife, Usha Dange, as one of its members. When the Communist International tried to intervene in these factional struggles through two American emissaries, each upheld a different faction.[93] As a result, the Comintern could not settle factional disputes in the city.

The Communist intellectuals who translated pamphlets were not just bilingual but multilingual. S. A. Dange, along with Gangadhar Adhikari and his brother Jagannath Adhikari, R. M. Jambhekar, S. G. Sardesai, and others were important to the process of translation and publication. Between them, these intellectuals were proficient not just in English and Marathi but also in Hindi, German, and Sanskrit. Dange, the Adhikari brothers, Sardesai, and many other Communists had studied in Bombay colleges. Gangadhar Adhikari had studied Sanskrit and German even

before leaving for Germany in 1922. *The Communist Manifesto* was translated by Gangadhar Adhikari in Meerut; the manuscript was edited by his
brother Jagannath Adhikari and R. M. Jambhekar, and published in October 1931 by N. S. Desai.[94] The Kamgar Vangmay Prasarak Mandal published the *Manifesto* (Kamyunista jahirnama) in 1931 and the Marksist
Vangmay Pracharak Mandal published *Wage Labour and Capital* in 1932.
Kamgar Vangmay also published two other pamphlets: *Comrade Lenin*
(Kamred Lenin) in 1933 and Alexandr Lozovsky's *Trade Union Movement
in the Colonies* (Vasahatintila desansathi treda uniyana calavalica onama),
possibly in the same year. All these pamphlets were banned by the government, but some copies circulated illegally.[95]

The Bombay Communists approached the Marxist texts they encountered as canonical, and Marx was often considered an ascetic or saint
(*rishi*). They treated the limited Marxist texts available to them at this time
as a coherent body of authoritative scriptures. In their minds, there was
never any doubt about the universal applicability of Marxist insights.
Marxism had taught Communists that the working class and peasantry
would be decisive in any struggle for national liberation.[96] Moreover, they
had figured out that Marx could be extracted from the European context
and made legible in India through domestication and translation. But in
the process of translation, the local erupted into the transnational (and the
universal) and registered its presence in Marathi Marxism. Take, for
instance, the *Manifesto*'s passage about the spatial transformation wrought
by capital, particularly the changing relationship between the city and the
country: "The bourgeoisie has subjected the country to the rule of the
towns. It has created enormous cities, has greatly increased the urban population as compared with the rural, and has thus rescued a considerable
part of the population from the idiocy of rural life."[97] The translators
emphasized this point by citing census reports on the rise in India's urban
population between 1871 and 1921. The population of Indian cities, according to the translators, increased from 4,321,917 to 8,211,704 in this period.
To make the change meaningful, the Marathi *Manifesto* emphasized that
the rate of increase in the urban population was higher than the increase
in rural areas.[98] Or consider this passage from *The Communist Manifesto*
on the revolutionary and destructive power of the bourgeoisie:

> The bourgeoisie cannot exist without constantly revolutionizing the
> instruments of production, and thereby the relations of production, and
> with them the whole relations of society. . . . All fixed fast-frozen relations,

with their train of ancient and venerable prejudices and opinions, are
swept away, all new formed ones become antiquated before they can
ossify. All that is solid melts into air, all that is holy is profaned, and man
is at last compelled to face with sober senses his real condition of life, and
his relation with his kind.[99]

In translating and explicating this passage—"all fixed fast-frozen relations, with their train of ancient and venerable prejudices and opinions,
are swept away"—their frame of reference was religion and caste.[100] For
them, what could be more ossified than caste or more prejudicial than religion? Their disquiet with the frozen relationships of caste was that particular castes performed specific occupations and therefore hindered the
creation of free labor, new social relationships, and a new mode of production. Caste and religion were thus encumbering the transformation to a
new mode of production. Marx and Engels probably did not have caste on
their minds when they spoke about "ossified relationships and venerable
prejudices,"[101] but these relationships were urgent for their Marathi translators. The translators believed (and hoped) that capitalism would overcome caste and other antiquated social relationships. They were in awe of
its revolutionary possibilities. Instead, capitalism attached itself to caste.
In fact, the strengthening of caste identities of the lower castes in the 1920s
and 1930s and the colonial government's attentiveness to caste-based
political representation for the Dalit castes in 1931 and 1932 rankled the
Meerut prisoners. In their statement to the judge during their trial, they
called the Dalit movement "artificial and ultimately reactionary."[102]

In the translation, abstract categories were rendered in Sanskrit or Sanskritized Marathi. The use of Sanskrit gave these terms the precision of lit-
urgy and the accuracy of scientism (*shastrashuddha*). It also linked Bombay
to the global world of Marxism. For instance, in the translation of *Wage
Labor and Capital*, "use value" is translated as *upyukta vastu*, "exchange
value" as *vikriya mola*, "labor power" as *srama sakti*, "commodity" as *kryavastu*, "value" as *mulya*, and "surplus value" as *varkada mola*. Similarly, in
the Marathi translation of *The Communist Manifesto* "production" was
utpadana; "overproduction," *atyutpadana*. In the Marathi *Manifesto*, the
publishers provided a glossary to help readers decipher these terms. The use
of a classical language for abstract categories also lent the text an authoritative power that only the translators could decode for their readers. The use
of Sanskrit allowed them to rise above the humdrum of Bombay and speak
down to newer activists and workers with authority. Sanskritized Marathi

fulfilled these various needs of translation, linking the universal to the particular and at the same time maintaining the importance of the interpreter for decoding texts.

Not all aspects of the translation carried the burden of synchronizing the universal with the particular. The decision to publish these pamphlets was often related to mundane factors like availability of text and ease of translation. According to the publishers of *Wage Labour and Capital* (Mola-majuri va bhandval), translated by R. M. Jambhekar, it was translated into Marathi because it was easy (*sopa*) and contained the essence (*sara*) of Marx's arguments in the three volumes of *Capital*. According to S. G. Sardesai, a Bombay Communist who wrote the foreword to the translation but was not jailed in Meerut at this time, Marx's *Capital* was not only voluminous (2,530 pages) but also "quite difficult." Sardesai praised Marx for cramming the essence of *Capital* in the twenty-five to thirty pages of *Wage Labour and Capital*.[103] He celebrated Marx as a sage blessed with clairvoyance, applauding him for simplifying the "immense confusion" (*gondhala*) created by Adam Smith and David Ricardo on the concepts of value (*mulya*) and price (*kimmat*) and eulogizing him for his crucial contribution to economic thought: the concepts of labor (*srama*) and labor power (*srama sakti*).[104] According to Sardesai, Marx and Engels had solved a mammoth puzzle of political economy by proving that wage labor is a commodity (*kryavastu*) and demonstrating how workers' wages operate in a capitalist system.[105] According to Sardesai, Marx and Engels's discovery provided an effective intellectual weapon (*baudhika hatyara*) for the workers' movement.[106] Marx's rendering of the difference between *srama* (labor) and *srama sakti* (labor power), according to Sardesai, was influential in demonstrating that the production of wealth under capitalism was not just about use value (*upyukta vastu*) or exchange value (*vikriya mola*) but about the production of surplus value (*varkada mola*). In his foreword, Sardesai argued that Marx laid out the inner workings of capitalism in coherent and simple language that would be accessible to all workers.[107] He hoped that a heightened awareness of the insidious workings of capitalism would rapidly (*jhapatyane*) produce class consciousness among workers.[108] Sardesai's hope must also be situated in the context of the steep decline in GKU membership in 1930, after the second strike of 1929. This and other Marathi translations were published after the arrest and incarceration of the leaders and the steep decline in union membership.

Kamgar Vangmay Prasarak Mandal's decision to publish Alexandr Lozovsky's *The Trade Union Movement in the Colonies* was quite likely an

effort to boost trade union membership. The pamphlet reveals the Comintern's rising influence on Communists in India, particularly at a time when
the stalwarts of the movement were in jail. Lozovsky, the head of the Red
International Labor Union, subscribed to the Comintern's opinion on
reformist unions. The pamphlet criticized reformers—national reformers,
capitalist reformers, and trade union reformers, who "wanted to make
Indian workers the handmaiden of the capitalist class."[109] According to
Lozovsky, reformers would eventually align with the state and support the
bourgeoisie in suppressing worker militancy.[110] It linked reformers to the
intellectual project of English liberalism and criticized the Indian National
Congress, arguing that the mainstream national movement wanted workers and peasants to be its appendages and desired trade unions to be the
instrument of class cooperation and capitalist dominance.[111] Lozovsky's
pamphlet displayed a close familiarity with current events, especially the
state of the labor unions in India and the national movement dominated
by the Congress Party. Lozovsky's intimate familiarity with various social
movements in India suggested the important role of Indian intellectuals in
providing information about the "Indian condition" and shaping the
Comintern's view of trade unions in the colonies. Thus, when Lozovsky
addresses Indian workers and criticizes leaders and movements seeking to
establish control over the working classes in the city, it would be a mistake
to simply read him as a European Communist talking down to Indians.
Instead, the text reflects the views of some Indian Communists addressing
Indian workers in the voice of the Communist International.

A pamphlet on the life of V. I. Lenin emphasized his heroism and
extended the critique of reformism. *Comrade Lenin* (Kamred Lenin) was
published by the Kamgar Vangmay Prasarak Mandal in 1933. This biography of Lenin suggested that class solidarity was possible only if the middle
classes and peasants aligned under the leadership of the workers.[112] The
pamphlet defined the alignment of workers, peasants, and the middle class
as "the multitude" (*bahujan samaj*).[113] The multitude led by the proletariat
constituted a revolutionary (*krantikaraka*) force that would lead the people
(*janata*) to freedom (*svatantra*). The notions of *janata* and *svatantra* were
deliberately capacious so that readers could pour their own meanings into
it. In the mind of the writer, who has not been identified,[114] the multitude
and the people are distinct categories, since the former would lead the latter to freedom. Freedom is an amorphous concept, encompassing independence from colonial rule as well as from capitalist dominance, reformist
union leaders, and the hegemonic posturing of the Indian National

Congress. The notion of freedom also suggests the people's unshackling from the influence of all reactionary thought: the pamphlet pointedly lists M. K. Gandhi's promotion of handwoven cloth and affirmation of village councils as examples of reactionary thought.[115] It exhorts Indian Communists to emulate Chinese Communists: "The Chinese workers also followed the same route and freed themselves from slavery and hunger."[116] Indian workers and peasants, like the Russian and Chinese people, would defeat the imperialist and capitalist forces and create a new society where there would be no "hunger, poverty, exploitation, and slavery."[117]

In these pamphlets, the translation of embodied categories did not have the precision or fixity of abstract categories. Embodied categories exceeded their boundaries and sometimes spilled over into one another. For instance, in the Marathi *Manifesto*, the term "Dalit" invokes two different groups of people. In the foreword, "Dalit" denotes "all other oppressed people apart from the working classes"[118] in India, who are asked to study the text and help the working class in their struggle. In the minds of the translators, Dalits were oppressed, but their experiences of oppression were distinct from the working class, and therefore they constituted a separate group of people who had an important but unequivocally supporting role to play in the Indian revolution led by the working class. But the translators also used "Dalit" to refer to the oppressed classes of medieval Europe under the sway of the feudal nobility, who became the bourgeoisie in modern times.[119] Thus the Dalits in the foreword and the Dalits in the *Manifesto* itself were distinct. The term "Dalit" was, of course, also used by another leader from Bombay city, B. R. Ambedkar, in 1928 to refer to the "untouchable" or "depressed" classes, as they were known then.

Similarly, the term for the lumpen proletariat (*mavali*) had no fixed referent. *Mavali* referred to people from the hilly regions of western parts of the Bombay Presidency and signified categories of people prone to create law-and-order problems for the colonial police.[120] In the key words appended to the *Manifesto*, the translators describe the *mavali* as "paupers" belonging to a class below the working class who lived in the city's slums.[121] The translators cited *Capital* to further emphasize the point: paupers who have been fired from their jobs and live in crowded slums in the cities, gaining notoriety as criminals, vagabonds, and lumpen proletariat. They have been permanently separated from the means of production and therefore do not think twice before selling themselves to counterrevolutionary forces for money. In Marx and Engels's formulation in *The Communist Manifesto*, the lumpen proletariat were an amorphous mass of underemployed, jobless criminals who aligned with the elite classes against the revolutions of 1848–49. In 1850, Marx and Engels appraised their estimation of them and hoped for an alliance between the proletariat and the lumpen proletariat. This category then largely disappeared from their writings.[122] It appears again in the first volume of *Capital* when Marx discusses the role of the lumpen proletariat in terms of surplus population, the reserve army of labor, and its importance for capitalist accumulation.[123] For Bombay's Marxists, the *mavali*, embodied the persistent threat of strikebreakers, who had a proclivity for violence and served the important function of driving down wages. The *Manifesto's mavali* was different from but also borrowed from the colonial use of the term. The unstableness of the category was further accentuated in the 1970s by the Dalit poet Namdeo Dhasal, who celebrated vagabonds, criminals, prostitutes, and Dalits in his work. The imprecision of embodied categories is clear from another term, "Negro slave," from *Wage Labor and Capital*. The Marathi translation renders "Negro" as Siddi and "slaves" as *ghulam*. The Siddis are an ethnic community deemed tribal by the Indian government in some parts of India. They were brought to India from Africa by the Portuguese after 1500, some of them as slaves. In the sixteenth and seventeenth centuries, some Siddis acquired political power and inaugurated a kingdom in the region called the Siddis of Janjira.[124] Siddis lived mostly in parts of southern and western India. For the translators of *Wage Labor*, the Siddis provided a frame of reference for slaves; they were Africans, their bodies were black, and they had been transported to India. The long and complex history of Siddi presence was compressed into slavery, ostensibly because it helped the translators make a point about workers' autonomy and also because it may have been comprehensible to readers in the Marathi public sphere. For instance, during the 1928 strikes in the textile mills, Communist leaders invoked the term "slavery" (*ghulami*), often asserting that workers were not the slaves of the capitalist or the colonial government.[125] Slavery serves here as a rhetorical device; conceptually it is the antithesis of workers' autonomy or popular sovereignty. The translators' assumption was that Bombay's workers were free to sell their labor power on the labor market to the capitalists, and the slaves were not.[126] The presumed slavery of the Siddis was the antithesis of the freedom of wage labor in the city, and that freedom needed to be protected from the machinations of capitalists and the state. Thus, the hierarchy of language that operated in the translation of abstract and embodied categories in these pamphlets reflects the

anxieties experienced by Communists in dealing with political movements organized around caste/ethnic solidarities at the time.

TRANSMISSIONS AND CONVERSIONS

Between 1929 and 1933 the Communist movement attracted new followers
in India. Jail was one source of new followers. Here nationalists like V. B.
Kulkarni became Marxists.[127] One convert to Marxism was a Dalit activist
from Bombay, R. B. More. More's initiation to Marxism was facilitated by
the city's institutions and public spaces, through oral communication; he
listened to the speeches of Communist trade union leaders in the working-
class localities of Bombay. The strike of 1928–29, in which Dalit workers
forced Communist leaders to recognize their demands for better-paying
jobs in the weaving departments of the mills, shaped his encounter with
Communism. More sought mentors in the leaders of the 1929 strike, B. T.
Ranadive, S.V. Deshpande, Jagannath Adhikari, and R. M. Jambhekar, for
an understanding of Marxism and Leninism.[128] As the secretary of a Dalit
caste organization, Mahar Samaj Seva Sangh (Organization for the Service
of the Mahar Community), More used his position to organize lectures on
Communism for Dalit workers. He encouraged Dalits to move beyond the
confines of caste and imagine an affinity with and inhabit the universal
categories of class.[129] More's mentors had assumed leadership of the Girni
Kamgar Union in 1929 in the absence of the incarcerated Communist leaders. They were instrumental in the translation and publication of Marxist
and Leninist literature. According to More, most activists of the Communist movement at the time belonged to the middle class (*madhyam varga*),
and their endeavors in the movement were financed by their families.[130]
Those activists who belonged to the lower middle class (*kanistha madhyam
varga*), such as Deshpande, supported themselves by working as teachers.
But a few activists who emerged from the working class were supported,
fed, and clothed by the workers themselves.[131] For More, social hierarchy
among Communist intellectuals, activists, and workers did not coincide
with the division of labor. For instance, the work of setting out tables and
chairs for events, making posters, printing and selling cyclostyle newspapers, organizing meetings in houses and public spaces, educating workers
in class politics, and leading processions and meetings was shared by all
leaders and activists. Yet the task of domesticating and translating Marxism was performed by a few multilingual intellectuals who were sought

out by younger activists to guide them in their comprehension of Marx and Lenin.

More identified with the Communist movement, especially the Ranadive faction of the Communist Party in the city, but did not abandon the Ambedkar-led Dalit movement. Dalit workers in the city were the target of various welfare schemes instituted by the Young Men's Christian Association and the Social Service League in the city. For instance, the YMCA opened a center to "experiment in welfare service among workers" and "to fill-up their leisure times . . . with worthwhile pursuits."[132] These pursuits included night school, indigenous games, and talks on hygiene, sanitation, thrift, and temperance. According to the Royal Commission on Labour in India, nearly all the members "served" by these associations belonged to Dalit castes. R. B. More organized classes on Marxism-Leninism for Dalit youths through these associations, often using translated texts or creating parallel institutions like the Friends Union.[133] One of the important focal points of his initiatives involved the chawls built by the BDD on Delisle Road. Here More was assisted by the Communist leader S. V. Deshpande and his friends in Delisle Road's Chawl No. 14, including Govind Tamhankar, Baburava Garud, and Bhargava Sonavane. Thus in central Bombay in the 1930s, public speeches and the translation of Marxist texts helped initiate Dalit workers into the Communist movement through face-to-face interactions.

Another Communist from the Dalit castes in the city in the 1920s and 1930s was P. Palan, known as Lingam. Lingam was born in Secunderabad in South India, from where he migrated to work in Bombay. Initially he worked in the textile mills and later joined General Motors. He joined the Communist movement in the 1920s. According to the police dossier on him, Lingam went to the Soviet Union to study the Soviet revolution and learn the "methods of struggle" in 1931, studying at the Eastern University in Moscow (possibly the Communist University of the Toilers of the East) for a year and a half before he returned to Bombay in 1932.[134] He was jailed in April 1932, contracted consumption there, and died in 1933. Thus, despite the reservations of the weekly *Samata* about Marxism, some Dalit leaders sought to inhabit the universality of class. But Dalits such as R. B. More did not relinquish the politics of caste. For instance, the Friends Union, of which More was a founder, in 1932 published a pamphlet titled *Forty Questions about the Untouchables* (Asprushyanche chalis saval), which demanded religious equality for Dalit castes.[135]

WHAT THE WORKERS READ AND WROTE

Bombay's Communists in 1924 had embraced the policy of translating and transmitting socialism in the vernacular. Even after 1934, when the Communist Party of India was banned and its members incorporated into the Congress Party, the Communists exhorted local units to "make technical arrangements for the production and distribution of literature."[136] They directed the provincial headquarters to publish political papers during the ban and instructed every district to have its "cyclostyle and producing and distributing arrangement for one-sheet agitational leaflets."[137] The intelligence agencies of the colonial state called this strategy "underground work" to "mobilize workers and peasants en masse" despite the ban on the Communist Party. The texts were produced and circulated in the working-class public sphere.

What was the cultural context of translations and their reception? What did the urban poor read, write, think, hear, and watch when they encountered Marathi Marxist texts? The Communist descriptions of the revolution that would result in adequate housing, better wages, and fewer hours of work were narrated in the vibrant public sphere of the working class. Here they showered abuses on capitalists in public speeches. An important reason for the intense and passionate confrontations between the city's industrialists and workers was the inability of the former to foster a culture of bargaining and negotiations with trade unions. When workers joined Communist-led unions like the GKU in 1928–29, mill owners locked out strikers and deployed strikebreakers rather than bargaining with them, because they believed that workers' strikes were unreasonable and trade unions were an undesirable mode of industrial organization. They did not want to give credence to workers or unions by negotiating with them.[138] The Communists weaponized language and vented vitriol on the industrialists. The narratives of revolution were popular and effective because they captured the experiences of workers and offered solutions to the impasse. In the public sphere, though, workers had developed social and cultural practices that were not completely in sync with the modernist temporality of Communism, though they were effective in mobilizing workers. For instance, workers recited religious tales (*kirtans*) and sermons (*pravachan*), and took part in folk performative traditions like *gondhala*, *povada*, *bharuda*, and plays. Similarly, at the Hanuman Theater in the Lal Baug area in Bombay's mill district, there were performances of *tamasha*, a popular musical folk tradition.[139] In the

1920s and 1930s, the rhetoric of class struggle paralleled the performative and folk traditions of popular culture, influencing each other in the process. This comingling of terms from the Marathi Marxist conceptual universe with popular culture can be discerned in novels and plays written and performed in the late 1920s and 1930s, which had workers as protagonists and were authored by writers who lived in or close to the mill districts of the city. Their audience mostly consisted of the urban poor.

The 1933 novel *The Flying Shuttle* (Dhavata Dhota). by Bhargavram Varerkar, or Mama Varerkar as he was popularly known, was an important landmark in the working-class public sphere. Early iterations took various forms. It was first serialized in 1930 in the Marathi weekly *Tutari* (Horn), edited by M. G. Rangnekar, but after ten installments the weekly shut down, leaving the novel incomplete. It was then performed as a play titled *The Golden Dome* (Sonyacha Kalas) in the first half of 1932 to much acclaim. It appeared as a novel toward the end of 1933. The Aryan Film Company commissioned a screenplay based on the novel, but the film was never released.[140] Thus *The Flying Shuttle* had multiple mediatized incarnations. The novel was set in Bombay in 1917–18, the last years of World War I. The war had increased the hours of work but not yielded higher wages for the city's workers, resulting in politicization of the working class and the rise of leaders from within the class. The protagonist of the novel, the wizened former mill worker and current security guard of a mill, Baba Shigvan, is one such leader. His protégés include a young man named Kanhu Krishna and young woman named Bijli (Lightning). Varerkar's decision to set the novel in 1917–18 bears explication. This was before leaders from the city identified themselves as Communists and when industry-wide strikes had not yet become the norm. It was also prior to the emergence of reformist or radical labor leaders who were not born in working-class families. In the novel, the leaders emerge from the working class. In fact, Baba Shigvan exhibits a particular disdain for middle-class leaders coming from the outside, calling them "bookish labor leaders." Even though the Communist-inspired discourse of class was absent in 1917–18, the novel's characters demonstrate an acute awareness of class (and caste). The novel valorizes the ethics of mill workers, criticizes white-collar employees who live in another part of the city (Girgaum), and distrusts capitalist classes. By situating the story in 1917–18, Varerkar ensures that Shigvan's class consciousness is untainted by Communist or reformist labor leaders. Instead, the making of a distinct class in Mumbai (as Varerkar calls it) is tied to the experiences of workers, as they live with and in dust, smoke, and trash in tenements made of cement in the mill district, suffer from hunger, wear worn-out clothes, experience rampant alcoholism, are subjected to arduous work in the mills and verbal or physical assaults and humiliation by mill authorities, and respond to this humiliation by going on strike. The home is an important site in *The Flying Shuttle*; Varerkar underlines the crisis in the domestic lives of mill workers. The production and reproduction of the labor force in homes is beset with many socioeconomic problems. For instance, Baba Shigvan emphasizes the alienation produced by laboring in the mills and highlights the estrangement of mill workers from their families because of the long hours of work.[141] Similarly, he says, the pent-up anger from humiliation at work finds a vent in domestic violence, particularly under the influence of alcohol.[142] Varerkar highlights the discord in domestic life through Bijli's life story: she loses her father in a mill accident when she is eleven or twelve, and her bereft mother dies of the shock soon afterward. The orphan Bijli is married off to a thirty-five-year-old mill worker who is alcoholic and violent. He dies of alcoholism when Bijli is fourteen.[143] In highlighting the discord, Varerkar presupposes the existence of a preindustrial domestic harmony shattered by industrial work. Varerkar's formulation of domestic discord is not uninformed by the Marxist theory of alienation, but by situating the play in this period, prior to the translation of Marxist texts and the mobilization of workers by Bombay's Communists, he posits that Marxists intervened in an existing working-class public sphere. In this public sphere, workers' literacy was rising and even the city's newspaper editors acknowledged their importance and wanted to cultivate them as a reading public.[144]

Varerkar's representation of the working-class public sphere in the 1910s and 1920s reveals historical insights. Recently, the historian Arun Kumar has confirmed that there was a vibrant literary culture among the working class in this period, as workers read and borrowed books from libraries. They "were voracious readers, library members, and intellectuals reading and writing poetic and political works."[145] One such writer was the playwright P. S. Sawant. Sawant was a mill worker who began writing a three-act play titled *In the Workers' Kingdom* (Majuranchya-samrajyat) during the strike of 1933. The play was performed at Damodar Thackersey Hall in Bombay, a venue for many workers' meetings, in October 1935, then published by Manohar Mitra Mandal (Manohar Friends Association), a group that addressed workers' issues in the Delisle Road area. Set in the sixth month of a strike at Mancharam Mill in the city, the play centers on

Ramchandra, a mill worker who has no money to feed his children, Indu and Madhu, or pay rent for his room in a chawl. He has recently been evicted by his landlord and is living on a city street. Ramchandra's world is fragile, "enveloped by darkness from all sides."[146] But despite the precariousness of his world, he has control over his moral compass. He does not want to be a strikebreaker and therefore does not seek employment in another mill. Enveloped in darkness, he urges his daughter Indu to pray to God and hopes that the jobbers Bhampakrao and Soka will find a solution to the impasse. Bhampak and Soka are lackeys of the mill owners, conniving to break the six-month strike. The jobbers address laborers derisively, using a term with caste and class connotations (*majurdya*, "son of a laborer"), and are impervious to their hunger. The author emphasizes their lack of morality. Bhampak, for instance, has an affair with Champa, a jobber herself. He lavishes money on her, humiliates his wife, Tara, and has stopped spending money on his children's education.[147] Apart from his ill treatment of workers and his own family, he is addicted to vices and sensual pleasures, including gambling, alcohol, and films. The play sets up a dichotomy between the morality of the workers who are on strike and the jobbers conniving to break it. Bhampak and Sopa represent one end of the moral spectrum; on the other are Ramchandra, Vishwas, Devdutt, and Trimbak—laborers who believe in the organization and unity of workers. As in Varerkar's play, God has an important presence in the lives of the mill workers in *In the Workers' Kingdom*: he (addressed in a masculine form in the play) is the object of their prayers, someone the workers turn to when they are in need. He is the remedy for the self-indulgence of the jobbers: he will transform them and guide them to the right path.[148]

In the Workers' Kingdom borrows terms from the conceptual apparatus of translated Marathi Marxist texts. The title of the play invokes a government led by workers, but the play ends in a Gandhian concord between mill workers and mill owners rather than a revolution.[149] The six-month strike is resolved after a meeting between the leaders of the workers and the owner of Mancharam Mill, Sumar Shet. The face-to-face interaction, without jobbers or managers, enables the mill owners and laborers to empathize with each other. Ramchandra hopes after the meeting with Sumar Shet that the demolition of the wall between the workers and mill owners will produce "truth, love, and justice . . . and workers' rule will become God's rule [*Ram Rajya*],"[150] the ideal society envisioned by M. K. Gandhi, where peasants and workers would come into their own and cohabit with other classes. Thus the play written by a mill worker relinquishes the Marxist dream of negating the authority of the capitalist class and the workers triumphing over mill owners. Instead, Sawant turns to Gandhian politics and its hope for reconciliation between mill workers and mill owners. This suggests that Gandhian politics remained an important political ideal for some workers at least in the mid-1930s. The appropriation of Marxian categories for Gandhian ends may also relate to the ban on the Communist Party of India in 1934. P. S. Sawant and Manohar Mitra Mandal probably did not want to face charges of sedition. Conversely, it could also mean that workers were exhausted by the long strikes of the past few years and desired reconciliation as a political solution to strikes.

The rising working-class readership of Bombay also consumed novels like *The Worker's Wife* (Majurachi bayko), which cost only four annas, a few pennies. Workers were its target audience, along with lower-middle and middle classes, judging from advertisements in the novel for an insurance company, a bookshop, a sweet shop, hair oil, and a brand of spices, items that presumed the financial resources to buy these goods. The novel offers a voyeuristic and titillating account of the lives of workers that uncannily corroborates sociological accounts of the working class in the city. *The Worker's Wife* was published in 1933.[151] The story centers on Gauri, the seventeen- or eighteen-year-old wife of a worker named Ganpati Lokhande. Gauri and Ganpati (the names have Hindu mythological resonance) work in the Dhanji Textile Mill, albeit in different departments. She migrated from the Konkan region of the Bombay Presidency.[152] *The Worker's Wife* also borrows from the conceptual universe of Marathi Marxism. For instance, while establishing the plot, the author discusses the technological inventions "that are appropriated by a handful of capitalists [*bhandwaldar*] to become more rich, but the workers [*majur*] are getting more and more hungry. . . . They [capitalists] live like kings in bungalows, drive motor cars, gamble on horses, enjoy dance shows . . . but to finance their leisure in the time of the Great Depression they exploit [*pilanuk*] workers more and more."[153] Apart from the conceptual and experiential categories of Marathi Marxism, embodied categories like *mavali* make their appearance too. In the novel, the workers and the urban poor are branded *mavali* at various moments, especially by those wielding power, such as the police. The capitalist's incessant exploitation of labor is the undergirding theme of the novel, and its tragic effects on Gauri's life the focus of the plot. Capitalist characters have a smaller albeit important presence in the story. In fact, Gauri's distress is brought about more by the violence of the urban poor and workers toward each other.

The novel presents the social relationship of power in the mills, including the jobbers who receive a percentage of the worker's pay and creditors who descend on the mills and tenements on payday to demand interest on their loans. Gauri is indebted to multiple people: her jobber, who claims a portion of her wages every month; a woman named Maina, a Pathan moneylender she borrowed money from for an illness in the family; and a creditor in the village who loaned her money for travel to the city, taking her cow as collateral. In a historical context in which wages were low, this means that Gauri and Ganpati need subtenants to reduce their rent. They share their tenement with another couple, Lakshmi and Narayan (also with Hindu mythological resonance).[154] Ganpati, Gauri's husband, earns twenty-eight to thirty rupees a month, almost three times as much as Gauri, but spends most of it on "liquor, gambling, paying old creditors, and an affair with Lakshmi,"[155] the other tenant. Ganpati and Lakshmi combine to physically and verbally assault Gauri, and Narayan molests her. Gauri's exploitation in the novel is overdetermined. Her suffering signifies the exploitation of the working class, her body standing in for the exploitation of a group. The reader explores the city through Gauri's eyes: the city's mills, the working-class neighborhoods and streets, the tenements, the places of working-class leisure like the *tamasha* theater, the gambling dens, the red-light district, and the interiors of working-class homes. The author's depiction of Gauri's Bombay corroborates sociological accounts of working-class lives. For instance, the author of *The Worker's Wife* shares the sociologist Pradhan's fascination with overcrowded tenements where two and sometimes more families share a room. The author ascribes a similar moral judgement to it, calling it foul and dirty (*hidis*), producing disgust (*kilas*). Consider G. R. Pradhan's description of living arrangements in a tenement: "If there are two or more than two families living in one room, there are as many chulas (stoves) as are the families."[156] Or take Pradhan's fascination with the sexual relationships of the people living there: "In some cases *I was told* if there are two or more married couples in the same room, each couple takes advantage of the room by turns or women sleep in the room and men outside the room and arrange anyhow for conjugal unions. . . . On account of insufficient space the natural sex functions of the married couples take place with the full consciousness of the presence of other inmates in the same room."[157] At the end of the novel, Gauri succumbs to the charms and riches of the mill owner, Dhanji Shet, and consents to a relationship with him. As the author puts it, "Dhanji Shet now possesses her . . . she is his property [*sampatti*]."[158] With Gauri's possession, the author signals the capitalist domination over labor at this moment. *The Worker's Wife* borrows from the conceptual oeuvre of Marathi Marxism but abstains from visons of overturning this social order. It establishes capital's suppression of labor but not the negation of the capital by labor.

Apart from these novels and plays, other texts in circulation at this time included hagiographies and pamphlets. One such was on the life of S. H. Jhabwala, a labor leader mentioned earlier in the chapter. The pamphlet, titled *Worker—Great Soul* (Majur-mahatma), was published in 1929 by his associate D. L. Nandurbarkar, at the time of Jhabwala's incarceration in the Meerut Conspiracy Case. The pamphlet lists Jhabwala's virtues, including commitment to workers' causes and sympathy for the downtrodden, to register a complaint with the colonial government for snatching away "the espouser of workers' causes and the lifeblood of the workers."[159] The pamphlet, not surprisingly, does not mention Jhabwala's Marxist influences but rather emphasizes Gandhi, Leo Tolstoy, Gautam Buddha, and Jesus Christ as key inspirations in his life. Without naming socialism, the pamphlet espouses his commitment to "workers' freedom from hunger, decent clothing, and better housing."[160]

CASTE AND ETHNIC BOUNDARIES IN THE PUBLIC SPHERE

Marxists relied on the shared experiences of hunger, low wages, long hours of work, and inadequate housing to mobilize workers for an Indian revolution. These experiences intersected with social practices of caste that undercut and sometimes obscured common experiences that could become the basis of class solidarities. In fact, caste practices among the workers and the urban poor shed light on the boundaries around the consumption of food and water and the use of caste, sometimes by workers themselves, to constrain access to employment and thus housing. Moreover, capitalists and the colonial states manipulated group identities by making them the basis of political representation and amplified these boundaries into fissures, particularly in times of political action. Caste therefore had an important presence in the public sphere. It was also constitutive of some texts. In the Marxist pamphlets, caste registered in the process of domestication and translation of experiential categories such as oppression or in the rendering of abstract or embodied categories in these texts. Some popular cultural texts invoked the social boundaries that existed in practice, boundaries that were drawn and renegotiated. Caste, in these texts, was important to the plot. In *The Flying Shuttle*, Baba Shigvan asks Kanhoba (the alias of the lead character Kanhu Krishna), "Tujhi jaat kona?" (What is your caste?). Kanhoba answers that he belongs to the Kulavadi or Kunbi caste, the same as Shigvan. He then invites him to stay in his one-room tenement in the mill district and helps him procure employment in Ruby Mills mill.[161] Shigvan represents Kunbi values for Kanhoba: "Always speak the truth, the unvarnished truth . . . our [Kunbi] conduct must be like a plow. Once it pierces the soil, it moves forward in a straight line."[162] The novel also highlights caste boundaries in everyday life. For instance, Kanhoba's jobber, Naru Parab, prefers employing people from his own caste, the Maratha caste, but makes an exception for Kanhoba based on Shigvan's recommendation.[163] Similarly, when Bijli offers Kanhoba lunch one day, it raises the question of caste and commensality. Bijli is from the Maratha caste, which is higher than the Kunbis, but she brushes Kanhoba off by saying she is from the Mahar (untouchable) caste.[164] Moreover, a tea shop owner in the mill district warns Kanhoba against intimacy between a Kunbi and a Maratha when he appears to be besotted with her.[165] Caste boundaries inundate the everyday life of mill workers in *The Flying Shuttle*, but they don't overwhelm it. In times of political action, mill workers overcome these boundaries.

According to the 1931 census of the city, a majority of workers in the textile industry and one-third of the city's population belonged to the Maratha-Kunbi caste cluster. The census acknowledged that the demographic heft of the caste cluster had a bearing on political culture in the city. There was friction within the cluster, as we saw with Bijli and Kanhoba's story in *The Flying Shuttle*, but there were possible solidarities along lines of caste (the anti-Brahmin movement) and class (the workers' movement) at particular historical junctures. But in a different conjuncture, the frictions of caste and class could become fissures, as we saw with Dange's revulsion at the anti-Brahmin movement. The anti-Brahmin movement's critique of Brahminism spilled over into the Communist movement of the 1920s and 30s too. For instance, two leaders of the Communist-led Girni Kamgar Union, Arjun Alwe and Govind Kasle, also participated in the non-Brahmin movement. Both Alwe and Kasle were jailed in Meerut and spoke critically of "communist Brahmins."[166] The friction between Communist and caste politics can also be discerned in the political rivalries between trade unions in the city. One important rival of the GKU in the

1920s was the Girni Kamgar Mahamandal (GKM; Organization of Mill Workers), led by S. K. Bole and R. S. Asavale. These leaders were representatives of labor in the Bombay Legislative Council at the time and, more importantly, were active in mobilizing the Maratha-Kunbi caste cluster in the city for the anti-Brahmin movement. In the words of the Bombay Communists, they "fostered strong anti-Brahmin feelings" among workers.[167]

In the hagiography of S. H. Jhabwala, caste leaps out of the text in the form of advertisements and sponsors of the pamphlets. The first advertisement in the pamphlet is for a mess, a boarding house (*Khanaval*) for Dakhshini (Deccan) Brahmins in the Shetye Building, at Poibavdi in the Parel area. The Shetye building housed the offices of the Red Flag Mill Workers Union (Lal Bavta Girnia Kamgar Union) in 1928, and it served as a meeting place for the B. T. Ranadive faction of the Bombay Communists and housed the offices of the Kamgar Vangmay Prasarak Mandal. Thus the Shetye building was both a place for the propagation of Marxism and a space for the practice of caste commensality. The Dakshini Brahmins include subcastes like Gaud Saraswat and Chitapavan Brahmins. The mess advertised cleanliness and timeliness as its virtues.[168] It was not just members of the mess who preferred to consume libations within the boundaries of caste. Anand Teltumbde has pointed out that K. N. Joglekar did not "eat food prepared by the people of other castes" and continued to be a member of the Brahmin Sabha, a caste organization, until the Communist Party asked him to resign this membership.[169]

Some Dalit intellectuals doubted Bolshevism's ability to transcend Brahminism. The anonymous author of a *Samata* article argued that Brahmin Communists

> have little knowledge of the strength of Brahminism. . . . I know Hindu comrades who insist that once capitalism is destroyed the disputes between Brahmin and non-Brahmin, touchable and untouchable would be rendered moot. Their shallow understanding of the social questions fills me with regret. Because of the shallowness, Sanatanists [those who believe in the everlasting influence of Hinduism] are not afraid of or bothered by communism. That is why I haven't found the occasion to praise communists. The untouchables are so poor, but in that class you'll find votaries of social equality but not among communists. When communists are produced in untouchable and backward castes only then will communism in India be self-reflexive.[170]

According to the *Samata* article, Communism could not be domesticated because its adherents in India, mostly upper-caste Hindus, could not comprehend or acknowledge caste. The article implies that the fragmented existence of most Indian Communists—with head in Russia and body in India—curtailed the efficacy of Marxism in India. The *Samata* article inverts the mind/body dyad to claim the impossibility of Communism's relevance to India. Indian Communists, it claims, are intellectually committed to equality but do not address the inequities of caste and particularly the indignities of untouchability. Yet, as we saw with More and Lingam, some Dalits overcame these reservations to embrace Marxism.

DANGE, INDOLOGY, AND BLIND SPOTS

Not surprisingly, the tension between caste and class persisted into the 1940s. S. A. Dange was incarcerated in Yerwada Jail, near the city of Pune, in 1942 and there began writing his book *India from Primitive Communism to Slavery: A Marxist Study of Ancient Indian History*. The book draws heavily on Friedrich Engels's *The Origin of the Family, Property, and the State*, and in Dange's own telling, "deals with the same subjects in Indian history."[171] Like Engels, he identifies five stages of Indian history, from primitive Communism to capitalism. In writing the book, Dange was responding to questions posed by fellow political prisoners in Yerwada Jail: What is class? When did it arise in India? What is the state? Dange's book provides an outline of "the rise of classes and State in Indian society from the viewpoint of historical materialism."[172] One notable feature of Dange's historical materialist understanding of India is the continued obfuscation of caste. For instance, he categorizes the Brahmin, the highest caste in the social hierarchy, not as a caste but as a mode of production in ancient India.

Dange holds that the early history of India is "a history mainly of the Aryan tribes and people, whose story later on becomes the history of India as a country."[173] Dange upholds the centrality of Aryans to the narrative of Indian history. He borrows these claims from Oriental scholarship in the eighteenth and nineteenth centuries. That scholarship sought to discover India's past, and the development of the science of race in the nineteenth century led to the conclusion that there was an Aryan race in India. The importance of the Aryan race to Indian history was propounded by two types of Orientalists: British Sanskritists and ethnographers and the German Orientalists like Max Müller. Both strands of Orientalism based their claims on the philological study of the Vedas, particularly the earliest Rigveda. As the historian of ancient India Romila Thapar notes, the Rigveda was viewed by these scholars "as the most ancient literature and the key to Sanskrit and the Hindu civilization."[174] The history of that civilization became the history of the Indian nation. Indian nationalists, eager for a sense of national identity under colonial dominance, borrowed this narrative to explain the origins of India society and history.[175] The Aryan theory was extremely important to the ideology of right-wing Hinduism, the Hindutva movement. In the Hindutva version of Aryan theory, the racially distinct Aryans were the progenitors of the modern Hindus. But to counter the lower-caste critique of Aryan foreignness, they posited an indigenous origin for the Aryans and sometimes tied themselves in knots to belabor their Indian origins. In one famous instance, the ideologue of the Hindutva movement, M. S. Golwalkar, argued in 1938 that even if Aryans were said to have originated at the North Pole, they were still indigenous because the North Pole during those times was located in the present-day Indian states of Bihar and Orissa. The Aryan theory also proved convenient to the Indian middle class, which included mostly upper-caste Hindus and became politically powerful during the Indian national movement. The theory explained the inherent superiority of those in the middle class. An important reworking of the Aryan theory was offered by the ideologues of the lower-caste movements. A pillar of Aryan theory—that fair-skinned Aryans conquered dark-skinned aborigines—was co-opted by Jyotirao Phule in the nineteenth century and B. R. Ambedkar in the twentieth century to explain the origins of the caste system. In their narrative, the Aryans conquered the aborigines and relegated them to low caste status.[176]

Dange's book is notable for what it says and what it does not. By making Aryans the central players in India's story, Dange summarily dismisses the archaeological evidence of a pre-Aryan urban culture excavated at Harappa and Mohenjo Daro in 1922–23. Since historical records of this culture are not available or not deciphered, he argues, they cannot be used to construct a historical account.[177] Furthermore, he refuses to engage with claims advanced by ideologues of the non-Brahmin movement that Aryans were preceded by a group of people known as Dravidians, who had a language distinct from the Sanskrit used by the Aryans and were defeated by the Aryans and subjugated as lower castes.[178] In an attendant move to avoid the thorny issue of temporalization, which would have disturbed his view of the Aryans as the primary actors of Indian history, he does not dismiss claims that Aryan society can be dated between 6000 and 4000 BCE. What Dange argues is equally interesting. He states that "Brahman is the commune of Aryan man and Yajna [ritual sacrifice] is its mode of production, the primitive commune with the collective mode of production. And the Vedas are the knowledge of this mode of production, of this way of life of the great Brahman, the commune. That is the way Aryan Hindu tradition puts history on record; and that is the key to the understanding of the earliest epoch of Aryan history, of its epoch of primitive communism."[179] In Dange's formulation, the ritual became the mode of production, and he did not revise this view in subsequent editions of the book. If Aryan society was a primitive commune, how does one explain the origin of the caste system? Dange's answer differs sharply from the non-Brahman movements' reading of caste. Here Dange goes back to his early writing in *The Socialist*. He contends that the caste system developed when the division of labor became hereditary. The caste system was the expression of Indian feudalism. Feudalism displaced the household community village, or *varnashram* village. It was an alternative to slavery and "best suited to the new forces of production." It started during the Maurya period (fourth century BCE) in Indian history and spread during the Gupta empire (200 CE), when it "became the unchanging rigid base of feudalism for all the centuries to come."[180] Thus the historical materialist lens Dange acquired from Marxism helped him read Aryan society as a primitive commune and caste as a division of labor. In the process of domesticating Marxism, with the help of nineteenth-century Orientalists and Indologists, he obscures caste. But caste was evident in the hierarchy of language, in the public sphere, in the practices of capitalists and some Communists, in the built environment, and in the social boundaries drawn in the everyday lives of workers.

3 URBAN PLANNING AND CULTURAL POLITICS, 1945-1971

IN THE EARLY 1940S, THE COMMUNIST PARTY OF INDIA (CPI) made its cultural turn. It was not that Communists were averse to culture before this moment. They read and published books and newspapers, domesticated socialism, translated Marxism, and articulated their desire for an Indian revolution that would end colonialism and overturn capitalism. Communists of the 1920s and 1930s were ardent participants in the world of ideas and stories of revolutionary transformation both in print and orally. These ideas and stories resonated in popular culture too. However, in 1942 the colonial government lifted the ban on the CPI after the party decided to support Britain's war effort. To popularize support for the war and mobilize writers and the masses, the CPI convened a meeting of the All-India Progressive Writers' Association (AIPWA) in 1943. The party congress of the CPI and the meeting of the AIPWA were held concurrently in May 1943. S. A. Dange was president of the CPI. At the meeting, the AIPWA headquarters was shifted from Lucknow to Bombay city, and Mama Varerkar was elected treasurer. The Indian People's Theater Association (IPTA) was instituted in 1943 to popularize Marxian and nationalist ideas, and its first meeting was also held concurrently with the congress of the CPI.[1] In 1944, a cultural troupe called the Lal Bavta Kalapathak (Red Flag Artists' Troupe) was founded in the city by Amar Shaikh, D. N. Gavhankar, and Tukaram (Annabhau) Sathe.[2]

Annabhau Sathe was one of the earliest icons of Dalit literature. Sathe's work sheds light on the politics of the urban poor and their occupation of public space to protest eviction from tenements, anxieties about the loss of class, and the machinations of the capitalists and political elites in Bombay of the 1940s. In his work, Sathe envisioned the upending of power hierarchies through mobilization of the poor in urban space. His work engaged with everyday life and took meaning from the historical context it indexed: the vibrant leftist movement in the city and the parallel processes of Bombay's urban transformation. Modern urban planning responded to the upsurge of the urban poor. The processes of urban change and the everyday life of the urban poor, in which caste played an important role, led to the production of literature advocating revolutionary transformation of society. The urban poor experienced everyday life in the city in terms of high rent, low wages, unaffordable housing, and lack of basic facilities such as water supply and sanitation. The state, city elites, and urban planners blamed burgeoning slums and inadequate housing, and their solution was urban transformation through planning. Sathe's plays, short stories, and poems depicted the effects of these processes on the urban poor and suggested a radical response. In his poem "A Ballad of Bombay" (Mumbaichi lavani), he exhorted the city's workers to unite under the banner of the Red Flag, declare revolution, and overcome the depredations of their lives.[3] His plays (loknatya; folk drama or people's theater), performed by the Red Flag troupe, are particularly relevant here.

Sathe's loknatyas were written between 1944 and 1955. They dealt with issues such as housing, unemployment, strikes, and wages—particularly nonpayment of bonus wages—as well as the politics of language, issues that were crucial to working-class politics in Bombay during this period. Sathe's depiction of everyday life, an ideal he shared with artists from AIPWA and IPTA, was lauded for its social realism. Social realism, like Marxism, was a transnational project translated by Indian authors to depict Indian social and political conditions. In India, social realism was harnessed to the anticolonial and antifascist movements of the 1930s and 1940s. It aspired to fashion a progressive national culture that was both rational and broadly socialist.[4] Sathe's loknatyas adapted social realism to the particularities of the struggles of the urban poor in Bombay. In Sathe's loknatya the dialectical relationship of the dominant and subordinate classes was well etched out. He accorded his characters precise class positions, and the categories deployed to situate them sociologically came from the conceptual oeuvre of Marathi Marxism. For instance, descriptors like "mill worker" (girni kamgar), "peasant" (shetkari), or "white collar/middle class" (pandharpesa) are frequently employed to identify protagonists in his plays. Characters embody class positions and the ideal of class struggle: peasants, mill workers, the lumpen proletariat, and the urban poor, on the one hand, encounter landlords, mill owners, merchants, bureaucrats, and ministers, on the other. The dialogues between dominant and subordinate characters demystify the social processes at work and reveal the construction and operation of class (and caste) dominance.

His work reveals the coconstitution of spatial and social hierarchy in Bombay. Urban planning was an important mode for the production of space, and Sathe's *loknatyas* were written at a conjuncture in which Bombay city was transformed to Greater Bombay through the Greater Bombay Law and the Bombay High Court Act of 1945. Urban planning accompanied the extension of the city's limits, and laws provided the legal accoutrements for city expansion. Laws relating to land use and demolition of slums were passed by the city municipal corporation and the regional state. Urban planning was as much about land use in Greater Bombay as it was a technocratic response to the social and political movements of the urban poor, including Dalits. In other words, urban planning was dreamed by technocrats and implemented by bureaucrats precisely because they thought it could be largely insulated from the politics of the city's poor, but this was short-circuited in practice. Dalits and the urban poor were not ideal subjects of urban planning who accepted slum demolition and eviction without protest. They responded by mobilizing in urban space, foot dragging, and using the legal apparatus of the state to contest evictions. All these had mixed results.

SATHE'S BOMBAY

Annabhau Sathe was born in a Matang/Mang Dalit caste in 1920 in the village of Wategaon in the Sangli district of Bombay Presidency. The Sathes migrated on foot to Bombay city from their village in 1931, a distance of approximately 350 kilometers. Along their long march to Bombay, they worked as casual laborers and stone breakers in cities such as Satara, Pune, and Kalyan. In 1933, they lived in the Byculla neighborhood in the mill district of Bombay city; Annabhau Sathe worked as a porter and errand boy in this neighborhood. Like R. B. More, he was influenced by the politics of the working-class districts in this period. He participated in political discussions, organized meetings, distributed pamphlets and handbills, wrote slogans on walls, and painted posters.[5] According to one legend, Sathe's friend helped him become literate 1934, but in his own rendering of his life he stated that he began reading Marathi translations of proscribed Marxist texts on his own that year, while residing in Matunga Labour Camp. Between 1934 and 1940, Sathe was employed in what we now call the informal sector—as a domestic servant, doorkeeper, boot polish boy, colliery worker, and porter. In all these jobs, caste and class intersected. According to a 1941 survey by Rasiklal Cholia, 98 percent of colliery workers in the Bombay docks belonged to the Dalit castes.[6] In 1942, Sathe joined the spinning department of Morbaug Mills, where he famously composed "The Ballad of Stalingrad" (Stalingradcha povada) on scraps of paper. He then founded the Red Flag Artists' Troupe (Lal Bavta Kalapathak). Sathe gained recognition from the Maharashtra state and won the state's literary award in 1961.[7] Seven of his novels were made into Marathi films, and his work was translated into several Indian and foreign languages.[8] Sathe's oeuvre set an important precedent for the content, form, and tropes of what came to be recognized as Dalit literature in the 1960s and 1970s.

SATHE AND *LOKNATYA*

The *loknatya* was a playful and spontaneous innovation by Sathe within a field of constraints. Sathe fashioned the genre by reworking a performative tradition based on the labor of women and low-caste men, the *tamasha*. In 1948, the Bombay government banned the *tamasha* on the grounds of indecency. Because of the ban, Sathe could not perform his famous *tamasha*, *My Bombay* (Majhi Mumbai), for his audience. Sathe responded by spontaneously calling it a *loknatya*, and the performance of *My Bombay* was staged with the police watching the proceedings.[9] Sathe drained the *tamasha* of its bawdiness and made it a vehicle for progressive politics. In reworking the *tamasha*, he drew inspiration from the anticaste Satyashodhak and Ambedkari *jalsas* of the 1920s and 1930s. Sathe retained the *tamasha*'s emphasis on competition between two contending philosophies. The *tamasha* was a vehicle for competition between the Shiva and Shakti schools of metaphysical speculation. In Sathe's *tamasha* Marxism and capitalism replaced metaphysical speculation. Similarly, he retained the element of *vag natya* (spontaneous theater), often satirical in content.

His *loknatyas* responded to the political moment. The last decade of colonial rule in India witnessed elections to provincial councils in 1937 and another election in 1946. These elections had a limited franchise—neither the urban nor the rural poor had the right to vote. Sathe perceived the 1946 elections in India as a site for the entrenchment of class power. In his 1946 play titled *The Financier's Election* (Shetjiche elecshan), Sathe depicts the financial considerations undergirding the Indian National Congress's decision to award a party ticket to the landlord and financier Seth Magarchand. Magarchand is a recurring archetypal character in Sathe's plays. The name was laced with satire—*magar* means "alligator" in Marathi. Magarchand has no moral or political claims to represent his poor constituents and has not participated in the anticolonial national movement, is known to market goods on the black market, and supported the British war effort during World War II. His nationalist credentials are thus thin. Similarly, he has no ideological compunctions. Magarchand has threatened to join the Hindu Mahasabha (the Hindu Grand Association) if he is not nominated by the Congress Party. He claims that he is an apt representative for peasants on the provincial council, a claim contested by Sattu, a small farmer; Dhondiba, Magarchand's man Friday; and his wife, Tara. Sattu, Dhondiba, and Tara point out that Magarchand would not disturb the banker-landlord nexus and, more importantly, would never advocate for the peasants and the working class.[10] One of the important demands of Sattu, the small farmer, is redistribution of land and relief from agrarian debt.[11] Eventually, Magarchand is forced to surrender the nomination, along with his claim to represent peasants and workers, and the peasants and workers shift their support to the Communist Party. In *The Financier's Election*, like most of Sathe's *loknatyas*, the claims of the dominant class to represent the subordinate classes are always contested. Sattu, Dhondiba, and Tara display a remarkable awareness of their class positions and an appreciation of the fact that electoral democracy is the site for the entrenchment of class power. Their political analysis is incisive: bankers and landlords are unlikely to pay heed to workers and peasants. Though the rural and urban poor did not have the right to vote in 1946, Sathe held that they had an important political voice. There are two possible readings of the denouement of Magarchand's candidacy. One is that the workers reject democracy tout court because it produces representatives like Magarchand. But the other reading could be that workers and peasants understand the possibilities of democracy and therefore prefer a representative attentive to their demand for land redistribution and debt relief.

In his 1947 play *Illegal* (Bekaydeshira), the character Magarchand reappears. He is again a financier, but this time he is also a minister in the provincial government. In the play, the workers have gone on strike, causing trepidation to the mill owner Raghunathmal (it is noteworthy that in Bombay there was a Raghunath Mills at the time); Magarchand is a close associate of the mill owner. They deem the strike illegal, an example of the volatility and recklessness of the working class. They attribute the strike to a Communist conspiracy to destabilize the recently elected Congress government. Raghunathmal comments, "If the strike was a disease we could have cured it with medicine, if it was an apparition, I could have countered it with magical incantation [Mantra Tantra], but there is no remedy for a strike."[12] Raghunathmal and Magarchand recommend patience, nonviolence, and constitutional methods as the mode for workers' politics. By contrast, the labor leaders Sattu and Dhondiba (who also appear in other plays) seize the possibility of the category illegal, recognize its potential to produce anxiety among the dominant classes, and dismiss the politics of constitutional procedures in favor of mobilizing and capturing public space. Magarchand and Raghunathmal accept the demands of the workers after ten thousand workers march on the mill and threaten to organize a larger march the following day. In Sathe's world, urban space is the key site for contesting power and formulating a politics of the urban poor. The urban poor and workers recognize each other as participants in political action in public space. The agitation enables them to transcend the particularities of caste, religion, and gender. In Sathe's view, sectional affinities of caste and religion remain important in the everyday life of the neighborhoods and tenements, but in the roads and streets of the city, they can be transcended, at least during political action.[13]

We see this dynamic in action in *Silent Procession* (Muka miravanuk), written in 1949 and set in a chawl in Parel, a working-class neighborhood in Bombay. The play responds to Bombay's spatial transformations in that historical moment. The play's protagonist, Vishnu, decodes the dense and mystifying node of housing, rents, tenancy, and private property for his wife, Putla. Vishnu, Putla, and Vishnu's brother Ramu are subtenants in a room in the chawl, which he rents from Dattu. Vishnu poses the mystification of private property, tenancy, and rent in the form of a puzzle. He asks Putla, "Which commodity belongs to two different owners?" He eventually answers his own question: "The room in the tenement [*kholi*]." Two simultaneous property rights operate in this instance: "The person who built/owned the commodity [tenement] and the person who leased the tenement [Dattu in this case]."[14] Sathe conceives of the room as a commodity, a thing (*vastu*) that can be traded and which embodies different property rights: the landlord and owner of the tenement has either sold or leased a room to Dattu. As a commodity, the tenement can be exchanged in a transaction and used by the people who live in it. It is interesting to note here that while Sathe delineates the commodification of a tenement, he does not dwell on the lived aspects of life in the *kholi*, as did the sociologists and social reformers we encountered earlier. The *kholi* is home to Vishnu, Putla, and Ramu. By not dwelling on their habitation, he dramatizes and heightens the fragility of their living arrangement and alerts us to their alienation from their home. Vishnu, Putla, and Ramu can only have a tenuous living arrangement and attenuated social relationships because of their living arrangements.

Dattu, who in all likelihood is a tenant, has subleased the tenement to Vishnu. Vishnu experiences the arrangement as two landlords or owners of a singular commodity: Dattu and the landlord who owns the tenement. The subtenant, Vishnu in this case, pays rent to the original tenant, Dattu, who in turn passes on a portion of that money to the landlord. In Bombay at the time, the tenant would sublet to a subtenant to supplement his income because rent was unaffordable in a low-wage economy and subletting generated an additional source of income. Putla has reservations about being a subtenant and encourages Vishnu to find a room of their own; Vishnu expresses his financial inability to afford a room or even rent one, because to rent he would have to pay a *pugree* (a large deposit) to the landlord. The agreement between tenants and subtenants was legally murky, even though it was a common housing practice. Vishnu thus reconciles himself to being a subtenant and internalizes the tenuousness of affordable housing for the working class.[15] He points out that if they cannot live as subtenants in a room, they will have to squat on land, "build a hut [*jhopdi*], and live there," surviving with the (un)certainty that the government would dismantle their home (*jhopdi*). He says, "The government has burned hundreds of slums in Worli and demolished five hundred hutments in Chembur [a suburb of the city]."[16] Sathe traces the continuum between subtenancy and slum habitation. Because the state and city government viewed slums as illegal, they were under constant threat of being dismantled. The state performed two important roles in Sathe's formulation: First, it guaranteed the property rights of the landlords and the contract between the landlord and the tenant, even though the agreement between Vishnu and Dattu had no legal basis. Second, it retained the right to demolish what it considered illegal—*jhopdi* or slums in this case.[17]

Vishnu explains the working of the housing market in Bombay to Putla: "Under capitalism the houses have not been built for people to live in, but for profit. The home is rented to people who can afford to pay the rent. And then came the *pugree* system, the house was only rented to the person who paid the *pugree*. This made it very difficult for some people to rent . . . and therefore they decided to build *jhopdis*."[18] Sathe places the hut and a room in a tenement on a linear continuum. The tenement is an improvement on the hutment, and he sees squatting and slums as a regression, a retraction from capitalism's promise of development. Sathe believes in the progression of human habitation, an evolution from caves in the hills to huts in the plains, to mud houses, to tenements under capitalism.[19] These stages of habitation map onto the Marxian teleology of socioeconomic development from primitive Communism to capitalism. In Sathe's estimation, the regression from tenements to huts diminished capitalism's sense of itself as a progressive force; the *jhopdi* was a reminder of capitalism's frayed dignity (*aabru*). Like the tenement, the hut is also a commodity. In Sathe's formulation, the hut diminishes the use and exchange value of tenements and prevents capitalists from profiting from the latter. Huts "bore a hole through the honor and profits of capitalists," so "they started burning hutments."[20]

Dattu informs Vishnu and Ramu that they will have to vacate the room because his "folks" are coming back to live there. He asks them to make alternative arrangements. But Dattu's announcement becomes moot when news arrives that all the tenants (and subtenants) have to relinquish their dwellings because the government has decided the chawl is in need of repairs.[21] According to the tenants, the landlord wants to get rid of them and has obtained the order for reconstruction to imbue the act of dispossession with the veneer of legality. In the play, the government and the landlords are in cahoots and are arrayed against the tenants and subtenants. The latter lead a silent procession (*muka miravanuk*) to the government headquarters to protest their ouster, but the silent procession eventually devolves into a violent confrontation between the protestors and the police. *Silent Procession* thus highlights the difficulty of nonviolent demonstrations by the urban poor as long as their nonviolence encounters police coercion. In fact, the play sheds light on the impossibility of nonviolence by poking fun at the naïveté and contradictions of the labor leader Upase (meaning "the one who fasts"). The play ends with the Putla, Vishu's wife, pushing Upase aside and confronting the police.[22]

Upase's real name is Girijashankar, but the workers address him as Upase. He is an object of ridicule and the subject of contradictions. The residents of the chawl know him and identify him with his political predilection to declare hunger strikes. Upase serves as a metaphor for Gandhian politics, providing a sharp critique of the workers' union affiliated with the ruling Congress Party, the Rashtriya Mill Mazdoor Sangh (RMMS; National Mill Workers' Association). The RMMS was founded in 1945, and by 1949 it had become the only union approved to represent workers and negotiate industrial disputes on their behalf.[23] It renounced strikes to get recognition as an approved union under the terms of the Bombay Industrial Dispute Act of 1946. The RMMS thus became an important presence in the lives of the workers by the end of the 1940s. Upase's politics center on conciliation. Upase naively believes that political parties of all ideological hues—the Indian National Congress, Socialists, Hindu Mahasabha, the Muslim League, and the Communists can unite on the issue of working-class housing.[24] Sathe's depiction of Upase's refutation by the residents of the Parel chawl in the heat of their confrontation with the police serves to convince his audience of the need for political action, beyond the limits imposed by the RMMS. The implication here is that the Communist union, which at this moment in the history of trade union politics in the city could not represent workers in negotiations with the mill owners, is better suited to lead workers in such an action.

There are two more important themes from the play I wish to highlight here. The first is the anxiety around categories that we saw in the Marathi Marxist universe of the 1920s and 1930s. In *Silent Procession*, the possibility of ouster from or loss of the category "working class" produces trepidation about losing one's sense of self. The ability or inability to rent a space in a tenement is tied to membership in the working class. The second is the relevance of space or the lack of it, which leads to fights and sometimes solidarities among the urban poor. In the play, the paucity of physical space and resultant lack of personal space lead to friction and occasionally violence. For instance, Ramu gets into a verbal altercation with Upase when he objects to Ramu taking an inordinately long bath at a public tap. According to Upase, public space and a public good—water from a tap operated by the civic authorities—are not for extensive private use. By contrast, Ramu insists that the water flowed in a trickle, when it eventually did, and therefore his ablutions needed more time.[25] Thus space and time are the crux of the conflict between Upase and Ramu. Similarly, Ramu gets into fisticuffs in an overcrowded train over a lack of personal space, and at night he confronts another person over a place to sleep on a public footpath.[26] Ramu endeavors to carve out personal space, albeit temporary, from congested public space, and this incites disputes. Friction over space thus has an everyday rhythm in the lives of the urban poor. Public spaces, such as the water tap or the sidewalk, are designed by urban planners and sanctioned by municipal authorities but are used in their own ways by people who live there. But the space also produces solidarity. For instance, the workers overcome their religious and caste differences when they confront the police in the silent procession.

Silent Procession reveals anxieties about the violence of categories and concerns among the urban poor over their eviction from the category of working class. A Muslim character in the play, Rahimu, asks Upase, "How will we be categorized? [Are we tenants?]."[27] They are legally neither landlords nor tenants; rather, some are subtenants and some of them, generally males, sleep on the sidewalk at night. Upase confesses that he has no term for them in his political vocabulary, but Marxists would categorize them as lumpen proletariat: those who have lost their property and their selves.[28] Rahimu protests the violence of categories: "How have we lost our selves? I work in the railways, Ramu is a peasant, and Dhondi is a porter."[29] *Silent Procession* links housing to status, social classification, and a sense of self; the loss of a rented room in a chawl and the resultant life as a squatter on the pavement or in slums signify a loss of status. Rahimu is angered by the precarious edifice of categorization and the loss of self.

The residents of the Parel chawl suggest that Upase declare a two-month fast to protest the eviction order. It is interesting to note here that the urban poor are dictating political tactics to a leader. Upase contends that the housing question, though an important one, does not merit a fast. Upase likely fasted for the anticolonial national movement, "which was a bigger question. The housing question is not that big. It can be solved through negotiations and bargaining with the government and the landlord. No fast required."[30] After Upase declines to fast, the residents suggest a rally (*morcha*) in lieu of a fast. Upase prefers writing letters and memorandums to authorities exhorting them to consider the demands of the residents. The urban poor do not budge, and Upase agrees to a rally but insists it must be silent and peaceful. When the procession nears the seat of government, the police ask them to disband and declare the procession illegal. Upase directs them to disperse, but the agitators do not want to abandon their claim on public space. They insist on moving ahead even if it leads to a confrontation. Upase brands them unpatriotic.[31] Vishnu points out that they have nothing to lose in their confrontation with the police; the police who are asking them to disperse will barge into their homes and evict them (in accordance with the order) in any case. The play ends with Putla, Vishnu's wife, pushing Upase aside and weathering the police assault. Thus the subtenants who had the most to lose from eviction, including their status as part of the working class, hurl themselves into an altercation with authorities. The confrontation with the police is their primary mode of interaction with the state, and these encounters shape their politics.[32] The neighborhoods of the urban poor and its built environment are key sites in this politics. The homes they rent, the public taps they use, the pavement they sleep on, the personal space they struggle to find in an overcrowded city, and their sense of self are all at stake in this confrontation.

Sathe responds to the restive politics of sanitation workers in the city in the 1940s in *The Minister's Tour* (Lokamantryancha daura). In the play, municipal workers in Bombay city go on strike to demand bonus wages. The strike results in overflowing sewage and choked drains.[33] There is also a possibility of textile workers joining the strike. Magarchand, a minister in the provincial government, tours the workers' neighborhoods to convince them to end the strike. This he does by threatening to incarcerate all eight thousand sanitation workers.[34] *The Minister's Tour*, like other plays by Sathe, reaffirms the nexus between the state and the mill owners. They bond over shared anxieties about disciplining the city's workers and their aversion to Communist unions. As labor historians have pointed out, the colonial state and Bombay capitalists attributed the lack of discipline among Indian workers to a "pre-capitalist culture"[35] and workers' inability to adapt to the temporality of industrial work.[36] The ideal laboring subjects for Magarchand are workers who do not go on strike or support the Communist Party. He idealizes the denizens of the mythological Ramrajya (the subjects of the kingdom of Lord Ram), who can take orders and endure hunger for the sake of the nation.[37] To counter the Communists' influence on workers, Magarchand visits working-class neighborhoods to propagate his vision of Ramrajya. He elaborates his vision: "Listen to your minister, stop going on strike, eat less, work more, be disciplined, unobtrusive, and obedient, embrace truth and nonviolence and strive to become like the mythological King Ram."[38] His other lessons in the neighborhood are farcical: when he advises them to plant trees, the workers take it as an opportunity to reclaim municipal land by planting trees. Magarchand amends his instructions to be more specific: the urban poor should plant trees in forests, on farms, and in villages and not in their neighborhoods.[39] He instructs the urban poor to grow food in boxes and flowerpots to help the Indian nation survive its food shortage. He asks them to eat less and switch to eating *penda*, fibers left after crushing and extracting oil from peanuts, because they are rich in protein.[40] Sathe foregrounds the disconnect between Magarchand and the workers; the votaries of Ramrajya appear tone deaf to the demands and aspirations of the striking workers. According to Sathe, Ramrajya is an ideological tool for the subjugation of the working class in a newly independent India. The play ends with incarceration. Two leaders of the urban poor, Vishnu and Hanmu, are jailed for disturbing Magarchand's vision of Ramrajya and publicly questioning its validity.

In Sathe's rendition, Bombay city is a site of contradictions. The city is a source of enchantment but also of unemployment, hunger, and lack of housing. In Bombay urban poor are marginalized, but here they stake a claim to public space and protest their marginalization. These contradictions seep into and are in fact foundational to the inner lives of its citizens. Thus, in his famous poem "My Parrot Has Remained in the Village" (Majhi maina gavavar rahili), Sathe laments the separation from his beloved, left behind in the village when he migrated to Bombay for work. Life in the city is harsh, but the industries, cars, and fashionable apparel—fine saris made of nylon and georgette—are alluring. In the city, unemployment is rampant. The city is also inhabited by capitalists, thieves, the reckless (sirajora), the slovenly, and the parasitical classes (aita khau).[41] For Sathe, everyday life in the city is bleak, especially for the poor. Housing is scarce, and the unemployed and underemployed can and do turn on each other. Sathe explores the theme of poor-on-poor violence in his famous poem "A Lavani for Bombay" (Mumbaichi lavani). In language redolent of his protégé Baburao Bagul, Sathe says:

Man eats man. Exploits and is exploited.
Three million people live here.
They get riled up and agitated occasionally,
And riot sometimes
And kill each other.[42]

To overcome the socioeconomic and spatial disparity, Sathe calls for a revolution led by the working class on behalf of the urban poor. The city enables solidarities of class but also unmakes them.

This play of enchantment with and alienation from the city is exemplified in "My Parrot Has Remained in the Village." After lamenting the separation from rural life and his relationships there, he urges the urban poor to pour themselves into the political movement that seeks to retain Bombay city as the capital of the Marathi-speaking state of Maharashtra in the

1950s. The psychic contradictions of life in Bombay dissolve into another contradiction: the political struggle to establish Bombay as the symbol of linguistic identity and cultural pride, as well as the administrative head-quarters of a regional state in which the working class and the urban poor play an important role. As the title of another poem suggests, "Finally, Bombay Is Now Maharashtra's" (Akher jhali Mumbai Maharashtrachi).[43] The Samyukta Maharashtra Samiti, formed in 1946, claimed Bombay city in the name of its cultural congruity with the Marathi-speaking state of Maharashtra, and gained traction in postcolonial India after the decision to reorganize Indian provinces on the basis of linguistic congruity. In the 1950s, only two-fifths of Bombay residents considered Marathi their native language. The city's Communists, who had hitherto avoided the question of cultural difference—particularly caste and religious difference—hurled themselves into the movement for an ethnic identity based on language.[44] The movement brought about a "remarkable ideological convergence"[45] between socialists, Communists, the leaders of the anti-Brahmin move-ment, Hindu nationalists, and even the Ambedkar-led Scheduled Caste Federation advocating for a Marathi-speaking state of Maharashtra with Bombay city as its capital. Alienation and ideological conflict were over-come, albeit temporarily, through participation in a movement in which the city itself was an important symbol of cultural identity. The city and its spaces enabled the alliance of these social movements and the mobiliza-tion of the urban poor.

URBAN PLANNING, SPACE, AND THE WRINKLES OF MODERNITY

Urban planning provided an administrative mechanism to manage Bom-bay's transformation in the face of this upsurge, in which the urban poor played an important role. As we saw in Sathe's *loknatyas* and poems writ-ten and performed for the urban poor, the subordinated classes in the city mobilized in public space to protest urban transformations that sought to marginalize them. Urban planning in Bombay at that time was as much about land use and efficient management of space as it was an administra-tive response to the mobilization of the urban poor in the 1940s and 1950s. Planning was the antidote to problems like overcrowding but had to be kept out of the purview of the masses overcrowding the city. In this sec-tion, I juxtapose the politics of planning with the upsurge of the urban poor to argue that urban planning was a response to the political conjunc-ture in the city. It was also in sync with global trends in postwar planning.

In the global conjuncture, planning was intended to renew the devastated urban fabric in Europe and America after World War II. In Britain this took the form of "stringent town and country planning legislation" that restricted suburbanization, while in the United States it involved rapid suburbanization.[46] In Bombay, suburbanization gained momentum in this context. Planning combined the prestige of science with confidence that it could rationally organize chaotic urban spaces. Bombay's postcolonial urban planning was enchanted by the possibility of ordering this chaotic city.[47] Planning for the city was essentially top down—dreamed by experts and implemented by bureaucrats.[48] Probably because it was considered a scientific enterprise, planners did not overtly invoke caste, even as they assumed and addressed class stratification. Like Marxism, class was haunted by caste in urban planning too. In fact, the plans utilized and exacerbated caste stratification in the city.

The visions of planning were different for technocrats—the urban planners themselves—and bureaucrats. For instance, when the municipal commissioner of Bombay waded into the process of planning, he sought legal power to reshape the built environment of the city. In 1943, for instance, he proposed amending the law to establish a Clearance Area, followed by a provision for clearance, a demolition order to knock down houses unfit for human habitation, a redevelopment order for congested areas, and a provision for compulsory acquisition of land.[49] He also asked for provisions establishing taxation on properties and loans to individual and housing associations to provide housing for the poor. Ironically, in the eyes of the municipal commissioner, the justification for clearance of congested areas and compulsory acquisition of land was to provide housing for the poor. According to the Bombay City and Suburbs Post-War Development Committee, "Housing and Slum clearance cannot be separated. Unless houses at cheap rents are made available for those living in slums, the slums cannot be cleared."[50] In the discourse of planning, then, slums were the conceptual other of the normative house. To symbolically and actually erase the former from the city, it was important to construct housing for the poor. The planners imagined a symbiotic relationship between the state and private capital to solve the housing question. The goal was to "bring it [a house] within the means of the working-class family."[51] In practice, the provision of housing and elimination of slums were not synchronous; the elimination of slums produced more slums.

From the early twentieth century, Bombay's planners envisioned suburbanization as the remedy for overcrowding and the proliferation of slums.

The Bombay government had recommended suburbanization in 1918 and reiterated it again in 1925, 1933, 1936, and 1938. The suggestion was to develop and incorporate Kurla, Trombay, and Salsette to the north of Bombay as suburbs. The government's rationale was that suburban sites would house the poor and middle classes of the city.[52] The proposals entailed reconstitution of the Bombay Municipal Corporation and extension of its legal and financial capacity to improve roads, public health, water supply, and drainage in suburban areas. The idea of expanding the city's limits met with an unenthusiastic response from the Bombay Municipal Corporation. The corporation, dominated by landlords, feared a tax increase to provide amenities in the suburbs. As a government committee mentioned in 1925, the suburbs were a menace to Bombay.[53] Even in 1946, when the Bombay Municipal Corporation agreed in principle to incorporate Bandra, Santa Cruz, Juhu, Kurla, Ghatkopar, Thana, and Trombay into the city, the question of taxation worried city councilors. According to J. A. Collaco, who opposed the integration of the suburbs into the city, "If you tax the people in the suburbs you will be killing them, if you tax us in the city, we shall have to commit suicide."[54] Thus, some elected representatives had reservations about suburbanization, but for urban planners it was the geographical fix to the problem of overcrowding.

The creation of Greater Bombay necessitated a comprehensive plan for the city. Like Marxism and Dalit literature, post–World War II urban planning had transnational links too. For instance, when the chief engineer of the Bombay Municipal Corporation was tasked with drafting a master plan for Bombay, he lamented the lack of urban planners in India. An invitation was extended to the American urban architect and town planner Albert Mayer to assist N. V. Modak in planning the city; by the end of 1947, they produced *An Outline of the Master Plan for Greater Bombay*.[55] The plan aspired to bring Bombay's housing, town planning, transportation, and communication lines in concert with modern times, finding its "inhuman overcrowding and its slums a menace to health, morals, and working efficiency" of the city.[56] In Modak and Mayer's view, slums and overcrowding were features of urban life that were not aligned with modernity, even though modernity had produced their preponderance in Bombay. The goal of town planning was to realign the asymmetry between urban life and modernity "to balance everyday requirements of the population in respect of work, industry, housing, recreation (both physical and mental), transport and communications and amenities. In addition to satisfying local conditions, it should also meet regional and national needs."[57] Planning thus was an ambitious endeavor. It would rectify the misalignments and synchronize modern life. It spanned the spectrum of spatial scales—local, regional, national, and transnational. Its focal point was the individual, who lived in a community and interacted with the city. Its primary goal was to provide "adequate living and working conditions to its population," and it would achieve this goal by prescribing practices of land use and ascertaining that every acre of the city's land was "rightly used to balance everyday requirements of the population."[58] To synchronize various aspects of urban expansion, a master plan was required for Bombay city, its suburbs, and the region surrounding the city. The committee conceived the master plan as the ur-text for other planning endeavors in the city, including transport, housing, and town planning.[59] Town planning was thus the conduit and the product of technocratic prescriptions, conveying their assumption that the contradictions of modernity could be dealt with through a measured response to processes not in tune with modern life. The planners did not articulate a critique of modern political economy or capitalism, but instead focused on its effects like slums. Moreover, their assumption that city life necessitated transformation in the individual and in society bore the imprint of modernism. The committee cited European models of city planning saying that planning should be "from the future towards the present and vice versa."[60]

In the present that Modak and Mayer sought to change, a hundred thousand people lived in small rooms that included anywhere between ten and nineteen people, and there were 400,000 people sleeping on sidewalks.[61] In response to that present, Sathe had proposed a political revolution. For their part, the planners imagined a spatial solution to Bombay's urbanity. In their own ways, both Sathe and the planners were responding to the problem of housing in the city. The planners envisioned the suburbs as localities for the middle class and urban poor and as a solution to the structural problems of the city. Modak and Mayer prescribed the creation of a legal architecture "to control the use of land and the density of its development."[62] The plan was touted as sound and realistic because it was based on the fusion of "Indian knowledge and foreign experience": the experience of Euro-American urban planners would help Bombay city tide over thirty years of trial and error in foreign lands. One of the errors that Modak and Mayer had at the back of their minds was the "divorce of housing from planning" in interwar Great Britain.[63] They encouraged the government to acquire land in advance to avoid much costlier acquisitions later and prevent dislocation and antagonism among the people.[64] The plan was tabled after Indian independence and partition, which resulted in a steep increase in refugees. In postcolonial India, city planning acquired a feverish urgency because the modernist endeavor of organizing space and time through urban planning was tied to the dream of creating a modern nation.

An important stated assumption of the planners was that all people aspired to live in "a Great City, a city of Dignity, Grace and Inspiration; not only an efficient city."[65] Housing, according to the Modak and Mayer report, was the "core of planning" and the city's "most crying need."[66] The plan identified housing for low-income and middle-income workers who lived in "frightfully overcrowded, ill-lighted, and insanitary homes."[67] It proposed 17,000 "low-income homes" to be built on vacant land, "not slum land," and recommended slum clearance only when there was a cache of new homes.[68] This was an important moment of synchronization of modern urban life; the plans of the 1940s stated that slums had a place in urban life. Slums and the lands on which they stood were granted legroom in the city, albeit temporarily, before being cleared after production of more low-income homes. Slums might be on a lower stage of evolution in housing and therefore not in sync with the imaginary of progress, but in twentieth-century Bombay they had an important role to play in urban life because they housed labor in the city. This was the context in which the Modak and Mayer plan specified that the bulk of low-income housing should be on vacant land (and not slum land) within Bombay city and not on land in Greater Bombay because "labour cannot afford the pay in and out of Bombay."[69] In their cautious approach to slum clearance, Modak and Mayer echoed Patrick Geddes's plans of an earlier vintage. In the 1910s, Geddes had opposed the large-scale razing of structures and favored selective clearance to open up cramped neighborhoods.[70] Modak and Mayer's long-term solution to the housing crisis was to decentralize industries: heavier industries would move to satellite towns outside Greater Bombay, leaving only light industry within Greater Bombay.[71] This prescription was in league with the Barlow Committee report in Great Britain, which had recommended the decentralization of industries from congested areas.[72] Decentralization of industries would also dissipate workers, controlling the upsurge of urban poor, a task that planning had performed in Europe and America in the late nineteenth and twentieth centuries. To reorganize the city, the planners and decision makers needed a legal apparatus to actualize it.

LAW AND URBAN PLANNING

Planning was buttressed by legal provisions. One provision to tackle the "acute shortage of housing" was the constitution of the Bombay Provincial Housing Board under the Bombay Housing Board Act of 1948. The board was granted the power to acquire and hold property, manage the lands and buildings vested in it, and frame and execute housing schemes. The creation of a legal architecture to plan the city created the space for legal disputes with various petitioners challenging the legality of provisions in the city's courts. These laws, along with institutions such as the Bombay Housing Board, shaped the relationship between the land and the built environment on the one hand, and individuals, groups, and institutions on the other. While the primary object of planning was imagining and sometimes reimagining the various uses of land in the city, the object of law was to shape the relationship of the individual to the land and the persons or institutions who controlled it. The courts were called upon to adjudicate these relationships. Take the case of Baburao Shantaram More, a resident of Sion Dharavi, who had "without authority or title . . . occupied" tenements in the Sion Dharavi camp. The Government of India had built the tenements during World War II for its use. In 1948, the Government of Bombay bought the camp from the Government of India and handed it over to the Bombay Provincial Housing Board in June 1949. More and some other people had squatted in the tenements before they were handed over to the Housing Board. More and the board sought to legalize the relationship by agreeing to a rent. The rent was fixed at fourteen rupees per month. In the meantime, the Government of Bombay refurbished the structure and revised More's rent to fifty-six rupees in early 1950, four times the rent agreed upon a few months earlier.[73] According to an economic survey of the city in 1963, most occupants of tenements or chawls paid anywhere between ten and forty rupees in rent, depending on the tenement's location and type.[74] Fifty-six rupees was thus steep rent in 1950. In February 1950, the board served notice to vacate the tenement unless More complied and paid the revised rent. More refused and did not vacate the tenements. The board then filed a case against him in Bombay's Small Causes Court, which eventually went to the Bombay High Court. More argued that protection against steep increases in rent offered by the Bombay Rent Act of 1947 was applicable in his case, but the High Court ruled against this claim in 1953.

The legal provisions for city planning invited litigation from tenants and landowners. For instance, the Bombay Land Requisition Act of 1948 and the Land Acquisition Act of 1894, which were deployed to acquire land for "public purposes," were litigated in court. The petitioner, in this case either the tenant or the owner of the land, contested the requisition on the ground that the actions violated fundamental rights guaranteed by the Constitution of India, such as the right to property or against discrimination on the basis of gender and caste.[75] In *Babu Barkya Thakur v. The State of Bombay and Others* in 1959–60, Thakur's land was about to be acquired by Bombay state to facilitate the construction of a factory by Mukund Iron and Steel Works. Thakur challenged the acquisition order, but the Supreme Court of India dismissed his petition. Apart from these acts, the Bombay Provincial Municipal Act of 1949 gave powers to the Municipal Commissioner of Bombay to acquire land or any building in the city for the purpose of implementing an improvement scheme like laying storm-water drains, sewers, or street lighting or construction of buildings for the poorer sections of the community.[76] The discourse of improvement in the name of the urban poor ended up displacing the urban poor. These provisions vested power in authorities like the State of Bombay, the Bombay Municipal Corporation, and the municipal commissioner to shape land use in the city by providing them with legal muscle. Shaping land use in the name of improvement had a colonial lineage and prefigured notions of the wasteful use of land and the goal of increasing the value of land.[77] But in the process, they encountered litigious tenants who countered the regime of improvement and the legal apparatus that supported it with a counterdiscourse highlighting the fundamental rights of independent India's citizens. The cases that were contested all the way up to the Supreme Court of India, for instance by petitioners like Babu Thakur, were lost. Thus, in the name of improvement, development, or housing for the poor, the city and the state, through their legal apparatus, placed an enormous burden on the same people they claimed to be helping.[78] Those who could not litigate responded by squatting on land owned by municipal or state authorities or private individuals. Thus urban planning, which was forged to manage the contradictions of city life and synchronize it with the time of global modernity, created other contradictions, namely the eviction of people in the name of housing and improvement of their lives.

Just as visions of urban planning were being laid out, the municipal workers, particularly city sweepers and scavengers, agitated for higher wages and better housing. Most of these workers belonged to various Dalit castes that had migrated to the city from the Gujarati- and Marathi-speaking areas of the Bombay state and also from regions beyond it. On July 1, 1948, nine thousand sweepers from Bombay and its suburbs went on strike, demanding increased wages and better housing.[79] That strike was called off on the assurance of speedy settlement of the issue. But on May 13, 1949, fifteen thousand municipal workers, mostly from the Conservancy Department, again went on strike, demanding free housing (not just better housing), a higher minimum wage, and a six-hour workday. In 1948–49, only 4,898 of these workers were housed in single-room tenements provided by the Health Department of Bombay Municipal Corporation; others lived in rented rooms or unauthorized hutments constructed on municipal land. Tenants paid ground rent of one rupee for the use of this municipal land.[80] The living conditions in municipal tenements in the Umarkhadi and Walpakhadi neighborhoods, with "privies full of night soil," "flushes out of order," bathrooms without water taps, and insufficient electric lights, were well documented.[81] The striking workers in 1949 were led by the Bombay Municipal Kamgar Sangh (Bombay Municipal Employees' Union), headed by B. R. Ambedkar, who was president of India's Constituent Assembly at the time. The vice president and secretary of the union were leaders of the Dalit movement in the city, P. T. Borale and Madke Buva.

The strike was notable for many reasons. The municipal employees were making demands on a municipal corporation that was the first civic body in the country to be elected by universal adult suffrage. The striking municipal employees hoped that a democratically elected body would be more responsive to the demands of the people, including its own employees, but instead they encountered a reticent employer. The strike lasted 140 days, a long time for the mostly poor conservancy workers in the city. In the initial days of the strike, the police jailed one hundred workers, hoping to intimidate the rest into ending the strike. They also restricted the movements of the union leader, P. T. Borale.[82] The workers responded by launching a sewage attack: they clogged sewage pipes near the residence of the chief minister and home minister of the Bombay state, thus encircling their official residences with overflowing human waste. Now the homes of the chief minister and home minister were surrounded with fecal matter, and not just the homes of Dalits described by sociologists and reformers. In this moment, then, the sanitation workers overturned the symbolic order of clean versus unclean, sanitary versus unsanitary. The strike was also significant because the demands of the sanitation workers included a minimum wage of forty-five to ninety-five rupees and a cost of living rate of fifty rupees per employee. In addition, the workers wanted a tenement with three rooms or an additional rent allowance of ten rupees if they were not allotted the desired tenement.[83] Most of these demands went unrequited at the time, and the strike collapsed after one worker died of malnutrition and the state deployed police, home guards, and nonunionized workers to take their places. But the strike had some long-term consequences favorable to the workers. For instance, the political party that controlled the municipal corporation, the Congress Party, lost the municipal elections in 1957, when it was defeated by an alliance of Communists, Socialists, and the Scheduled Caste Federation. P. T. Borale was elected mayor. The Municipal Corporation nominated a wage commission, and the Bombay state set up a committee to investigate the living conditions of sweepers and scavengers. The committee recommended a minimum housing accommodation of two rooms, including a living room and a kitchen, with the total floor area not less than two hundred square feet.[84] It also recommended a housing allowance of ten rupees per month to the head of the family, one of the demands of the strikers in 1949, and an additional five rupees for each employee of the corporation living in the household. Moreover, the committee encouraged the corporation to help staff "own decent houses" and recommended they make use of the provisions under the Backward Class Co-operative Housing Scheme, also known as Post-War Reconstruction Scheme (PWR) No. 219.[85]

Here the state was addressing the caste question, at least as it pertained to the housing of conservancy staff in Bombay city, through the logic of property. PWR 219, it must be noted, was "for the improvement of the housing conditions" of all backward classes or Dalits and not just scavengers and sweepers.[86] Under this scheme, the government offered interest-free loans of up to 75 percent, on an amount not exceeding two thousand rupees, for the construction of a dwelling. The loan was repayable over twenty years. More importantly, the government promised to give land, free of cost, to the housing society, and each member of the society could lease the land for ninety-nine years at a nominal rent of four annas per year.[87] The government justified the acquisition of property in the name of social welfare and improvement of the living conditions of its conservancy workers. Workers could acquire property by approaching the state as a member of the backward classes or a group that labored in city sanitation, including handling and disposing of garbage and excrement. Their ability to own or rent a room in Bombay city was tied to their continued consent to handle waste.[88] Social welfare was the ideology for this transaction and an important arena in which the postcolonial state sought legitimacy. PWR 219 made them owners of property, but in the bargain, the twenty-year loan tied them to the property. And since property passed from father to son, the work of scavenging also passed from one generation to the next. Thus, apart from ensuring its own legitimacy by providing welfare for its backward subjects, the state also guaranteed the reproduction of labor in what it saw as an important service—scavenging. At the same time, the acquisition of property, because it was attained through identification with scavenging and untouchability, did not disturb the symbolic order of repugnance felt toward scavengers and Dalits.[89]

The author Daya Pawar's autobiography, *Village Servant* (Baluta), sheds light on the everydayness of revulsion in the city at this time. Pawar remembers his childhood experiences of caste in Bombay during this period. Pawar was born to a family of Mahar Dalits. He once came to visit Bombay from his village along with older boys and men from the Maratha caste; Pawar wanted to visit his uncle in the Kawakhana neighborhood. Pawar accompanied his friend Vithoba, identified as a Warkari (a religious sect known for its deep devotion to the deity Vithoba) from the Maratha caste. Vithoba visited his family and friends in Sangappa Chawl in the mill district of Parel before accompanying Pawar to his destination, Kawakhana. Sangappa Chawl and its vicinity, where Vithoba's relatives lived, was home to many Marathas from their village. When they reached the chawl, Pawar was asked to sit outside the building and brought a plate of food there.[90] Pawar narrates his experience: "I ate with my eyes downcast. . . . I was dying to get away . . . to Kawakhana"[91]

There are two distinct but interconnected strands at work here that shed light on the everyday experience of caste. At one level, caste (and class) shaped the spatial arrangement of localities, chawls, slums, and schools. Sangappa Chawl had many Marathas who did not want Pawar to partake in libations in the tenement. Pawar experienced the visit with Vithoba's family as humiliation; the practice was, after all, designed to exclude Pawar and put him in his place outside the building, reminding him that he was socially inferior to the Maratha caste. Caste (and class, because Pawar was not as well off) informed this humiliating experience. Caste and class also shaped the experience of schooling. The economist Naredra Jadhav described his schooling in the Bombay Port Trust School, where "most of our teachers were also Dalits; some of them had converted to Christianity."[92] Similarly, Pawar reminisced about Kawakhana, where children from the Mahar Dalit castes were sent to a school in the ironically named Sundar Gully (Beautiful Lane), a "filthy area . . . covered with piles of rubbish [and] puddles of dirty water."[93]

PWR 219 enabled some Dalits to acquire a home, but the reproduction of the conservancy staff did not diminish the significance or experience of caste and class. The tenement and a sanitation job passed from father to son. To illustrate with an example from the 1970s, Ramesh Haralkar, who painted banners for the Dalit Panther movement after arriving in Bombay in 1971, was one such twin beneficiary of a job and a tenement. His father, Hari Vithu, was a sanitation worker in the city and lived in a tenement for conservancy workers in the suburb of Sion in Dharavi. That tenement had been allotted to him by the Bombay Municipal Corporation. Haralkar dreamed of being an artist and enrolling in the city's famous J. J. School of Arts. In his rendition of the story, Haralkar discarded the paintbrush and picked up the broom in order to inherit the tenement.[94] To retain the tenement, he embraced the symbolic order of repugnance associated with sanitation work. He felt revulsion for his work, and the everydayness of revulsion eventually deadened him to it. For instance, he describes in detail the routine of picking up "mountains" of dead rats with his bare hands from a research laboratory in the city, as well as the day he was covered with menstrual blood from used sanitary pads.[95] It is important for Haralkar to communicate this revulsion to his audience as background for his work as political activist in the 1970s and 1980s. Haralkar inverts the order of repugnance and propagates a politics of self-respect (atma-samman). For him the politics of the Ambedkarite movement after the death of B. R. Ambedkar was preoccupied with the symbolic politics of erecting statues at the expense of substantive issues like self-respect, housing, and education. He credits his association with the Dalit Panther movement for his worldview. For Haralkar, the reproduction of labor and property created the conditions for experiencing more revulsion. He was attracted to the transformative politics of self-respect to escape the cycle of revulsion. But to cultivate self-respect and overcome the debilities of repugnance, one needed a worldview that foregrounded the symbolic and substantive demands of Dalits. In the 1970s, he was attracted to the Dalit Panther movement for this reason.

SLUMS AND ALTERNATE HOUSING

Even as the state offered some Dalits a chance to acquire property through PWR 219, the slums and tenements that housed many Dalits and urban poor continued to fester in the eyes of the urban planners. In 1946, there were 88 slums in the city; in 1957, the number increased to 144, covering 877 acres across various wards in the city. The total population of slum dwellers in the city was 415,875.[96] Bombay's population had increased dramatically in the intervening period from 1.49 million in 1941 to 2.3 million in 1951; one reason was the influx of refugees after the partition of India in 1947. According to a 1956 survey conducted by the Bombay Municipal Corporation, almost 29 percent of the 131,662 tenements in the city were overcrowded and failed to meet the minimum occupancy rate of twenty-five square feet per person.[97] A Bombay Municipal Corporation survey conducted in 1957 concluded that 83,451 families lived in slums.[98] Industrial workers constituted more than one-fourth of the total slum population. The survey suggested that more than two-thirds of the slum population did not have manufacturing jobs. The figures thus provided an early indication that the urban population, particularly those living in the slums, grew at a faster rate than workers in the manufacturing sector.[99]

Slums were built on various types of land tenures. For instance, Kamathipura, in the E ward of the city, had the largest slum on privately owned land, while Dharavi in G ward, which was the biggest slum in the city, was built mostly on municipal land and consisted predominantly of huts.[100] In 1954, the municipal corporation amended the Bombay Municipal Corporation Act to enable slum clearance.[101] Since the slums were built mostly on state, municipal, and private land, few slum dwellers had title deeds to the places they inhabited. In theory, therefore, they could be evicted and the slums demolished. In practice, though, this did not come to pass. In 1958, the Bombay Municipal Corporation began a pilot project in the Kamathipura slums under the aegis of the amended act, but this project failed, in the municipal corporation's estimation because of inadequate government support for rehabilitation and redevelopment, reluctance of slum dwellers to shift to suburban locations, and refusal of shopkeepers to move out of the city.[102] According to the Bombay Development Plan, the "socio-economic aspects" of clearance and rehabilitation had undercut implementation of the plan, and therefore "progress ha[d] not been satisfactory."[103] The cost of the Kamathipura scheme was prohibitive, the government subsidy for construction and land acquisition was inadequate, the wages of the tenants were low, and often more than one family lived in a tenement, making it difficult to identify the person or family to be rehoused. This made it difficult to implement the scheme. One of the founders of the Dalit Panther movement, Namdeo Dhasal, moved to Kamathipura from a village near Pune in 1957. In 1959, planners said the city still needed three hundred thousand tenements.[104] Apart from state support, the Development Plan of 1964 blamed the "natural apathy" of the people for the failure of the Kamathipura scheme. It lamented the inability of slum dwellers to treat planning, slum clearance, and rehabilitation as an act of God, just as they would the collapse of a house.[105] If they saw it as a divine act, they would consent and submit to the process. The slum dwellers' resistance to the Kamathipura clearance scheme thus needed the intervention of an extraterrestrial being, God, for its success. It was an ironic recognition on the part of the Bombay Development Plan that the temporal and spatial authority of the state and capital could not create perfect subjects of urban planning who would consent to slum clearance and resettlement in the suburbs. That consent needed a divine spark that would magically transform recalcitrance. This recalcitrance—the lack of fatalism of slum dwellers—was a political act, and political parties and social movements had to attend to the slum dwellers' reluctance to accept slum clearance and resettlement in the suburbs.

Both Dalit politics and leftist movements responded to the politics of slum clearance. Their constituents experienced the possibility of eviction as marginalization from the city, a city they had agitated for in the Samyukta Maharashtra Movement a few years before. The issue of slums was important to the Dalit social movement. In fact, the Republican Party of India (RPI) was the first party to organize slum dwellers on the issue of shelter (*nivara*), starting the Republican Zopadi Sangh (Republican Hutment Association) in 1958.[106] The president of the RPI, B. K. Gaikwad, linked slums to the larger issues of landlessness and land redistribution in the country. He petitioned the Bombay state and the central government to redistribute fallow land to landless laborers. Gaikwad articulated his demands in the language of the rights of the citizen; he argued that the urban poor "should be provided jobs and homes."[107] He stated that hutment dwellers were "mostly . . . Scheduled Castes (Dalits) and Other Backward Class" and demanded that their huts not be demolished until they were provided alternate housing. According to Gaikwad, the political response to housing vulnerabilities and the marginalization of lower-caste and lower-class groups was redistribution of state resources.

The leftist movement also demanded alternate housing for slum clearance in the 1950s and 1960s. The Bombay Municipal Corporation undertook projects of slum demolition similar to the Kamathipura project in 1960.[108] The leftists elected to the municipal corporation opposed the demolition and bargained for alternate housing for slum dwellers. The BMC, with financial assistance from the Indian government, agreed to construct one-room tenements for slum dwellers at suburban sites, fixing the monthly rent at forty rupees. The residents of the slums paid twenty rupees as rent; the difference was treated as financial assistance from the central government.[109] Some of the slum residents of south and central Bombay were moved to Kannamvarnagar in Vikhroli, Motilal Nagar in Goregaon, Shivajinagar near Trombay, and Malvani near Malad, all suburbs to the north and east of Bombay that been incorporated a few years earlier.[110]

THE CASTE AND CLASS OF SUBURBAN SLUMS

The removal of a slum from the city to the suburbs produced slums in the suburbs. One such slum was the Janata Squatters Colony in the suburb of Jogeshwari in North Bombay.[111] The colony made use of the Indian government's slum clearance scheme; land was made available in the suburbs for resettlement, and the land containing the original slum in the city was earmarked for residential complexes, bus terminals, and milk dairies.[112] The BMC moved 1,957 families from south and central Bombay to Janata Squatters Colony. They were given a title deed known as a Vacant Land Tenancy (VLT) for land measuring fifteen by twenty feet (three hundred square feet). The tenants had to pay a monthly rent of three rupees and twenty-five paisa on the land and sixteen rupees in annual property tax.[113] The BMC could terminate the tenancy rights on short notice. By the 1960s and 1970s, though, many original tenants of the BMC encroached upon land in their vicinity and built tenements there to house subtenants. In the process, VLT holders became landlords. The tenements that subtenants lived in were approximately 15 by 7.5 feet, or 112.5 square feet, and the "walls were made of jute bags or reed and the roofs of broken pots and mud. There was no electricity, drainage, or water supply."[114] In the 1960s and 1970s there was a huge influx of migrants to the Janata Squatters Colony, many of whom became subtenants of the VLT holders. In this way VLT rights became a commodity, like housing, that could be traded, exchanged, or used to create more commodities (albeit without adequate legal protection) for subtenants. This arrangement created intense conflict between VLT holders and subtenants, with many disputes adjudicated by the small causes court in the city.

It is important here to pay attention to the sociohistorical condition of the residents of Janata Colony. Both the tenants and subtenants worked mostly in the informal sectors of the city's economy. Many men were carpenters, masons, painters, artisans, hawkers, or laborers in small manufacturing units, while women worked in home-based industries or as domestic servants in middle- and upper middle-class households. VLT served as an important structuring hierarchy. But another feature of social stratification—caste—also operated here. The residents of the colony predominantly identified themselves as "backward castes."[115] It is significant to note that within the Janata Squatters Colony one locality was named Harijan Nagar; Harijan was a caste marker imposed on the Dalit castes by M. K. Gandhi.[116] Within the backward castes, then, there was a further spatial segmentation between Dalits and non-Dalits.

Segregation by caste in slums and tenements was not a novel feature of the 1960s. It shaped urban habitations (and employment) throughout the late nineteenth and twentieth centuries. Let us consider this point with another example from the 1950s referenced in the previous paragraph—domestic service. Domestic servants in Bombay city were stratified along lines of class, caste, ethnicity, and gender. Domestic servants were "unprotected by any legislation . . . and left out of any scheme of social security."[117] In the 1950s, most domestic servants identified as backward castes. There was also a gender dimension to caste stratification. Male domestic servants belonged to the higher ranks of the backward castes. For instance, among Marathi-speaking domestic servants in the city, men from the peasant Kunbi caste comprised 46.5 percent of domestic workers while almost 90 percent of female domestic servants were from the Dalit castes.[118] According to the sociologist Aban Mehta, who surveyed domestic workers in the 1950s, many "domestic workers are housed in some of the poorest slums of the city . . . areas hardly fit for human habitation!"[119] But even though they were not fit for habitation, there was caste segmentation within them. The domestic servants he studied lived in chawls segregated by caste. Even within Dalit castes, for instance, domestic servants lived in clusters segmented by subcastes, for instance the "Mang chawl at Mahim and Chamar Chawls at Dadar and the Matunga Labour Camp."[120]

Thus slums, as a commodity, housed labor that helped produce other commodities for the city. Slums therefore continued to grow in the 1950s and 1960s. The BMC and the state sought to clear slums from some places and resettled them elsewhere. But clearance and resettlement in alternate sites produced more slums. The economic historian Morris D. Morris points out an important feature of the labor market in the city. In his study of the textile industry, he points out that the industry required very large amounts of minimally trained labor that could be easily sourced in the city, temporarily employed, and summarily dismissed, without any notice.[121] Trade unions in Bombay city had been created in response to this feature of the labor market, where job security was minimal. In 1961, there were 703,542 workers registered in unions in the city across all industries. Most of these industrial workers lived either in slums or chawls. In that same year, according to the census, there were 445,000 wage employees in the informal or unorganized sector. The economists Heather Joshi and Vijay Joshi estimate that wage employees constituted only half of the total number of workers in the informal sector. The other half were either self-employed or "unpaid family workers" in household industries.[122] Jobs in this sector included household servants and cooks, hawkers of commodities, scrap dealers, shoe shiners, barbers, tobacco workers, workers in soap, salt, and matches manufactures, and bicycle and motor repairers. The steady waning of jobs in the textile industry was matched by a steep increase in the informal sector. In the informal sector wages were even lower than the textile industry, employment was casual and intermittent, and workers did not have the protection that trade unions had offered some textile workers.[123] Workers in the informal sector lived in slums with two insecurities: the constant threat of eviction because the slum was illegally built on public or privately owned land and the fear of loss of employment. It is no surprise, then, that the city had the highest rate of unemployment in India and there was a burgeoning population of surplus labor in the city.[124] The formal and the informal sectors of the city's economy were intricately connected. The informal sector provided cheap products and services, including domestic service, to city residents.[125] Slums therefore proliferated in the city.

The Bombay Development Plan of 1964 addressed this problem. Urban planning once again encountered a complex reality and tried to resolve it through abstract mechanisms. It registered its disquiet with the "prevailing conditions of congestion in the City with slums, shortage of housing accommodation, dearth of open spaces and other social facilities and heavy traffic loads."[126] It lamented that "present building activity . . . is not sufficient . . . for accommodating the natural increase in population."[127] Its imagined future city was the "*Urbs Prima in Indis*, a worthy capital of

Maharashtra, a port of international fame, a commercial and industrial centre and above all a cherished home for its teeming millions."[128] The 1964 plan was, however, significant for other reasons. It marked a shift in the government's endeavor to produce space through technocratic and bureaucratic means, by inaugurating two spatial parameters—one vertical and one horizontal expansion. The 1964 plan introduced abstract mechanisms such as the floor space index, which worked out a formula for height, number of floors, and number of units in a building in a particular locality vis-à-vis the total area of the plot of land on which the building stood.[129] The exact floor space index of a particular locality or zone in the city depended on various considerations, including water supply to the area, drainage system, transport and communication, community facilities, total land for residential development, and the total population of the metropolitan area.[130] In effect, the plan attempted to address the housing question by regulating (and increasing) the height of buildings and therefore the number of tenements within them. The plan projected a requirement of 539,943 additional tenements by 1971, and 911,034 by 1981.[131] The urban historians Sharda Dwivedi and Rahul Mehrotra have pointed out that urban planning now became a "numbers game," and statisticians and economists played an increasingly important role in urban planning.[132]

The other contribution of the plan—the horizontal fix, so to speak—was its recommendation of regional planning, not just city planning. The Gadgil Committee Plan of 1966, which addressed the metropolitan region of Bombay, was an important outcome of this change. The plan discouraged locating industries in Bombay city and proposed new commercial centers in the suburbs, like the Bandra Kurla complex, and envisioned a "multinucleated Metropolitan Region" with many new towns that would reduce the pressure on Bombay city.[133] As a result, the Bombay Metropolitan Regional Planning Board (BMRPB) was set up in 1967. The BMRPB came up with its own plans. It fixed the spatial coordinates of the Bombay region,[134] which now comprised 3,965 square kilometers. The plan's rhetorical thrust focused on housing deficits and slums in the city, which it likened to a cancerous growth, and deterioration of the built environment, which ensured that "Bombay the beautiful is no more beautiful."[135] The plan's response to the stain on the city's beauty was to highlight the need for 757,000 new tenements at the expense of 8,450 million rupees.[136] Most of these tenements were designated for the "economically weaker sections." The estimate, which was "very moderate" in the plan's reckoning, was dependent on the "social control of urban land values" to ensure adequate availability of land for housing poorer classes.[137] Since the Regional Planning Board was created in accordance with a provision of the Maharashtra Regional and Town Planning Act of 1966, the state of Maharashtra was to play an important role in the social control of urban land values. The state thus openly acknowledged its crucial function: it would play an important role in determining land values, just as it played a key role in guaranteeing private property. It was another technocratic response to the housing question, where land required for lower-income housing was to "be subsidized from the profits realized from the sales of other types of land, namely industrial and commercial land and housing lands sold for higher income housing."[138] The plan thus laid the groundwork for deindustrialization and the sale of industrial land. The state, in its rhetoric at least, acknowledged the contradictory political, economic, and social pressures it faced in its attempt to provide land and housing to poor city dwellers and at the same time respond to the call to restore the city's beauty. To escape this contradiction, the state proposed the creation of New Bombay, Bombay's doppelganger in name but not in practice, and sought a spatial solution to the growth of Greater Bombay.

Thus, in twenty-five years, the city had expanded horizontally from Bombay city to Greater Bombay, and by the 1960s planners had mooted the idea of New Bombay. Urban planning was the modality for the spatial solution to overcrowding, and housing for the poorer classes was its rationale. But urban planning was also isolated, as much as possible, from the politics of the urban poor. Slum clearance attended the processes of urban transformation and ended up creating more slums in the city and in the suburbs. Slums were not only home to many Dalit writers but also an important referent and site of depiction in Dalit literature.

4 REVOLUTIONARY LINEAGES OF DALIT LITERATURE, 1950-1972

BY 1972, BOMBAY CITY HAD EXPERIENCED THREE TRANSITIONS. The first was horizontal spatial change, from Bombay to Greater Bombay, which accelerated the process of suburbanization. Urban planning attended this transformation. The second was in the modalities of planning itself, from city planning to regional planning, including the proposed creation of Bombay's doppelganger, New Bombay. New Bombay was imagined as a "counter-magnet" to the old city's chaotic growth. Work on New Bombay started in 1971 on the mainland across Thane Creek. It was built on approximately 343.79 square kilometers and included portions of two districts adjoining Bombay city, Thane and Raigarh.[1] Part of the area that became New Bombay was already the rural-urban fringe of Greater Bombay in the 1960s. It displayed the characteristic features of this formation—partially urbanized villages, polluting chemical- and petroleum-based industrial plants, and declining agrarian use of land.[2] The acquisition of land to make a new city was a long and contentious process that the Maharashtra state government accomplished by notifying villages of its decision to acquire land under the Land Acquisition Act of 1894.[3] This laid the groundwork for social conflict between the villagers, the state, and the new settlers in the city. New Bombay's intended goal of decongesting Bombay and attracting new migrants to the city did not have the desired effect. The population density of Bombay kept increasing— from 9,901 persons per square kilometer in 1971, to 13,671 in 1981, and 16,461 in 1991.[4] Moreover, 50 percent of Bombay's population, or 8.2 million people, lived in slums in 1984.

The third transition was the attitude toward slums of city, regional, and the national governments. In the 1950s, slum clearance was the solution.

But slum clearance schemes had limited success. Some of the biggest opponents of slum clearance were shopkeepers whose customers were slum
dwellers. Slum clearance was then supplemented with slum rehabilitation.
The cost of relocating the slum was prohibitive not only for the state but
also for the people being relocated.[5] By the end of the 1960s, the government shifted attention to slum improvement, upgrading the built environment of existing slums by providing basic facilities such as sewerage and
water supply. The Maharashtra government passed the Maharashtra Slum
Areas (Improvement, Clearance and Redevelopment) Act of 1971 as an
alternative to slum clearance. Because of this act, at least some slum dwellers who fulfilled the residency requirements and could provide documented proof were awarded a modicum of security from the displacement
that accompanied slum clearance.[6]

Dalit literature thrived in the context of the production of urban space
and the everyday lives of Dalits in the 1960s, 1970s, and 1980s. During this
time the city's political economy changed: its textile mills began shutting
down, and the economy shifted to services, commodities, land, and financial investments.[7] More slums accompanied these transformations. Most
Dalit writers grew up in spaces designated as slums, and they depicted life
in the slums in their writings. These writers declared a revolution to transform the sociopolitical conjuncture in which they were situated. Their
notions of revolution borrowed from world-historical events like the
French Revolution of 1789 and the Russian Revolution of 1917, situating
Dalit literature and Dalit social movements in this lineage. They were also
inspired by the global movements of 1968; some icons of these movements
were also icons of Dalit literature, like Mao Tse-tung and Frantz Fanon.
Thus the revolutionary space invoked in Dalit literature was transregional
and not bounded by the particularities of a linguistic region or nation-
state.[8] The political, socioeconomic, and spatial changes in this region, fostered the conditions of possibility for the symbolic and substantive politics
of recognition that Dalits fashioned in the city. Contemporary spatial and
social transformations of the city informed Dalit literature, which constructed its own genealogy of revolutionary movements and revolutionary
writing. The spatial transformation intersected with the literary formation; thus slums adorned Dalit literature as a metaphor of Dalit lives in
the city and as real spaces inhabited by characters in stories and poems.
But this intersection also created a paradox. In particular, how would the
revolutionary break imagined in Dalit literature and by Dalit political

movements fructify when the lives of the revolutionaries were enmeshed in webs of property, tenancy, subtenancy, VLT, and recognition? Housing, particularly tenure rights of slum dwellers, and employment were demands of the Dalit social movements, including the radical Dalit Panthers and its splintering factions. Their radicalism forced the municipal government and the state to concede some of their demands; they did so by guaranteeing some slum dwellers the right to stay in the slums and providing them with municipal services like water and sanitation, while ignoring the demands of other slum dwellers. For the state, this was a way of co-opting some of the Dalit Panther leaders.

HUMILIATION AND RECOGNITION

The social welfare provisions of the postcolonial state, like the PWR 219 scheme, had enabled some Dalits to acquire property, but they had not overturned the symbolic order of repugnance. In fact, the *Government of India Report of the Committee on Untouchability, Economic and Educational Development of the Scheduled Castes*, tabled in 1969 and published in 1971, documented its persistence. The report demonstrated that this structure of repugnance had material effects. The report, popularly known as the Elayaperumal Report after the chairman of the committee, maintained that "untouchability as a propensity on the part of the caste Hindus to discriminate against the Scheduled Castes (Dalits) is not vanishing either in towns or in villages."[9] The report provided substantive data on the economic backwardness of Dalits in various parts of India and the negligence of the state in addressing these issues. Another material effect of the symbolic order was the obliteration of Dalit bodies with impunity. One of the most incriminating sets of data presented in the report was the killing of 1,117 Dalits in various parts of India in the year before the tabling of the report.

Dalit writers and intellectuals, many of whom lived in slums, invoked the Elayaperumal Report in the following year. The event was the twenty-fifth anniversary of India's independence in August 1972. On that day, black flags that symbolized mourning rather than celebration were hoisted in Dalit neighborhoods in the city.[10] In anticipation of the silver jubilee there was a profusion of public stock taking of India's postcolonial past. Two Bombay-based poets reflected on this history; both were unequivocal in their assessments. One of them, Raja Dhale, in an article in the Marathi weekly *Sadhana* (Study), declared the silver jubilee of India's independence

Black Independence Day (Kala Svantantrata Divas). In this article, Dhale caustically observed that the Indian national flag was merely a piece of cloth. Dhale's friend at the time, the poet Namdeo Dhasal, had published a collection of poems called *Golpitha* a few months earlier. *Golpitha*, named after a neighborhood in the red-light district of Bombay, included a poem on the twenty-fifth anniversary of independence titled "On the Occasion of August 15" (Nimita 15 August). In this poem, Dhasal memorably questioned the significance of the end of British colonialism for Dalits in India. He asked, "Where is this donkey named independence? In which tenement of Ramrajya do we live?"[11] Dhasal's invocation of Ramrajya, the realm of the mythological King Ram, an imagined oasis of prosperity, peace, and good governance, was a critique of the postcolonial reality of India, particularly the policies of the Congress Party–led government of India and also of M. K. Gandhi, a propagator of the idea of Ramrajya. Before Dhasal, Annabhau Sathe had deployed a similar reference in his "Mumbai's Mill Worker" (Mumbaicha girnikamgar) to narrate the violence faced by striking mill workers in 1950:

When the Mouth of Ramrajya Opened
It revealed the teeth of Raavan
Batons and Bullets flew
And everywhere there was outrage.[12]

The ideal of Ramrajya thus devolved into violence in practice. Gandhi's idea of India encompassed another contradiction: he condemned the practice of untouchability—the stigma associated with the touch of a person belonging to a Dalit caste—but the caste system that justified the stigma was left untouched. In other words, the foundation and façade of the structure that produced everyday humiliation were left intact. Moreover, Gandhi's idea of India did not address the substantive social, political, and economic problems faced by Dalits who were landless agricultural laborers in many regions of India or were employed in low-paying jobs in towns and cities where they often lived in slums. Dalits experienced everyday humiliations but were also subjected to spectacular acts of violence. The Elayaperumal Report documented these acts, in which burning, lynching, and rape acquired a tedious regularity. Dhale's and Dhasal's criticisms of the postcolonial nation-state referenced the promise of substantive change augured by independence that was foreclosed for many Dalits.

Dhale and Dhasal became iconic figures in Dalit Sahitya. They also, in 1972, founded the short-lived Dalit Panther movement in the city. The Dalit Panthers, named after and inspired by the Black Panthers in the United States, aimed "to begin an armed struggle in literature and outside the field of literature."[13] The Dalit Panthers' call for an insurrection within and without literature must be situated in the long history of radical social imaginaries, with transnational lineages, that operated in Bombay city in the twentieth century. But there were two important regional—Marathi-language—antecedents to this imaginary. The movement was shaped by the militant workers' movements as well as by the anticaste/anti-Brahmin movements. Both of these aimed to upend social hierarchy, in their rhetoric if not always in practice. The workers' movement, particularly under the influence of Marxist trade union leaders and intellectuals in the late 1920s, sought to do so by overcoming capitalism and the anticaste movement by toppling caste hierarchy. The revolutionary imaginary of the post-colonial Dalit movements was heir to these lineages. Thus two distinct temporalities of radical thought—one Marxian and the other harkening back to Ambedkar and Phule—intersected at this conjuncture in postcolonial Bombay. The articulation was worked out in the arena of political practices as a response to the historical moment. Both these movements had created a cultural corpus in which the *tamasha* (loosely translated as "spectacle") was harnessed and reworked to transmit messages of dissent. In the Ambedkar movement, the reworked *tamasha* was called *jalsa*, where radical imaginaries were translated into songs. By 1930, there were many *jalsa* troupes in Bombay city, including groups led by Bhimrao Kardak and Dadasaheb Pagare. These troupes apprised their audience of current political developments such as temple entry campaigns and dialogues or disagreements with the Indian National Congress, propagated Ambedkar's ideas, and addressed alcoholism and domestic violence within Dalit communities.[14] Bombay's workers had a similarly long history of dissent; many Dalit workers had been politicized in the labor movement and supported leftist groups. Thus the rhetoric of the annihilation of caste and capital resonated in this public sphere.

The Dalit Panthers and Dalit Sahitya emerged in this vibrant public sphere. This public sphere also reaffirmed the connection between urban and rural Dalits that was established during the Ambedkar movement, and a response to the violence and humiliation documented by the Elayaperumal Report was fashioned here. As J. V. Pawar, one of the founders of the Dalit Panther movement, explains,

Dalits from all over western India had migrated to Mumbai to escape
poverty and hunger. Apart from struggling to stave off hunger in the city,
the Dalits have been constantly striving to analyze and make sense of the
world around them. Humans do not just live on food; they also need
fodder for their intellect. Newspapers provide them with the fodder; the
newspapers report stories about rape and atrocities on women, social
boycott of Dalits in villages, forced appropriation of land, and lack of
access to wells. These atrocities on rural Dalits produced the Panthers.
They wanted to crush the structures that produced Dalit humiliation in
the villages.[15]

To combat humiliation in the villages, the Panthers wanted to form an
army of urban youth that would respond to atrocities in villages. As Raja
Dhale said on his visit to the village of Brahmanwada, where two Dalit
women were paraded naked in 1972, "We will fight and kill the village
thugs who commit such crimes."
For the literary war, Marathi was armed with rural Marathi dialects
and buttressed with urban slang that consisted of words loaned from
Hindi, Urdu, Gujarati, and English. The literary jousting was playful and
joyous but also intended to be caustic and scathing at the same time. It
interpellated, shocked, and scalded its readers. It did not fuss with the
purity of a literary language; the unfussiness was also reflected in its pro-
miscuity regarding literary and intellectual influences. It devised metaphors and an imagery that remained unalloyed to the exaltation of regional
identity or national glory. For example, in Dhale's article, he also said that
if the flag feels insulted, "shall I shove it up somebody's arse?"[16] Or consider
this stanza from Dhasal's poem: "The day came, the day went; the day that
came I lived it; the day that went, I shat it out."[17] The vivid possibilities of
anatomy and bodily functions revolutionized Marathi literature. A significant aspect of the revolution was the writers' assertion of mastery over
time—the day that was lived and flushed like excrement—and space. The
space it invoked was not just the transnational space of revolutionary
movements but also the space that urban planning designated as slums.
Dhasal describes this built form, sometimes voyeuristically, for his readers. Dhale's and Dhasal's assertions in these passages must be situated in
the context of the wider corpus of Dalit Sahitya, in which mastery over
space and time is a desirable goal but still a distant dream. In fact, contrary
to Dhasal's assertions, a recurrent trope in Dalit literature is the impossibility of mastery over space and time, where life itself is often precarious

and fragile. And the space in which one lives in this literature—the slums in Bombay city—is also marked by this fragility. That life, precarious to begin with, can be rent asunder by events.

BOMBAY CITY AND ITS NEW LITERATURES

Some of the preliminary conversations on Dalit literature were held not in Bombay but in Nagpur. The Sahitya Charcha Mandali (Society for the Discussion of Literature) was instituted in Nagpur in 1941, and the first meeting of Dalit poets was organized in 1947 under the stewardship of Revaram Kavade.[18] Around the same time as the preliminary discussions of Dalit literature, new trends appeared in Marathi literature. These two movements, despite different histories, shared a common assumption: they were self-aware about the need for a rupture from old Marathi literature. Bombay city generated the new trends in Marathi literature: the Nava Kavya (New Poetry) movement of the 1940s and 1950s was created there. Nava Kavya was punctuated with critiques of traditional literature, rejecting the British Victorian norms that had percolated and dominated Marathi literature from the late nineteenth century until the 1940s. Nava Kavya included poets such as B. S. Mardhekar, Mangesh Padgaonkar, and P. S. Rege, who had, between them, written poems on various modern objects, including clocks, machines, and daily routines.[19] Another movement in the city was Sathottari poetry (post-1960s poetry). These trends either immediately preceded or were coterminous with the rise of Dalit Sahitya, and some Dalit writers from the city (and the region) were in conversation with or participated in the production of these literatures. For instance, Namdeo Dhasal and Raja Dhale participated in the Sathottari movement and edited little magazines that were an important feature of its literary expression. Thus the social and cultural networks that produced Nava Kavya, Sathottari, and Dalit literature overlapped and intersected. All these strands of Marathi literature articulated a critique of tradition and a broad invocation of realism in literature. Sathottari poetry experimented with plebian language and brought it into "the elite halls of poetry."[20] Thus, traditional or established (*prasthapit*) Marathi literature was subjected to critical scrutiny before the emergence of Dalit literature in the city. What made Dalit literature distinct was its unapologetic embrace of the Dalit social movement and its commitment to a political response to the conjuncture, its centering of the question of caste along with class, and its embrace of a distinct Dalit identity as well as its dialectical other, the endeavor to annihilate caste.[21] Dalit literature aspired to make its audience aware of the distinctness of the group, even as the term "Dalit" itself was open to varied interpretations. Some Marxist writers, such as Annabhau Sathe, considered "Dalit" to be a collective defined by class, while others foregrounded the disadvantages of caste and its importance to the making of a Dalit self. Moreover, Dalit literature invoked Ambedkar's ideas at a time when he was a marginal presence in postcolonial India,[22] at the same time borrowing insights from Marxist critiques of modern life and conceptual terms from Marathi Marxism.

Dalits who were part of these literary movements in the city played an important role in debates on the making of Dalit literature. Dalit literature was based on important assumptions shared and expressly stated by its early proponents: As a part of society, literature is influenced by society and should in turn influence it. Society changes, but in societies shaped by caste the change is not as dynamic or perceptible as it should be. Social change needs to be hastened, and literature can speed up this transformation.[23] From its inception, therefore, Dalit literature was opposed to a type of formalism that separated literature from society. In fact, an important early advocate of Dalit literature, M. N. Wankhede, anticipated in 1966 that literary critics of the time, who were formalists in his estimation, would be unable to make sense of literature that stemmed from the experiences of Dalits in Indian society.[24] What form did the transcendence of formalism take? In one account, Dalit literature worked like the quintessential counterpublic. It provided the space where a counterideology was formulated and then deployed by Dalit social movements to address the material conditions of Dalits.[25]

The creation of Dalit Sahitya was thus a cultural revolution and necessitated the conscious acquisition of culture and the production of a worldview. The construction of a conscious Dalit self was a long process. It assumed a radical transformation not just in the relation of a person to themselves, but also a social transformation that would sustain the newly created self. The transformation of the self and the social in which the self was embedded could only be achieved through a revolution. These transformations and the contingent process of acquiring culture presumed self-reflexivity, an important feature of modernity.[26] The processes of modernity also produced contradictions. Dalits *inhabited* modernity and recognized its radical possibilities; simultaneously, they also experienced and understood that their subordinate position in Bombay's postcolonial urban formation was a *consequence* of this modernity. For instance, they favored the annihilation of caste and yet at the same time had to present themselves as objects of caste indignities to partake of the welfare provisions of the state. For many Dalits, industrial capitalism in Bombay city entailed subordinate positions in the labor market and a marginal status in the projects of town planners, who deemed their dwellings in slums and tenements a blot on a beautiful city. It also entailed visions of social equality, but the promise of social equality guaranteed to them by the Indian Constitution, which abolished untouchability and granted them the right to vote, did not lead to legal endowments for social equality in everyday life. It is in this context that Dalit writers and the Dalit Panthers declared an armed insurrection inside and outside literature to obliterate these contradictions and hasten the promise of modernity—understood here as razing the structures that inhibited social equality. For Dalit writers and activists, revolution was a political horizon available to them at this historical juncture; they could make this declaration because of the existence of a global revolutionary conjuncture. They proclaimed a revolution to transcend the schism between the promises and practices of modernity. That revolution would, they believed, help them gain more control over time and space in everyday life.

DALIT LITERATURE AND THE GLOBAL REVOLUTIONARY CONJUNCTURE

The literary practices of Dalits in the city got a boost from the educational institutions and magazines started by B. R. Ambedkar.[27] Students and faculty associated with Siddharth College in Bombay, an educational institution founded by Ambedkar in 1946, initiated the short-lived Siddharth Literary Association (Siddarth Sahitya Sangh) in 1950. The Sangh discussed the content and form of Dalit literary expression. One of the most important points of discussions was the recognition of literature by Dalits as Dalit literature. Could Dalit literature survive and thrive within the aesthetics and values propagated by the dominant castes? If it did not, would it get recognition?[28] Some of this foundational dialogue played out in the early 1950s in *Janata* (People) and *Prabuddha Bharata* (Awakened India), weeklies that Ambedkar had started, and in issues of magazines released on the occasion of his birthday on April 14. According to the writer and critic Arjun Dangle, Dalit Sahitya could not establish an independent identity in the 1950s because it remained confined within the aesthetics of the dominant Marathi writers of the period.

Dalit intellectuals trained in institutions started by Ambedkar initiated a dialogue on the formation of Dalit literature, which was taken farther by writers living in Bombay's slums. These writers included Annabhau Sathe, Baburao Bagul, and Namdeo Dhasal, who had little formal education but had close associations with leftist writers and activists in the city. A sociological study published in 1974 confirmed that Dalits were "underrepresented in education" in Greater Bombay, and their enrollment rate in primary and secondary education was below the state average.[29] Annabhau Sathe, in his presidential address to the Dalit Literary Meeting (Sahitya Sammelan) in 1958, envisioned Dalit literature not as an extant body of work but as literature to be produced in the future. He hoped it would not only be revolutionary but also raise the self-awareness of Dalits. Sathe predicated his vision of Dalit Sahitya on *difference*: the essential difference in the experiences and ways of being a Dalit. Sathe held that labor was an important universal category through which readers would grasp this difference. Dalits had a heroic capacity for labor/hardship (*kashta*). Sathe's notion of Dalits was capacious, encompassing not just the Dalit castes but all those involved in manual labor. For him, the capacity to labor and the hardships borne by the Dalits produced wealth. Production and accumulation of wealth was predicated on the alienation of Dalit labor. In other words, being Dalit was synonymous with belonging to the working class. According to Sathe, Dalit literature should not only be revolutionary but also raise consciousness of Dalit hardship. In language evocative of *The Communist Manifesto*, Sathe passionately argued that Dalits should become aware that they were not slaves but, in fact, the proprietors of the world.[30] Slavery, as for Marathi Marxists of the 1920s and 1930s, was the metaphor for highlighting the oppression of a group, including Dalits. While he did not specify whether a writer needed to be born Dalit, Sathe did insist that the writer be wholeheartedly devoted to the *cause of Dalits*. Once again, in language redolent of the Communist Party's thesis on the relationship between intellectuals and the masses, he argued that the writer should always be with the Dalit masses, should strive to understand them and not invent literature in the comfort of home. Sathe's notion of Dalit literature prefigured a critique of mainstream Marathi literature of the time, which, he argued, did not offer an insightful representation of Dalit hardships or aspirations.

Sathe's notion of Dalit Sahitya was reworked by his protégé Baburao Bagul in the 1960s, who did so by introducing a new ontological category—humiliation—in addition to using terms from Marathi Marxism such as "exploitation," "pain," and "suffering." Dalit humiliation was a result of the structures and practices of insult (*apman*) and contempt or repugnance (*tiraskara*). Humiliation, he suggested, was constitutive of being a Dalit.[31] Bagul, in his collection of stories *When I Concealed My Caste* (Jevha mi jat chorali hoti) of 1963, argued that Dalit literature emerged from the need felt by writers like him for a "new and rebellious" type of literature.[32] While Sathe wanted Dalit literature to offer a clear depiction of the everyday lives of Dalits, Bagul did not want it to merely reflect their pain, humiliation, and poverty. He prescribed that writers move beyond simple representations of Dalit suffering to address the socioeconomic and cultural structures that produced humiliation. An appraisal of the structures of humiliation would trigger a revolt within and beyond Dalit literature. In Bagul's view, Dalit literature was a revolt against structures that were *faceless* but a fecund source of indignity and exploitation.[33] A notable aspect of Bagul's understanding of Dalit literature was the conjugation of humiliation and exploitation rather the melding of one into the other. Exploitation might create the conditions of possibility for humiliation, but the Marxian category of exploitation could not fully account for Dalit humiliation. To grasp humiliation, one needed to understand the complex workings of untouchability. Dalit Sahitya sprang from the experiences of untouchability.[34] Therefore, its intellectual progenitor was B. R. Ambedkar and not Karl Marx.[35] Marx and socialism were important and generative of some Dalit literature but not the totality of it. Dalit literature, then, was a product of the conjugation of two distinct temporalities in that historical conjuncture: of anticaste/anti-Brahmin politics and the radical politics of the working class and the urban poor informed by Marxism. One did not subsume the other. In fact, for Bagul the anticaste/anti-Brahmin tradition of Dalit politics took precedence in the making of Dalit literature.

For Dalit literature to emerge and gain recognition, it needed to transcend the hegemonic Marathi literature of that time. Bagul termed the dominant literature "Hindu" or "Sadashiv Pethi literature," referring to a neighborhood in Pune associated with elite culture. Dalit literature needed to commit itself to a social revolution that would end exploitation and humiliation by overcoming capitalism and the caste system. Dalit literature was thus synonymous with a just revolution.[36] And because it was revolutionary, its lineage, in the minds of its forebears, went back to transregional revolutionary movements.[37] Thus the space of hegemonic Marathi literature was identified with a locality—Sadashiv Peth. As Michel de Certeau points out, the locality denotes stability, a place where things are in their proper place.[38] On the other hand the space of revolutionary literature is global and dynamic, comprising the lineage of world revolutions across time and space.

Crafting a revolutionary worldview stimulated the search for models of revolutionary action. Translation played an important role in the transmission of these ideals. Dalit writers considered the French Revolution of the late eighteenth century and the Russian and Chinese Revolutions of the twentieth as exemplars of successful social revolutions. An important feature of these revolutions for Bagul was that the revolutionaries of these periods questioned the intellectual credibility of the hegemonic formations of their time and regions. They fostered new ways of seeing the world and produced a culture that reflected and augmented these transformations. Dalit writers harnessed this revolutionary spirit and included them as chapters in their genealogy of revolutions. For Bagul, this entailed a secular assault on religious traditions to generate "new ideas, new inventions, new knowledge and science, and new modes of productions."[39] In other words, Bagul harkened back to and claimed the radical Enlightenment tradition for himself and Dalit literature. He extracted Enlightenment from its history as a bourgeois cultural revolution and embedded it in postcolonial Bombay to craft a literature of outcastes and urban poor. His rationale was the inability of the Indian intellectual class to effect a radical transformation because they were enmeshed in the rigidities of religion and caste. As a result, intellectual life was claustrophobic and backward-looking rather than focused on the futurity of revolution.[40] For him, the Dalit literary revolution was a cultural revolution.

Within literature, Dalit writers borrowed from and translated Russian realism of the late nineteenth and early twentieth centuries, and African American literature of the second half of the twentieth century to serve as models for Dalit literature. The novels of Russian realism and short stories, plays, and poems of LeRoi Jones and Richard Wright, for instance, were dissimilar in form. But where they became equivalent for Dalit writers, and their formal differences resolved, was in their ability to demystify and highlight the persistence of caste and class in society. Bagul was an admirer of Maxim Gorky, Anton Chekhov, and the Bengali writer Sarat Chandra Chatterjee. He was part of the Marathi public that had read these writers in Marathi translations published by the Communist Party of India in the 1940s and 1950s and circulated in newspapers and periodicals started by B. R. Ambedkar. Maxim Gorky, for instance, was published in serialized form in the weekly *Janata* (People) in the 1930s. Bagul explicitly claimed

this genealogy for Dalit Sahitya: "Dalit Sahitya's lineage is world revolutionary literature because that literature gives agency to the common man
and propagates socialism."[41] The place of Dalit literature in this genealogy
was demonstrated by its rejection of Indian traditions that did not advocate notions such as equality (*samata*), socialism (*samajvad*), independence (*svatantrya*), and brotherhood (*bandhubhav*).[42]

Bagul's validation of a secular assault on religious tradition bears explication, especially because an influential strand of scholarship traces Dalit
Sahitya to the religious conversion of Dalits from Hinduism to Buddhism.
Votaries of this view argued that Dalit conversion to Buddhism, starting
from Ambedkar's conversion in 1956, was the catalyst for the efflorescence
of Dalit literature.[43] For many converts, conversion was a protest against
"discrimination and exploitation" and a journey toward a new beginning,
a step celebrated in paintings, music, songs, and essays.[44] In Dalit literature, though, conversion and Buddhism remained peripheral, at least in
the 1950s and 1960s. Eleanor Zelliot confirmed in her later writings that
"Dalit Sahitya seems to be only marginally concerned with the Buddhist
conversion."[45] Bagul attributed this to the newness of the event, "some-
thing must be completely absorbed and understood before it can be written
about."[46] But he did concede that Buddhist conversion set the untouchable
free to be creative.[47] Even as conversion brought freedom to be creative, cre-
ativity itself sprouted from other sources, most importantly Dalit experiences of untouchability and the interrogation of religious traditions. As
Bagul acknowledged, untouchability did not lapse with religious conversion; religion and religious conversions had played an important role in
Zelliot's understanding of historical change. Zelliot, unlike the makers
of Dalit literature, traced the *longue durée* of Dalit Sahitya to the
fourteenth-century Mahar saint Chokhamela and the prominent role
played by Mahar Dalits in the formation of *tamasha*. The Dalit writers
and intellectuals of the 1960s and 1970s chafed against this lineage, particularly the religious tradition of saints, explicitly trying to distance
themselves from it.

There was a gender dimension to the disquiet with religious traditions.
The decision to convert to Buddhism caused turmoil within families. For
some women in Dalit families, the prospect of conversion was experienced
as a loss of control over time and space, because all that was familiar in
their relationship with Hindu gods was upended in conversion. Consider
the debates between Damodar Runjaji Jadhav and his wife, Sonu, Dalits
from the Mahar caste, who lived in Bombay Port Trust tenements of

central Bombay. Damodar, a follower of B. R. Ambedkar, said of the conversion: "Whatever Babasaheb said had to be followed."[48] Damodar announced his decision to convert in 1956 in this way: "We are the masters of our destiny and have to reclaim our rightful place in society. We shall renounce Hinduism. Hail Babasaheb, the great one, who is our visionary, our savior!"[49] Sonu, by contrast, was circumspect and apprehensive about "tampering with God and religion."[50] Renouncing Hinduism, she believed, would lead to the collapse of Dalit spiritual life. The practice of religion for Sonu involved devotion to deities like the goddess Mariaai and the gods Khandoba and Vithoba. Vithoba was also worshiped by saints such as Chokhamela. With these deities Sonu had a relationship of intimacy, trust, and fear—fear at the prospect of incurring their wrath. She worshiped brass idols of these gods every day, and in times of adversity she "prayed to them when any problem worried me. I beseeched them when my man had no job. I implored them to make my man well when he was in hospital. I washed them with my tears when my children suffered ill health."[51] With conversion, that practice would now be gone, and Sonu was circumspect. But it was not just Sonu; many women from her caste in her neighborhood were also apprehensive: "When I went to fetch water [from a local tap] all the women there were heatedly talking about the same thing: none of them were prepared to give up Hinduism, but they did not dare voice their opinion to their men."[52] Damodar and Sonu converted to Buddhism in a public ceremony on October 14, 1956. Sonu returned from the ceremony with an idol of Buddha; she hid the idols of Hindu gods "in the lowermost mattress of my bed" and asked for their forgiveness.[53] Religious conversion was a poignant moment and an emotional process for Sonu and other Dalit women in the city. Conversions continued in Bombay over the next few years. For instance, some Dalit sex workers in the Thirteenth Lane of Kamathipura converted to Buddhism on March 15, 1959, under the leadership of Kisan Jadhav, two and a half years after Sonu's conversion.[54] The votaries of Dalit literature recognized that religious transformation was important, but in Bagul's own words they had not comprehended and narrated it in literature. Instead, Dalit literature fashioned its own genealogy and a utopian future that would overcome a present filled with misery and shape a new social harmony, a new life, and a new Dalit self.[55]

African American literature was an important landmark in the social space of Dalit literature. Like Russian realism, translation and vernacularization helped in its propagation, but the relevance of African American writers to Dalit literature was amplified by travel and personal

connections. A key figure in shaping the intellectual horizon of Dalit literature was M. N. Wankhede. Wankhede was one of fourteen students
selected by B. R. Ambedkar to study abroad in 1953 on a scholarship for
Dalit students. At that time, Ambedkar's goal was to create an intellectual
class of Dalits in India. In 1953, Wankhede could not travel because of ill
health, but he eventually arrived in the United States on a Fulbright Fellowship in 1962. He earned a master's degree from Indiana University in
1963 and completed his doctorate at the University of Florida, Gainesville,
in 1965. In America, Wankhede studied Black literature or "nigro sahitya," as he called it, adding it to the horizon of world revolutionary (*vis-
vavidrohi*) literature constructed by Dalit writers. He was impressed by
the cultural history of the civil rights movement and the aspirations of
the Black literary movement.

After returning to India in 1966, he wrote a programmatic article in
Prabuddha Bharata. In this article, titled "Dalits Write Rebellious Literature" (Dalitano vidrohi vangmay liha), Wankhede describes the violent
imagery and provocative writings of African American writers and
explains the connection between literature and African American history.
But the lineage he constructs for this literature is temporally compressed.
He offers a brief history of the representation of Black characters in
nineteenth-century America as mean (*dushta*), scheming (*labada*), or cari-
caturized and clownish.[56] He describes Harriet Beecher Stowe's *Uncle
Tom's Cabin* as a novel that generated sympathy for African Americans in
the nineteenth century. He presents the character of Nigger Jim from Mark
Twain's *The Adventures of Huckleberry Finn* as one who experienced many
humiliations because of the color of his skin. But it was Richard Wright's
1940 novel *Native Son* that offered the first realistic portrayal of Black life
in the United States. Wankhede calls Wright a Communist but adds that
Native Son does not reveal the impress of Communist ideology but is a
testament to Wright's fidelity to the realistic depiction of African American lives. He describes the character of Bigger Thomas and his trial for
Mary's murder, saying that Wright had offered a startling depiction of the
inhumanity of race relations through them.[57] Wankhede also describes the
writings of James Baldwin, particularly *Go Tell It on the Mountain* and *The
Fire Next Time*. He finds the latter book more explosive (*sphotaka*). He particularly focuses on the culture wars or, as he calls it, the "cultural dual-
ism" of white and Black culture and supports the call for a Black Nation.[58]
Moreover, he discusses Elijah Mohammed's Black Muslim movement and
celebrates the consciousness-raising work of the dramatist LeRoi Jones

(Amiri Baraka) and the revolutionary demands of the Black Power movement.[59] After telescoping the almost two-hundred-year history of the depiction of Blackness in American literature and celebrating the realist turn after Richard Wright and the radical demands of the Black movements of the 1960s, he poses a direct question: Why don't Marathi writers from the lower castes capture the rebelliousness and anger of their castes? He attributes this to writers' inability to find a true voice and true identity because they are beholden to the middle-class ideals of Marathi literature. That is why Dalit writing is tasteless (*bechav*) and bland (*milamilita*).[60] He encourages Dalit writers to stay true to the inherent difference of Dalit experience if they seek to create a separate Dalit literature with a unique identity.[61] Wankhede's highlighting of African American literature as worthy of emulation was adopted in spirit but not in form. Wankhede promotes novels, semiautobiographical novels, and plays as examples of Black literature, but Dalit literature's initial corpus, which helped it gain recognition, included mostly poems, short stories, and autobiographies. The novel as a form remained relatively less developed in this literature.

Wankhede's exhortations were persuasive, and his influence was bolstered by his ability to create and nurture institutions. He was one of the founders of the quarterly literary journal *Asmita* (Identity) renamed *Asmitadarsh* (Mirror of identity) in 1966.[62] The journal was not based in Bombay city, but rather in Aurangabad, where Ambedkar had started Milind College. Most Dalit writers from Bombay published in this journal. After 1969, Wankhede himself moved to Bombay after he was appointed chairman of the Maharashtra Public Service Commission. *Asmitadarsh* became an important avenue for the discussion and propagation of Dalit literature in Marathi. The journal was founded with some financial assistance from the newly created state of Maharashtra, which saw the promotion of Marathi as a matter of regional identity and Dalit identity as a social welfare initiative.[63] Many writers now identified with the corpus of Dalit Sahitya, including Baburao Bagul, Namdeo Dhasal, Raja Dhale, Keshav Meshram, Daya Pawar, Vaman Nimbalkar, and M. N. Wankhede himself, published in the magazine during its first few years. Wankhede had offered an important definition of Dalit literature: literature written by Dalits for Dalits from the standpoint of revolt and rebellion of Dalits against the existing social hierarchy.[64]

Wankhede was not the only emissary of African American literature. There were other interlocutors too, many of them not Dalits. The Marathi writer and critic Waman Lakshman Kulkarni, like Wankhede, believed

LeRoi Jones's plays were peerless and worthy of emulation by Dalit writers. On a visit to Los Angeles in the 1960s, Kulkarni saw a performance of Jones's *The Dutchman and the Slave* and was enraptured by it. He visualized Dalit Sahitya through the lens of LeRoi Jones's plays. *The Dutchman* gave Kulkarni "goose flesh. The play shocked me."[65] He wanted Dalit Sahitya to similarly "shock" its audience. Moreover, he wanted Dalit writers to emulate Jones's rage. "It's better to be angry than depressed," he said.[66] The ability to express anger assumed a self-confidence that Kulkarni believed Dalit writers lacked: "The Dalit writers that are being produced [today] lack the necessary self-confidence."[67] Kulkarni equated lack of self-confidence and the inability to express rage through literature with lack of dignity. He argued that building self-confidence was a historical process. According to him, at that historical moment confidence was only available to middle-class and upper-caste writers like the poet and essayist Dilip Chitre. Chitre embodied the defiance he found desirable, and he urged Dalit writers to emulate him. Kulkarni located Chitre's self-confidence in his habitus, particularly in the consciousness of dignity among sections of the Marathi middle class. In other words, people who experienced humiliation everyday, such as Dalits, do not have the confidence to articulate their rage and should emulate their middle-class and upper-caste peers who have learned to express anger.

Dilip Chitre was an important interlocutor for Dalit Sahitya. Chitre, Satish Kalsekar, Ashok Shahane, and Bhau Padhye were icons of the Sathottari movement and had started *Little Magazines*, a series of short-lived publications that challenged the literary establishment of the time. Some founders of the Dalit Panthers and Dalit Sahitya, including Namdeo Dhasal, were part of this movement too.[68] Chitre's influence on Dalit Sahitya, particularly on Dhasal, was also literary. He introduced Dhasal to modern urban poetry, including Charles Baudelaire's *Les fleurs du mal* and Arthur Rimbaud's *Une saison en enfer*. Chitre had written essays on these poets and translated their poems into Marathi in the late 1960s and said that acquaintance with their work "opened his [Dhasal's] eyes to possibilities of poetry untapped by Marathi poets."[69] Chitre and Kalsekar were inspired by Herbert Marcuse's notion of "sexual, moral, intellectual and political rebellion ... directed against the system as a whole."[70] The stated goal of this rebellion was to recalibrate everyday life in the wake of a revolution. Temporality, particularly futurity, was important to it. Their practice, however, did not match their rhetoric; their opposition remained circumscribed either to "an individual, institution, or a literary journal."[71]

Dhasal's intellectual heroes were also icons of the global 1960s. He admired Frantz Fanon and, like him, believed that the wretched of the earth could be mobilized for a political and cultural revolution. Dhasal imagined that the lumpen proletariat, the sex worker and the pimp, and the gangsters could also revolt in that historical moment. In one of the little magazines, *Vidroh* (Revolt), which he launched and edited, he laid out his vision for a magazine for "the man who wants to begin armed struggle in literature and outside the field of literature."[72] This vision resembled Fanon's *littérature de combat*. But unlike Fanon's call for a literature that formulated and expressed a new Algerian culture and national identity while contesting French colonial rule, Dhasal's revolt was against the postcolonial Indian nation that had overthrown colonial rule but not the depredations of caste and class.

In the early 1970s Mao became an important idol for the Dalit Panthers and by extension Dalit literature. This again was in line with political culture of the 1960s, in which Maoists all over the world, including India, had taken over the radical initiative from established leftist parties aligned with the Soviet Union. The momentum of revolution shifted to parties and actors who identified with Maoism and the ideals of China's Cultural Revolution.[73] In Bombay city ultraleftists (*ati davya*) started collaborating with Namdeo Dhasal and Arjun Dangle. The Marathi magazine *Magova* (Hunt), edited and published in Bombay by Sudhir Bedekar, a self-identified Maoist, acquired a strong readership among Dalit youth in the city.[74] *Magova's* critique of traditional Marathi literary values dovetailed with similar critiques by writers associated with Dalit Sahitya. *Magova* also supported Dalit social and political movements, thus contributing to their popularity among Dalit writers.[75] Arjun Dangle, however, writing in 1978, after Dalit Sahitya had become a recognizable object of analysis, argued that "the separatist tendency of the far Left pulled *Magova* away from the concerns of Dalit Sahitya."[76]

Another important milestone in Dalit literature's turn to realism, radicalism, and revolution was its embrace of social anthropology. Wankhede promoted this encounter. Because in India social anthropology bore the taint of an association with colonialism, it struggled to prove its relevance to the new political moment.[77] The virtues of social anthropology, according to its foremost proponent and practitioner in India in the 1950s and 1960s, M. N. Srinivas, included a holistic analysis of the totality of society and its social institutions, including caste, intensive fieldwork involving total immersion and language learning, and a comparative perspective that was not ethnocentric.[78] According to Srinivas, social anthropology produced a certain charity and tolerance toward ways of life different from one's own. Wankhede perhaps had this in mind when he argued that tools from social anthropology would help Dalit writers, and more importantly its critics, appreciate a literature that linked art with life.[79] In India, social anthropology's turn away from studying primitive tribes to the study of caste in Indian villages, as was the academic fashion in the 1950s and 1960s, may have led Wankhede to believe that it could link Dalit literature with Dalit everyday life. Wankhede's invocation of social anthropology was also functional. He invested the discipline with modernist hopes of rejecting older traditions and myths and inventing new ones. The aspiration was noteworthy because many Dalits, particularly Mahar Dalits, at the time were converting to Buddhism and abandoning Hindu traditions and myths. Social anthropology would help Dalits create new myths.

SLUMS AND URBAN PLANNING

The road to social anthropology and realism in Dalit literature led to Bombay's slums. The geographical space of the city intersected with the literary space of Dalit Sahitya here. Realism's claim to depict the truth made slums the material referent for Dalit literature. In other words, literature and infrastructure were conjoined in the depiction of and the space of the slums. An important trope of Dalit literature was that everyday life was rent asunder by events in the lives of its protagonists, be they the sex worker who loses her son or a neighborhood ruffian murdered in a street brawl. Dalit writers captured the humanity of their characters in the midst of the inhuman events they encountered. The precarity in the lives of these literary characters matched the uncertainty faced by residents of the city's slums. The slum was a precarious formation because of its illegality, and in urban planning it often invited the prescription of its own demolition. The threat of the bulldozer sanctioned by the postcolonial state and its prescription of eradicating slums and evicting slum dwellers were a presence in their lives. The threat may not have always materialized in practice. In the postcolonial period, political parties, including Dalit social movements, mobilized slum residents to protest slum demolition. Annabhau Sathe had alluded to this pressure from the urban poor in *Silent Procession* in the 1940s. But with the institution of universal adult franchise in postcolonial India, the state and municipal officials had to appear responsive to these pressures from below.[80] As a result, some slums became durable, and dwellers who met the criteria for residency, and produced documents to support it, got tenurial rights to the slum.

For instance, in December 1964, Dadasaheb Gaikwad, along with another leader of the Republican Party of India, Rajabhau Khobargade, organized a nonviolent demonstration in Delhi demanding protection from slum demolition, as well as adequate water, electricity, and sanitation facilities for slum dwellers. Political mobilization and pressure from hutment associations such as the Republican Zopadi Sangh eventually led to a change in social policy; slum dwellers in the city were guaranteed protection if their huts were constructed before 1964. Moreover, slum protection and improvement were codified in law with the passage of the Maharashtra Slum Areas (Improvement, Clearance, and Redevelopment) Act of 1971 and the Slum Board Act of 1973. The 1971 act defined the slum as "an area that is or may be a source of danger to the health, safety or convenience of the public of that area or of its neighborhood, by reason of the area having inadequate or no basic amenities, or being unsanitary, squalid or overcrowded."[81] The recommendation was to improve the built environment. For instance, the Slum Board Act authorized the state government to install taps, bathing areas, covered drains, and toilets. It must be noted, however, that these acts did not provide for reconstructing individual houses nor did they encourage community participation in slum improvement. They represented "a purely technical approach to slum development" prescribed by the state.[82] In 1976, India's federal government passed the Urban Land Ceiling and Regulation Act of 1976, which provided for the acquisition and redistribution of vacant land in excess of five hundred square meters. The acts did not address the issue of the legality of slums, and many of the provisions of the act remained unenforced. A 1976 amendment to the Slum Board Act, however, ensured that inhabitants of slums constructed on lands owned by the Maharashtra state would qualify for alternative accommodation in the eventuality of slum demolition if the dweller held a photo identity card issued by the state. The photo identity cards accompanied a census of slums held the same year, 1976. But this selective recognition of the rights of some slum dwellers created a split among the urban poor and resonated in Dalit literature as violence by the urban poor on the urban poor.

The intellectual history of Dalit literature resides at the intersection of political-economic and spatial changes in Bombay city and the transregional political conjuncture of the 1950s, 1960s, and 1970s. Dalit writers, particular those affiliated with the Dalit Panther movement, responded to this conjuncture by declaring a revolution in literature and beyond. The revolution outside literature was a response to the violence and humiliation of Dalits, particularly in rural India. The context of the revolution was the global revolutionary conjuncture of the 1960s and early 1970s and the disquiet with the postcolonial Indian government. In Bombay, this revolutionary fervor demanded responsiveness from the democratically elected municipal, state, and federal government in meeting Dalit demands, which included housing and employment.[83] Slum improvement for some was a concession to these radical demands. The revolution in literature required a radical genealogy of its own. Some writers situated Dalit literature as the new chapter in a genealogy going back to the French and Russian Revolutions and translated the ideals of Russian realism and African American literature to create Dalit literature. They distanced themselves from a lineage confined to the tradition of saintly literature from the Marathi-speaking region. These literary and political revolutions intersected in the city's slums. Many Dalit writers, as well as founders of the Dalit Panther movement, lived in slums. Slums animated the imagination of the city's bureaucrats and technocrats, for whom this built form was a blot on a beautiful city. Slum dwellers faced the threat of evictions and slum clearance in the twentieth century. But slums also housed Bombay's workers and were thus important to producing and reproducing the workforce for industrial capitalism in the city. Similarly, with universal adult suffrage, slums were home to an important segment of Bombay's voters. Therefore, some slums became durable.

5 SLUMS, SEX, AND THE FIELD
OF POWER, 1960-1984

DALIT LITERATURE EMERGED IN THE CHANGING POLITICAL AND
economic context of postcolonial Bombay, in which slums proliferated.
Slums served as a metaphor and a material referent for Dalit lives in this
literature. The new field of literature sought recognition from its public.
Writers of Dalit literature located the impulse for revolutionary transformation in Dalit experiences of marginalization and oppression. The recognition they sought was, in the first instance, acknowledgment of the
validity of these experiences. Dalit literature desired validation not just
from a Dalit public but also from the state and society that played an
important role in the marginalization. Moreover, they aspired for recognition from the Marathi literati, or at least a section of it, who would judge
the value of this new literature. To enable the literati to critically appreciate
Dalit literature, M. N. Wankhede had proposed social anthropology as a
model for crafting the narrative of Dalit experiences. Social science and science, presumably because of their emphasis on evidence, became the ideal
for Dalit literature, particularly in the 1960s and 1970s. They were writing
literature, however, not social science, and Dalit writers hoped that this lit-
erariness would be acknowledged favorably by their public and the literati.
This created a paradox: the objects of revolutionary transformation—state,
society, and Marathi literature—were the sources of both recognition of
Dalit literature and the subordination of Dalits.

Dalit literature was not alone in encountering this contradiction. The
regional state also faced a dilemma and in turn exacerbated the paradox
for Dalit literature. In 1960, a new regional state, Maharashtra, was created
on the basis of a common language, Marathi. The demand for a Marathi-
speaking state and for the linguistic reorganization of Indian provinces
hitherto divided into multilingual presidencies was an old one. In fact, the
census commissioner of India in 1901, Herbert Risley, who had played an

influential role in elaborating caste, also had a role in establishing language as the basis for reorganizing Indian regions. In 1903, Risley, and before him John Bright in the 1890s, had identified language as the basis for restructuring Britain's Indian territories.[1] The Congress Party had upheld this principle: in fact, in 1921 it had reorganized the party along linguistic lines.[2] In the 1940s and 1950s, however, when the Congress Party held political power in the region and at the center, leaders dithered, fearing fragmentation of the newly independent Indian state. Their vacillation was contested by large political and social movements demanding monolingual states. The Samyukta Maharashtra Samiti (SMS; Association for a United Maharashtra) had been formed in 1946. The SMS brought about a remarkable alliance of socialists, Communists, right-wing leaders, and various caste groups, including Dalits. The idea of a province for Marathi-language speakers enticed leaders and their constituents to traverse social and political boundaries and linked them in an alliance in the 1940s and 1950s. Perhaps such an alliance was possible in this moment because of a thriving public sphere in Marathi that had come into being in the nineteenth century, when there were fractious debates. These debates amplified feelings of caste, community, and class differences, but they also deepened the identification of these groups with the Marathi language. The colonial state and the Congress Party's proposals to establish language as the principle for restructuring India therefore met with an enthusiastic response and further augmented the ties of language and region. This did not mean that linguistic affinity trumped differences of caste or class.

It was not just the social space of Marathi language that divided the SMS; it was also the position of Bombay city within that space. Both proponents and opponents of the city in a new Marathi-language state deployed the rhetoric of caste and class.[3] For instance, some of the older disputes in the Marathi public sphere between the region's Brahmins and the non-Brahmin movement animated the struggle for control over the Congress Party in the Bombay Presidency in the 1930s and 1940s and were recalibrated in the 1950s in the formation of the Marathi-speaking state. The heightened affinity for language and an appreciation of the economic importance of the city, coupled with dissatisfaction with class and caste factions that did not want Bombay city in Maharashtra, laid the groundwork for the extraordinary alliance of the SMS. Bombay city was important to a Marathi-language state because of its economic importance. Greater Bombay accounted for 75 percent of the industries in the Marathi-speaking region of the province. Its hinterland had strong economic and social ties with the city. Bombay was also a place to migrate for work for the region's Marathi-speaking middle and lower classes. SMS wanted Bombay city in the new province, but the Congress Party toyed with the idea of making it a city-state administered by the Union of India, or possibly the common capital of both the Marathi and non-Marathi (mostly Gujarati) parts of the Bombay Presidency. The SMS deemed the idea perfidious and attributed it to the influence of the city's industrial and mercantile groups and the region's politically dominant Brahmin castes. In 1957, the SMS won a majority in the elections to the Bombay Municipal Corporation and passed a resolution supporting inclusion of the city in Maharashtra.[4] The Marathi-speaking state of Maharashtra was created in 1960; by then the SMS had fragmented owing to the weight of its contradictions and had exited the political scene.

The SMS movement and the creation of Maharashtra produced a contradiction for Dalit politics and Dalit literature. B. R. Ambedkar, when he was alive, had reservations about a Marathi-speaking state. He had feared a worsening of repression of Dalit castes by politically dominant groups in the new state.[5] After his death in 1956, however, many Dalit leaders and intellectuals supported the movement for a monolingual state. Writers like Baburao Bagul comprehended this moment as a revolutionary conjuncture. Bagul believed that the SMS provided the vehicle for Dalits in the region to transcend the isolation of caste by joining the movement for a united Marathi-speaking region. A common language, Marathi, became the path to overcoming Dalit marginalization and the grounds for participating in a broader political movement for a linguistically defined region. Many Communists and Socialists had embraced this politics in the 1950s, and Bagul believed in its power to bridge the particularities of caste. For Bagul, language permeated caste and class boundaries. He therefore regarded this as a historic alliance.[6] Once Maharashtra was formed, Ambedkar's anticipation of violent repression came to fruition, a development captured in Bagul's stories. In fact, in Bagul's stories, the violence toward Dalit castes became severe precisely when they transcended caste boundaries.

The new state was positioned as a patron of the Marathi language and the upholder of its culture. Within a few months, the government set up the Maharashtra State Board for Literature and Culture in November 1960 to promote regional culture by commissioning and publishing works on the history, culture, and literature of the region. Marathi culture, which the new state claimed to patronize, was an important site for government efforts to construct its own legitimacy. The Maharashtra State Board saw its work as protecting the rich heritage of Maharashtra and modernizing the "language and literature of Maharashtra."[7] Moreover, the board saw itself as the upholder of the revolutionary legacy of nineteenth- and twentieth-century thinkers, including Jyotirao Phule, Gopal Krishna Gokhale, and B. R. Ambedkar, and tasked itself with the intellectual regeneration of Maharashtra.[8] Karl Marx was another important icon in this pantheon; the board translated and published two of his works, including his mammoth *Capital*. One effect of the state's attention to Marathi culture was that *tamasha*, the performative practice the state had found morally repugnant in the 1940s and 1950s, was recognized in the 1960s as an important folk tradition of Maharashtra, after it had been suitably sanitized by draining it of erotic content. Many *tamasha* performers were from the Dalit castes. In fact, by the 1960s, state patronage enabled the revival of *tamasha* in cities like Bombay, where it also enjoyed support among the middle class. The government also commissioned a Marathi encyclopedia, modeled on the lines of *Encyclopedia Britannica*, in twenty volumes of one thousand pages each, with an emphasis on Maharashtra and India.[9] Dalit literature, however, posed a conundrum for the state. Its foundational impulse in the 1960s was to criticize established Marathi literature—the literature patronized by the board—and to create a new literature beyond the Marathi canon. The writers of the new literature were critics of state policies and advocates of the view that untouchability had not yet been exterminated, even though laws against untouchability had been passed within a few years of India's independence. These writers aspired to a revolutionary social and political transformation. The patronage of this literature could pose a conundrum for the state, particularly because Dalit Sahitya's instinct at this time was to distance itself from dominant Marathi literature and establish parallel institutions. The writers of Dalit literature had formed alternative organizations, such as the Maharashtra Boudh Sahitya Sabha (Maharashtra Buddhist Literary Association), in the early 1960s, which held annual conferences to flesh out their vision for a separate literature. But their vision of the distinction of Dalit literature from Marathi literature did not consistently hold in practice. For instance, M. N. Wankhede, one of the proponents of a separate Dalit literature, said in his foreword to Baburao Bagul's 1970 book *Quest* (Suda) that "Dalit literature was a river that joined the sea of Marathi literature."[10] Indeed, by 1978, the board published an edited volume on Dalit literature, and its head, Lakshmanshastri Joshi, while acknowledging the desire for separation, hoped that in the future Dalit literature would merge with Marathi literature.[11]

This chapter situates the work of two important Dalit writers of this period, Baburao Bagul and Namdeo Dhasal, in relation to the tensions in Marathi literature. It maps the push for separation in the 1960s, but also the parallel and contradictory impulse for recognition from the literati and the state. This recognition took the form of patronage and delineated the field of power within which Dalit literature was suspended. The chapter focuses on the field of power and the strategies adopted by some Dalit writers to navigate it. One important theme I highlight in the works of these writers is their understanding of social relationships in the city. In the works of Bagul and Dhasal, social relationships are shaped by their characters' understanding of themselves and each other as things—or commodities—and not just as friends, lovers, sons, daughters, or parents. This trope—which borrows from the writers' understanding of Marxist notions of commodity and commodification in circulation in the 1950s, 1960s, and 1970s—is pronounced in the depiction of Dalit characters, particularly Dalit women. The depiction of life in Bombay's slums helped the writers gain recognition from the Marathi literati. For instance, Namdeo Dhasal took the iconic Marathi writer Vijay Tendulkar on a tour of the slums of Kamathipura, including its red-light district, and decoded his literary language and urban slang for Tendulkar in return for a foreword to his groundbreaking collection of poems, *Golpitha*. Thus slumming for the real experience of city life became a tradable commodity for some writers in the recognition of this literature.

DALIT LITERATURE

Dalits did not begin writing in the 1950s and 1960s. Neither were depictions of Dalit lives by Dalits and non-Dalit writers novel at this time.[12] In fact, in the 1920s, the term "Dalit" itself was popularized by writers like S. G. Tipnis and P. N. Rajbhoj, in a newspaper started by Ambedkar, *Bahishkrut Bharat* (Outcaste India).[13] The list of first-generation writers of Dalit literature from the 1930s, 1940s, and 1950s included names such as Tukaram Purohit, N. R. Shende, Bandhu Madhav, Vishvas Bhonsale, Vasant Rajas, Dinesh Lakhmapurkat, Sharad Mahatekar, B. V. Varale, Annabhau Sathe, and Shankarrao Kharat.[14] These writers published in newspapers and magazines started by Ambedkar, including *Bahishkrut Bharat*, *Janata*, and *Prabuddha Bharata*, and were associates in the political and social movements he started.[15] This list of male writers was amended by Urmila Pawar and Meenakshi Moon with their account of women who published in some of the same publications in the same period. These included women writers mostly from cities like Bombay, Pune, and Nashik. The articles and short stories written by women addressed themes like women's political participation (Shantabai Gondane and Kausalya Nandesvar), equality between the sexes (Nalini Jagtap), Dalit death rituals (Sharda Shevale, Draupadi Kamble, and Shanta Jadhav), intercaste relationships and marriage between Dalit castes (Sheela Shejval), and women's education (Pankabai Wankhede and Nalini Jagtap), along with other topics raised by the Dalit social movement. For instance, in the early 1950s, the topic of death rituals among Dalits sparked a debate when Sharda Shevale wrote in *People* that Dalits should not bury but instead cremate the dead. Cremation was practiced by many upper-caste Hindus in the region. Draupadi Kamble responded by pointing out the expenses involved in incinerating a body. Shanta Jadhav pointed out that cremation was merely an imitation of upper-caste rituals.[16] Shevale defended her initial proposal, articulating that her goal was social reform of the Dalits to match the political progress they had made as a result of Ambedkar's movement.

This unacknowledged history of the literary and political participation of women in Dalit literature highlighted by Pawar and Moon alerts us to the field of power constitutive of Dalit literature itself. For instance, the recognition and awards conferred on Dalit literature in the 1960s and 1970s, after Maharashtra was created, accrued mostly to male writers: both Annabhau Sathe and Baburao Bagul won state awards in the 1960s. Dalit literature became synonymous with the literary output of male writers, particularly in the generation after Ambedkar and his associates exited the scene. The male writers themselves were suspended within a power hierarchy. For recognition, awards, and sometimes an apartment in the city, they relied on the state government and the Marathi literati. The latter saw in Dalit literature newer possibilities of narrative, thought, and depiction of social realities. The literati could grasp these new stories through language, especially because they could not experience or produce it on their own. Only the Dalit male could do so. In other words, the stories themselves became commodities savored by the literati and its public, which also included non-Dalit readers. The literary scholar Aniket Jaaware has rebuked this consumption. He mocks the upper-caste readership for consuming Dalit literature as a means of assuaging their caste guilt without making radical changes that would have brought the practice of caste to a point of crisis: "We could now begin to undo the sins of our ancestors . . . by reading and praising Dalit poetry, only so long as we are not forced to eat with them, or marry our daughter to one of them."[17]

What were some tropes of this literature? One important point that demarcated it from an earlier generation of literature *on* Dalits, and not *by* Dalits, was the residence of these writers in cities, many in Bombay, and their discussion of life in the city. The lumpen proletariat, the built form of the city, casteism not just in the city but also in villages of the region, and prostitution and sex workers provided the stories with drama, tragedy, and titillation. Dalit literature was different from earlier writings on Dalits because these earlier works were set mostly in villages and highlighted the suffering of the Dalit castes. By contrast, the new writers were revolutionaries bristling with the possibility of a political and social revolution, not just a literary transformation. In their writing, they dwelled on the inner lives and social relationships of their subjects: the lumpen was not just a tool of opponents of the workers' movement but was also a father struggling to feed his children. Similarly, the sex worker had dependents that she supported through her work and had relationships that were not merely transactional but also affective. Their lives were shaped by their treatment as commodities, used and abused by others in the city. Therefore, in some situations their relations with each other had also been commodified: they existed because they generated money. Thus, a father forces his daughter into sex work for the money. Did these male writers appropriate the figure of the sex worker and make her stand in for the plight of Dalits in the city and the region? We will explore this question as we turn to a close reading of some of these writers, Baburao Bagul and Namdeo Dhasal particularly, and highlight the literary innovations that received recognition as Dalit literature.

BABURAO BAGUL'S MUMBAI

In *Golpitha*, Dhasal described in vivid detail the world of sex workers, pimps, and underworld dons in the city. Writers before Dhasal, including Baburao Bagul, had explored these characters in short stories. Before Bagul, Saadat Hasan Manto, a writer from the 1940s who wrote on the city in Urdu, had also depicted this world.[18] Annabhau Sathe had similarly represented everyday life in the overcrowded tenements and slums in the 1940s and 1950s. One of Bagul's contemporaries, the Marathi novelist Bhau Padhye, wrote about these spaces in his 1965 classic *Vasunaka*. But M. N.

Wankhede critiqued *Vasunaka*, saying the everyday life and language depicted there "was from the point of view of the middle class," and the turn to the slum "was motivated by the desire to shock, to claim novelty, and emphasize the writers' youthfulness,"[19] vis-à-vis the dominant Marathi literati of the time. Bagul was a protégé of Annabhau Sathe and, like him, had grown up in the slums of the Matunga Labour Camp after migrating to Bombay as a child. His memories from childhood in the tin chawls of the camp during the 1930s and 1940s are redolent with Communist sloganeering, caste conflict leading to fisticuffs even among the Dalit castes, and the presence of the *mavali* who ran betting and other illegal operations.[20] Bagul grew up reading translations of Maxim Gorky, Lenin, B. R. Ambedkar, and Karl Marx and, in his teens and youth, attended meetings of the Scheduled Castes Federation, the Communist Party of India, and the Socialist Party.[21] Bagul's stories display a tension between Marathi Marxist understandings of the lumpen proletariat and his own struggles to transcend the limitations of the concept. His empathy for the lumpen men was tinged with the assumption, shared by many Marxists in the city, that they were prone to violence and their actions could not be folded into the politics of the working class. At the same time, he humanized them, recognizing their presence on the streets of the city and in their homes in the slums. His investment in humans and humanity was informed by Marxism and by Ambedkar's ideas. Thus, when he foregrounds the humanity of the dehumanized, he emphasizes the social relationships that dehumanize them, like Marx, and assumes, like Ambedkar, that every human has rights. These rights are denied to outcastes in societies where caste norms are predominant.

The protagonist of *Ruffian* (Gund) exemplifies this struggle for the recognition of his humanity. *Ruffian* appeared in his path-breaking collection of short stories *When I Concealed My Caste* (Jevha mi jat chorali hoti), published in 1963. The protagonist is a nameless Ethiopian man with a transnational itinerary of work with gangs. Like the transnational genealogy of ideas that shaped Dalit literature, slum dwellers moved beyond national boundaries too. The protagonist has spent time with gangs in Hong Kong and Singapore before arriving in Bombay via Karachi. His appearance—racial markers like the color of his skin and hair—and his imposing physique mark his difference. Fellow gang members do not let him step out of the den for fear he will be identified by authorities and rival gang members and thus reveal their hiding places. He lives a cloistered life in Hong Kong and Singapore. His appearance instills dread in his rivals and revulsion among many. Sex workers in Hong Kong and Singapore loathe him: a German prostitute in Singapore is contemptuous of his demonic appearance.[22] As a result, he yearns for female companionship and intimacy. In Bombay, a widowed woman, Jayantiben, approaches him seeking help for the funeral of her mother. Jayantiben's ability to overcome revulsion and appeal to his humanity moves him. He agrees to help her, robs a rich merchant, gives the money to Jayantiben, and organizes her mother's funeral. Jayantiben's transcendence of derision and her ability to acknowledge and appeal to the ruffian's humanity match Bagul's ability to transcend stereotypes of the lumpen proletariat. Bagul reveals the tension in the outcaste: the ruffian terrorizes and robs a merchant to assist a widowed woman who has lost her mother. In Bagul's world, the space of the slum is not insular. It enables unlikely bonds: an African ruffian and Jayantiben are brought together by acknowledging each other's humanness. As Bagul summarizes in a commentary on Dalit literature, it is the literature of humans and humanity.[23]

Unlike Jayantiben, who rises above racial disdain in a Bombay slum, villagers succumb to caste and gender prejudice. In Bagul's stories from the 1950s and 1960s, casteism and caste oppression are mostly but not exclusively rural. There is no romance for pastoral life: for Dalits it is a space of violence and despair. This formulation echoes B. R. Ambedkar and Marathi Marxist understandings of the village as the receptacle of caste prejudice. In the 1950s, when Bagul was a young man, he had discussed with his friends the possibility of an armed revolution in India and dreamed of blowing up every village where Dalit women were oppressed by the upper castes.[24] The rural association with caste prejudice is evident in *Prisoners of Darkness* (Kalokhyache qaidi). In the story, Banu, a beautiful woman born in an untouchable caste, becomes the second wife of an upper-caste landlord, Ramrao Deshmukh. After Ramrao's death, Devaram, his son from his first wife who resents Banu, wants to kill her. Devaram's resentment also has a sexual charge: he also wants to rape Banu. His antipathy is shared by most of the village: they encourage him to humiliate and kill her. Bagul sketches the system of rural oppression by portraying the drama of the village ganging up on Banu and her son Daulat within a few hours of Ramrao's death. The drama highlights the predatory nature of caste violence, as if Banu were an animal being hunted. She is cornered and helpless, with no escape; even the village temple denies her sanctuary. The story ends in horrific violence, with the deaths of Banu, Daulat, and Devaram. In Bagul's rendering, the upper castes in the village are complicit in the violence that kills Banu and Daulat, who has been scorned since his birth as the product of caste miscegenation. For the villagers, Banu and Daulat are less than human. In *Prisoners of Darkness*, Bagul reworks the narrative device of intercaste marriage—which he argues had become formulaic at the time he was writing the story—to highlight the degradation, humiliation, adversities, and violence that inform caste relationships, particularly untouchability, in rural society.[25]

Bagul again explores casteism, particularly the depredations of untouchability, in the title story. The narrator of the story is a Dalit man who has grown up in Bombay. He relishes the opportunity provided by the city to transcend caste; he experiences the anonymity afforded by city life as "gamboling in the river of humanity."[26] The city obscures his caste. The protagonist gets a job in the railways and is assigned to a small town, Udhana, in a Gujarati-speaking area of western India. He is joyous when he lands there, baggage in one hand and a book by the Russian poet Vladimir Mayakovsky in the other. The Mayakovsky book depicts its protagonist as a person in tune with the Russian poet's politics of rejecting tradition. But the possibilities of Bombay evaporate as soon as he lands in Udhana. When he meets his colleague Ranchod, identified as belonging to the Kshatriya (warrior) caste, he inquires about housing. Ranchod asks him, "What is your caste . . . we ask strangers their caste?"[27] The narrator is affronted, conceals his caste, and identifies himself as a citizen of Bombay (Mumbaikar). In his self-representation, the particularity of caste dissolves in his identification as a Mumbaikar. His comportment, his dress, and the Mayakovsky book mark him as upper caste in Ranchod's eyes. "Why would a man like you stay in the house of Dheds and Dublas [Dalit castes]?" he asks, justifying his appraisal of the narrator as an upper-caste man. The narrator does not disabuse Ranchod of his (mis)conception. His concealment of caste, however, splits his sense of self: he feels compelled to hide his caste from his public persona. Within a few minutes of his arrival in Udhana, his joyousness has given way to a claustrophobic timidity and fissured his sense of self. The split self is the prerequisite for passing as a man with a dignified caste in the eyes of his colleagues.

The author's bind is exacerbated when another worker from Bombay, Kashinath Sapkal, self-identifies as a Mahar Dalit at a tea shop. His declaration is greeted with outrage and violence. Bagul employs a possibility in the caste system—that travel from one place to another, Bombay to Udhana in this case, could obscure one's caste at least for some time, because people from one language community may not be familiar with the last name that reveals one's caste in another setting. Kashinath's confident self-assertion invites contempt from his colleagues, and he is ostracized. He begins carrying a knife in his pocket, fearing an eminent attack. By contrast, the narrator is regarded as a good Mumbaikar; his fondness for poetry marks him as a man of culture. His boss, Tiwari, a Brahmin man, considers the narrator to be his poetic mentor. Tiwari insists that the protagonist visit his home for a meal. However, commensality across caste boundaries is restricted by the caste system. The protagonist dodges the invitation. He surreptitiously allies with Kashinath, offering him sage counsel, but is unable to reveal his caste to him either. On payday, the author decides to end the charade, quit his job, and return to Bombay. Kashinath has similar ideas. On the last evening of his stay in Udhana, the author yields to Tiwari's relentless invitations and goes to his house for dinner. After a sumptuous dinner, he falls asleep there, only to be woken up by blows. His hosts and his colleagues have discovered his caste. The narrator is eventually rescued by a knife-wielding Kashinath, and they both escape to Bombay, where they will apparently be at home, leaving the claustrophobia of caste and Udhana behind them.

Violence, particularly against women, was also urban, and women were complicit in it. Bagul narrates these relationships in terms of competition among women. Women, their bodies commodified, are compelled to compete and sell their bodies. In "Streetwalker" (Vatervarchi), the protagonist is a sex worker named Girija. She lives in a room in a Bombay slum. Girija has just returned from a pilgrimage to the shrine of a Sufi saint, Haji Malang, on the outskirts of Bombay city. In Bagul's world the ritual practices of outcastes and slum dwellers are eclectic; they are not purists and visit shrines, temples, and churches for blessings. An important reason for Girija's visit to the shrine is to solicit benediction to counter the competition from a younger sex worker. Girija devotedly performs her rituals: she feeds a mendicant, offers flowers at the tomb of the saint, and feels confident that she will be rewarded for her devotion. The blessing of the saint should work like a charm in this competition. After returning home, Girija distributes benediction from the shrine, *prasad*, to her acquaintances in the slum, including the moneylenders and creditors. One such creditor is the owner of the betel nut shop in the neighborhood; Girija needed the betel nut to color her lips red. She also owes money to Kasam, the owner of the restaurant where she generally has breakfast. She has accrued a debt to Kasam, and she receives letters there from her family in the village. A wire from her village, which Kasam hands her that morning, informs her that her young son in the village is seriously ill. Girija's good cheer evaporates. In her grief, she begins planning her day. Her plan is to accumulate as much money as possible that day to visit her son. To get money, she is compelled to do sex work.

Bagul lingers on Girija's emotions. Her grief is accentuated by the mundane rituals of getting ready for work—washing her face, combing her hair, and applying the dot worn by married women to her forehead. She breaks down while dressing but eventually gathers herself and makes her way to the betel nut shop. Sadness envelops her as she reaches her place of work, a public garden. She smiles to attract clients but without much luck. In the afternoon, Girija spots a familiar client, an abuser, and the memories of previous abuse by him scare her. If he solicited her for sex, she would not be able to deny him since she needs the money. As he approaches her, Girija is paralyzed by fear. He interprets this as a sign of refusal and passes her by. She chastises herself for losing a client. Later she sees another familiar client, Narayan Shetty, and bargains for a higher price, five rupees. Despite her grief, she is satisfied with her ability to strike a good deal. After Shetty, she hopes to service a few more clients, at the same high price, before leaving for the village. But things don't work out as planned: some prospective clients humiliate her after she tells them her rates, and by late afternoon she is very hungry and desperate for money. Eventually Girija finds a client who is only willing to pay her two rupees. She relents. Bagul juxtaposes the thought processes of Girija and her client. She needs the money; the client knows it and plans to take advantage of her need and decamp with her money. He torments her; she relents to his fantasies because he keeps paying her more money, over and above the initial bargain. At the end of the session, Girija is tired. He beats her up and leaves with the money. She learns in the evening that her son has died. Girija's swindling and torture exemplify the abjection of the lives of gendered bodies of urban outcastes in the city slums. In Bagul's account, prostitution is a metaphor for and the site where class, caste, gender, and the built environment intersect. The depredations of Girija's life stand in for the devastations inflicted by capitalism and caste. The commodification of women's bodies and the competition among sex workers, fostered by their clients, stymie solidarity among them. Through Girija's story, Bagul shows the precarity, isolation, and alienation of urban life. She has no control over space and time.

Competition among women is the theme of another story by Bagul, "Competition" (Spardha). Yamuna, an old woman, peddles bananas opposite a textile mill. In the nineteenth century, the hawkers of Bombay registered their presence in the city streets, and their peddling of commodities has been regarded since then as a nuisance by the city's middle classes and elite.[28] Bagul looks beyond the nuisance and peers into the lives of two women. The mill workers treat Yamuna like a mother figure; she enjoys this role and proffers life advice to some of them. Yamuna encourages her niece Chandra (the wife of Yamuna's nephew) to hawk bananas opposite her mill because the young woman's husband is suffering from tuberculosis and she needs the money. They are both selling the same commodity, bananas, to the same customers, which eventually leads to competition between them. But the competition involves not just the quality and quantity of bananas sold in the day, but also the use of women's bodies to sell bananas. The matronly Yamuna cannot compete with the youthful and pretty Chandra, who encourages the attention of the male workers by flirting with them. Yamuna realizes that she is being edged out of her business. The competition leads to squabbles between them and ends with Yamuna moving back to the village to spend time with her family. But before leaving, Yamuna sheds light on the logical outcome of the competition. Chandra, she says, will have to up the ante and either find a new suitor (a mill worker named Kisan always hovers around her) or be prepared to have the mill workers treat her like a sex worker.[29] Thus the figure of the sex worker haunts the competition between two women hawkers.

What should we make of this collection of stories? Bagul provides an insight into his intellectual scaffolding in the afterword to *When I Concealed My Caste*. He locates naked casteism in villages where the upper castes lust for blood and desire to exterminate lower-caste bodies, particularly if they are perceived as crossing caste boundaries. Similarly, his decision to highlight the marginalization and fragility of outcastes in the city through the figure of the sex worker needs explanation too. In his own telling, some critics of the Dalit castes criticized "Streetwalker" as disgraceful and insulting.[30] Girija's story was read as a story about a woman of the Dalit castes, even though Bagul never identifies her caste, as he does in his other stories. It could be that Girija belongs to the same caste as Banu from *Prisoners of Darkness*. To understand the stories of Banu and Girija, both victims of violence, one in the village and the other in Bombay, we need to locate them in the context of the political moment of the 1950s and 1960s, which shaped Bagul and in which he intervened as a writer and an activist. Bagul had noted the revolutionary possibilities of the Samyukta Maharashtra Movement, which led to the making of a monolingual state.

This possibility of transformation disappeared along with the organization upon the creation of the new state. The dream of effecting change and transcending caste boundaries invited violence against Dalits. Violence was important to maintaining the social and political boundaries that Dalits sought to transcend.[31] Bagul thus depicts the shattering of this revolutionary possibility. In *Prisoners of Darkness*, for instance, the metaphors of imprisonment (*qaidi*) and darkness (*kalokh*) heighten the fragility of this moment. Banu's beauty and her desire to avoid sex work, coupled with Deshmukh's lust, result in a relationship between the two that lasts for twenty years. In a way, Banu has shielded herself from the depredations of sex work by consenting to a relationship with a powerful man in the village. In the process, Banu has insulated herself within the shield and has not fathomed the antipathy she faces from villagers. Her son, Daulat, has, however, experienced the hatred and is bitter toward his mother. After Deshmukh's death the darkness of caste envelops Banu and Daulat and extinguishes their lives. In Bagul's thinking, the village is the graveyard of the dreams of social, particularly caste, transformation in 1950s; the city is not the site of naked casteism, at least in his early writings.

Caste was not absent from the city, as we saw in *When I Concealed My Caste*. It hid behind and haunted the category of the sex worker. In fact, caste, class, and gender intersected in the figure of the prostitute. She bore the burden of enunciating this intersection and stood in for outcastes in the city. Girija's life is upended as easily as Banu's. Like Banu in the village, Girija is not at home in the city. Only a radical transformation could make both Banu and Girija feel at home. In lieu of this change, mundane life hurtles into horrifying violence within a few minutes. In Bagul's stories, this is the lived experience of Dalits and all subordinate groups in the city and the villages. Girija, Banu, and Kashinath are not unaware of their subordinate positions in the relationships and networks they foster or find themselves in, but the volatility of these relationships surprises them; their lives are engulfed and often extinguished by shifts in the delicate equilibrium of everyday life. The protagonists have limited ability to control these transformations. In other words, power is "deeply structured" in these relationships, and a trigger produces displays of extravagant brutality.[32] To paraphrase Marx, the little that was solid in those relationships, including the protagonists' sense of self, also melted into air. Bagul aspired to convey the tragedy and brutality of the moment in which the structure caves in on subordinate groups. His stated goal was to evoke compassion (*karuna*) and anger in his readers and provide artistic renditions of real-life oppression.[33]

Along with this narration, the writer, in his view, needed to pose probing questions: "What were people [oppressors and the oppressed] thinking? What and who shaped their mentality? What was the social, cultural and economic situation at the time? How did people regard humans and women [in that context]?"[34] In Bagul's view, when the writer poses these questions and accepts responsibility for answering them, he becomes a scientist (*shastragnya*). And because he is a scientist, he surpasses the partisanship of ethnic and national identity.[35] The investigation of social conditions leads to a reckoning with institutions that justify caste, class, and gender oppression.

This was Bagul's manifesto for Dalit literature. He believed that the writer of Dalit literature must combine the method of a scientist with the skill of an artist in evoking compassion and rage. The author must commit to transformation of the deep structures that subjugate the outcastes and advocate for a social revolution. Bagul's invocation of a scientific method, revolutionary fervor, and affinity for oppressed groups reflects the influence of Marathi Marxism and Ambedkar's ideas. Bagul draws a conceptual equivalence between Marxism and Dalit literature. After all, "Marxism is opposed to poverty, suffering, and servitude."[36] He asks the Communist and Socialist to advocate for Dalits. The real Indian revolution, he believes, will sprout from untouchables and untouchability, and therefore Communism and Socialism should focus on the low castes and outcastes and consider them as the vanguards of their political movements.[37] He suggests that if leftists realign their politics to focus on untouchability and outcastes, they will realize that a focus on caste automatically enables an emphasis on the "economic, political, cultural, and social" issues that they have long been agitating for. According to Bagul, Dalit writers must never detach themselves from the people, in particular the marginalized groups. They must transcend the boundaries of caste, community, race, and religion to write about the "Muslim, Christian, Negroes."[38] In sum, the Dalit in Dalit literature is not just an expression of the identity of untouchable castes but also a recognition of the marginalization of various groups. Bagul imagines an affinity with these groups born of a shared experience of marginalization. The affinity may collapse in practice, revealing the working of class, caste, and patriarchy, but it is still an ideal the author must aspire to. According to him, the identification of the writer with marginalized groups and of the people with the writer must be strong. *When I Concealed My Caste* is peopled with characters from these groups. We also see such characters in his second collection of short stories, many of them again set in the slums of Bombay.

In Bagul's second collection of stories, *Death Is Becoming Cheap* (Maran swast hot ahe), published in 1969, he again deploys the trope of competition among sex workers and the commodification of body and sex. In "Plunder" (Lutalut), he depicts the relationships between Gangu, the brothel keeper, and sex workers Putli, Vanchala, and Soni, who have been sold to the brothel by men they were intimate with. Intimacy crumbles in the face of monetary want and greed. The brothel keeper, Gangu, and her husband have migrated to Bombay in the hope of accumulating money to buy back land in the village they have pledged to a moneylender. Unable to do so, Gangu's husband sells her to a brothel, where she eventually becomes the brothel keeper. Soni abandons the village and her husband to escape poverty and arrives in the city with another man, who sells her to Gangu. Her resourcefulness in leaving the village and her husband, and her dreams of escaping poverty by migrating to the city, lead her to sex work. Bagul sketches a direct link between rural and urban poverty. The choices characters make as well as their relationships are shaped by their poverty. Every aspect of their lives, including their relationships, is commodified. Plunder and violence underwrite these relationships. The liaisons among characters in the story are extractive: the women in the brothel, the partners who sold them, the world beyond the brothel inhabited by clients who throng the place on payday, the pimp and enforcer summoned by Gangu to discipline a recalcitrant Vanchala, and the police all want to profit from each other. Human relationships have been reduced to transactions of body and money. The commodification of bodies and relationships amplifies the desolation of life in the city for the sex worker.

It is easier for men to cultivate camaraderie, even though that is also precarious. They can rise above the limitations of caste, religion, and language, even as their amity may shatter in an instant. Bagul's characters have the ability to speak in multiple tongues and dialects. In "Hard Labor" (Sakta majuri), Fernandes, a three-card trickster, along with his friends Sikandar Sindhi, Kasam Ali, and Sambha, are hustling workers. The lumpen proletariat and the worker are antagonists, with the former trying to trick the latter. Sindhi impersonates a man speaking Gujarati; Kasam Ali, a North Indian man who speaks Hindi, Urdu, and the dialects Awadhi and Bhojpuri; and Sambha, various dialects of Marathi. Together, they solicit workers to bet their wages. One day, after Fernandes has fought with his wife and spent the rest of the night drinking in the slums, he moves with his accomplices from one street corner to another and then from the gate of one textile mill to the other, in the hope of executing a con and getting money for his hungry and ailing kids. They need capital for the three-card trick, so Fernandes borrows money from a money-lender. They solicit workers without any luck. Kasam Ali beckons a North Indian worker, referring to him as Bhaiyya (Brother): "O, Maiku, ava, ava [Come on, Maiku].[39] Fernandes and his accomplices hustle all day without any luck. Their hunger, disappointment, and anxiety about not getting any money for their families agitate them. Fernandes and Sikandar begin to fight, blaming each other. A crowd gathers, and police arrive on the scene. The police beat up all of them, threaten to arrest them, and relieve them of the capital they borrowed from the moneylender. The accomplices return to the slum dejected and empty-handed, their abjection enhanced by the failure of their collective resourcefulness. At the end of the story, Fernandes has not resolved the issues of hunger and anxiety that informed his actions that day and has sunk further into debt.

Bagul explores further the fragile camaraderie of the lumpen proletariat in "Outcaste" (Mavali). Five *mavalis* are hiding in a desolate cemetery in the city after a fight with a rival street gang. The leader of the group, Columbus, is grievously injured. Peter, Lalya, Raphael, and Kashinath are his accomplices. At the beginning of the story they address each other as "brother" and "comrade"; their language is an amalgam of Hindi, Urdu, English, and Marathi. For instance, Raphael instructs Kashinath, "Baradar . . . comrade Kolambasla jaldise durust [Urdu] karun [Marathi] apnala ithun satakla paije. Nay tar punha Vanda [Gujarati] Vhaycha, haryap [English]" (Brother, let's repair comrade Columbus quickly and decamp from here before any more trouble, hurry up).[40] The argot is of the street; a linguistic purist would not claim it. The language heightens the sense of the protagonists' being of the street and at the margins of respectable society. Moreover, they have lost respect in the street, because they, particularly their leader, have been thrashed by a rival gang. They want revenge. In "Outcaste," the brothers ride an emotional roller coaster, and their camaraderie begins to unravel. Raphael feels bad for Columbus, but Peter resents his leadership, his ability to attract women, his inability to fight in the street, and his failure to diversify the sources of the gang's income through smuggling. Peter's irreverence angers the other gang members. Peter and the others are grappling with questions that are important to them: how to regain their respect in the street, assuage their aggrieved sense of masculine pride, and diffuse the tension among them.

Bagul introduces a sex worker in the story. Kanchan is a maid by day and a sex worker by night. She arrives in the vicinity of the cemetery with a client. Kashinath points them out, and Peter follows them, beating up the client and trying to molest Kanchan. Raphael and Kashinath intervene, as does Columbus, who regains consciousness and rouses himself to save Kanchan. But Peter tries to rape Kanchan. The sex worker induces a complete breakdown in their camaraderie, and they end up killing each other. As the title of the book notes, "Death is becoming cheap."

The violence of the urban poor toward each other and the relevance of group boundaries, particularly caste restrictions, which inform it, provide the theme of another story, "People on an Open Tract of Land" (Maidanatil manse). In this story, Bagul focuses on the lives of a motley group squatting on public land in the city adjacent to an electric power company, where they are spending a cold night struggling to stay warm. They are so poor they cannot afford a rudimentary shelter in a slum that would shield them from the cold. The group includes David, a neighborhood ruffian who was assaulted that day and abandoned there; Abdul Karim, who is unemployed and suffering from tuberculosis; Jhunkavu and Supad, an old married couple who pick rags for a living; a leper identified as "Madrasi" (a derogatory term for South Indians); and members of the nomadic Phase Pardhi tribe, considered criminal by the British. All of them struggle to stay warm and deploy strategies, including intimacy and sex, to ward off the cold. The narrator offers the reader a voyeuristic account of intimacies and squabbles among partners in public space. One such sexual encounter—between Sona, a young girl from the Phase Pardhi tribe, and an unknown man—degenerates into a brawl. Group boundaries are drawn on the bodies of women: having sex with a person outside one's ethnic group is seen as caste taboo. As the Phase Pardhis pummel Sona's partner, David, who is himself recovering from a thrashing, intervenes. The group turns its anger on him and beats him until he is unconscious or possibly dead. Bagul's depiction of sexual encounters among squatters harkens back to the social reformers' and sociologists' fascination with the intimate lives of the urban poor. But there are important differences too: whereas sex in public spaces was intended to shock and possibly titillate the reader in these stories, Bagul does not pass judgment on the morality of the people he describes. Bagul narrates public sex as a need born of the destitute person's desire to stay warm as well as a desire for companionship in the city. Intercourse here is not devoid of feelings of lust and pleasure, missing in the reformers' dreary accounts. The drama of sex in public spaces and violence among the outcastes draws our attention not just to the abjectness of the poor but also to the importance of caste in violence and of sexual taboos in maintaining group boundaries. Taboos do not disappear in the city.

In the title story, "Death Is Becoming Cheap" (Maran swast hot ahe), Bagul narrates the stories of Bombay's slum dwellers through the eyes of a poet friend visiting the author in a slum for a dialogue on literature. The friends work in different forms: one short stories, the other poetry. Both write on Bombay, addressing a common topic: death is cheap in Mumbai. Their literary collaboration is, however, foiled by writer's block. They decide to step out for a walk in the slum for recreation and inspiration. By the end of the walk, they are saturated with stories. The poet synthesizes these in verse:

> This is Mumbai.
> Here humans eat humans and
> Death is cheap!

Through the stories of slum dwellers, Bagul offers his readers a geography of slum demolition in Bombay city. The 1960s heralded both horizontal and vertical expansion of the city as the solution to overcrowding and slums. As a result, many slums were demolished and moved to the north and east of the city. The slum where the two friends from "Death Is Becoming Cheap" are strolling is a recent habitation in northern Bombay and includes residents who have been pushed out of slums farther south. For instance, one character, Bheemu Kadam, arrives in the narrator's slum from Bandra, a suburb that became part of the city in the 1950s, after the creation of Greater Bombay. Bheemu's hut in Bandra was washed away by the sea, and the replacement he erected was demolished by the Bombay Municipal Corporation. Bagul offers a backstory to Bheemu's presence in Bombay and its slums. He was born in a prestigious rural family of the Maratha caste[41] and is an accomplished wrestler. One day, he discovers his wife is having an affair with his arch rival. He hacks up both of them with an axe and surrenders to the police. Upon his release from jail, he migrates to Bombay. For five years he squats on city streets doing petty jobs, becoming an alcoholic and a substance abuser. After five years, he meets a Dalit woman from the sweeper caste and starts living with her in the Bandra slum. Bagul dwells on the woman (she is nameless in the story), contrasting her physical beauty with her work. She cleans toilets in the apartments of the neighboring buildings. The symbolism of a man from the higher Maratha caste cohabiting with a woman from the Dalit caste in a city slum is not without significance. For the woman, love transcends caste, while for Bheemu the degradation of life in the slum makes caste hierarchies redundant. Kadam finds work in an slaughterhouse[42] but cannot hold onto it and is eventually abandoned by the woman.

The narrator introduces the poet (and the reader) to an elderly Muslim man. His presence in the slum is marked by social descent, much like Bheemu. The old man was a schoolteacher in Hyderabad proficient in Urdu and Persian. After his retirement and his wife's death, he comes to Bombay to be close to his three sons. In the city, following a series of unfortunate events, he is saddled with the responsibility for his ten grandchildren after their father abandons them. He has to sell his home in the city to feed them and now lives on the street. Unable to take care of the children, he starts either selling them to rich people or abandoning them at restaurants. His journey from South-Central Bombay's Bhendi Bazaar neighborhood to the slum in north Bombay takes seven to eight years. Like Bheemu, who moves from street to slum and from slum to slum, the old man is itinerant in his destitution. He is now left with only one grandson, who begs on the streets to feed himself and his grandfather. For the old man as well as Bheemu, Bombay hastens his destitution, and the slum signifies a steep decline in social status. The descent and the accompanying torment in their everyday lives shape their interaction with the city. Bombay and its slums produce a dramatic psychosocial transformation in the lives of these characters.

Bagul emphasizes the link between migration to the city and the alteration of the material and moral lives of the outcastes through the story of Barku. Barku is a Dalit man from the Mahar caste who digs wells for a living in the village, but an accident leaves him paraplegic. His family, particularly his brother, do not want to bear the burden of his dependency. Barku migrates to the city and arrives in the slum with his wife and two children, determined to buy property in the village and reclaim his social status. His resourcefulness entails pushing his son into begging and his daughter into sex work. He makes his son dress like an upper-caste Brahmin boy, with bodily markers such as the tuft of hair (*shendi*) and sacred thread (*janeyu*), and has him seek alms outside a temple in the hope of benefiting from worshippers' generosity. Barku hoards the money from their work to buy property in the village. He refuses to buy, rent, or build a hut in the slum, so the family continues to live on the street. Bagul depicts

Barku's greed. The city commodifies everything: his children and their bodies are sources of money. Even a hut in the slum is deemed an unnecessary expense, and its absence a sign of abjection. The wretchedness in the city sustains private property and status in the village. The two children eventually abandon Barku, but in the meantime his wife has produced other children, and they become vehicles for his aspirations. "Death Is Becoming Cheap" ends with the narrator and the poet witnessing the rape and murder of a woman.

The slum dwellers relieve the artists of their writer's block. Inspiration is outside their door. In this collection of stories, the lines between fiction and reality, rational and irrational, camaraderie and hostility, love and revulsion are murky. The city and the slum upend the lives of the people; all that was solid in their lives melts into air, including their sense of self, making the boundaries redundant and murkiness the new reality. In this new reality family relationships are commodified, and they trade each other for money. Bombay produces this moral murkiness, commodification, and debasement of life. The debasement of the lives of the outcastes shocked the sensibilities of Bagul's readers and critics and upended the status quo in Marathi literature. In *Death Is Becoming Cheap*, Bagul's depiction of life in Bombay city, particularly for the urban poor, is bleak. The poor, by exchanging their bodies for money, become aware of their value as commodities. They relate to each other as things, not as friends and lovers or father, daughter, and mother. Camaraderie and love are ephemeral, since commodities cannot love each other. People are indifferent to each other. They have lost their humanity.[43] Bagul captures the wretchedness produced by this loss of humanity and the new understanding of the self. Bombay and its slums serve as sites for the production of this new self. People arrive there for various reasons, including personal tragedies and failing class and caste status. The slum absorbs and equalizes them inasmuch as they know they are all commodities. Their humanity is shrouded by their indifference to each other and the indifference of others, particularly the elites, to them. This indifference does not erase but rather relies on caste, class, and gender boundaries. Its effects are most pronounced among the marginalized, especially Dalit women and men. In fact, the sex worker experiences not only abuse and indifference but also humiliation by the client and the brothel keeper. According to Bagul, apathy and humiliation result from caste, untouchability, class, and gender continuing to reside "in the thoughts and hearts" of dominant groups.[44] Because of apathy and indifference toward them and among them, characters in the stories cannot pull themselves out of the slum. They are unable to overcome the murkiness and see what is right or wrong. They cannot comprehend or confront the forces that have reduced them to this status. Bagul asks, "How did this happen? Why do humans behave like animals?"[45]

Bagul inherited Marx and Ambedkar's focus on humans and their omission of nonhuman species. For Bagul, if humans are inhuman to each other, they are animals. For Marx, humanity is not an abstraction but rather is embedded in concrete social relationships. Humanity and society share a dynamic relationship, and therefore to change humans and stop them from acting inhumanely, it is important to transform society.[46] According to Ambedkar, humans are capable of reason, have rights, and must be attentive to the needs of others. Bagul grapples with these two strands of thinking, seeking to synthesize them. He depicts the social relationships that make his characters behave like animals. He describes in vivid detail the brutishness of everyday life in the slums and the indifference with which humans, now commodities, treat each other. These depictions, according to the makers of Dalit literature, are dramatized narratives of the lives of historical Dalits in the city and the region. Government reports like the Elayaperumal Report, journalistic accounts, and social movements documented the violence and humiliations that were part of the everyday lives of Dalits in the region. Bagul advocated a social and political revolution that would transform the apparatus of indifference and violence. That revolution would ostensibly end caste and erase class hierarchies, spark the imagination of the outcastes, and enable them to develop a new sense of self. Bagul believed that the revolution was already under way, because time itself was revolutionary. According to him, the time—that is, modernity—had bestowed us with a scientific temper, industrial cities, the working class, democracy, and socialism.[47] It had enabled Ambedkar (and Dalits) imagine and bring about many transformations. But this revolution was incomplete: "The social organization, culture, Brahminism, and the casteist way of thinking are intact."[48] Dalits—using an expansive definition of Dalits that includes untouchables, Indian tribals, all oppressed people including Black Americans and Africans, and people of all hues and colors—would complete this revolution.[49] Bagul was writing in and channeling the revolutionary conjuncture of the global 1960s. He alerted his readers to the deep hole that Dalits were in and the need to fashion a new cultural imagination and sense of self. Only the hastening of the revolution already under way would help them create a new world in the future. Dalits would be the vanguard of this transformation.

Bagul played a role in the creation of the Dalit Panthers. On May 27, 1972, he chaired a meeting at Worli in Bombay that had been organized to articulate a response to the sexual abuse and humiliation of two Dalit women in Brahmangaon village in Parbhani district of Maharashtra and to protest the social and economic boycott of Dalits in Bavda village in the region. That boycott was led by the brother of a Maharashtra government minister, Shankarrao Patil.[50] The meeting highlighted the complicity of the Maharashtra state in the sexual abuse and social boycott of Dalits. Bagul urged the city's Dalit youth to respond to these atrocities and destroy the foundation of the caste order. According to the poet J. V. Pawar, though, Bagul refused to play an active role in crafting a response to the government. He turned down a request from writers to sign a memorandum to the government that envisaged violence by Dalits to counter state-supported violence.[51] Within a few days of Bagul's refusal, on May 29, 1972, Pawar and Dhasal came up with the idea of the Dalit Panthers. The Panthers took on the work of responding to violence against Dalits and organizing in the streets of the city. Some early supporters of the Panthers were young men from the slums and tenements of central Bombay, including Dhor (Cattle) Chawl and Siddarth Nagar in Kamathipura. The megaphone used for the propaganda was provided by the Communist Party of India.[52] The year 1972 is also notable for Namdeo Dhasal's publication of his collection of poems, *Golpitha*.

NAMDEO DHASAL'S MUMBAI

Namdeo Dhasal, like Baburao Bagul, was born in a Mahar Dalit caste in 1949 in a village in Pune district. He arrived in Bombay in 1955 to join his father, Lakshman Dhasal, who lived in Dhor (Cattle) Chawl in Kamathipura, which has a long history of Dalit political activism. Almost 75 percent of Dalit political rallies in the city in the 1920s and 1930s were held in this neighborhood;[53] it was here that Dalit leadership emerged to advocate for housing in the 1920s. In the 1950s, Lakshman Dhasal worked in a butcher's shop in the vicinity, and leftover scraps of meat, mostly beef, were the family's staple food.[54] Dhasal's *Golpitha* is set in the red-light district of Bombay. *Golpitha* depicts what Dhasal saw—everyday life in the neighborhood—and what he wanted the reader to see. Dhasal invites us to see and imagine sex work and the life of the sex worker. Here the sex worker is the "ultimate symbol of human degradation—an object of exploitation through sexual possession, and an otherwise loathed non-person, left to living decay after use."[55] Dhasal's depiction of sexual possession, loathing, and decay shocked his readers' sensibilities but also enthralled them, and foregrounded the plight of Dalits in the city. For Dhasal, "Dalit" signified all urban outcastes, including untouchables.

If the narration of decay elicited pity among his readers, Dhasal recommended a corrective. The first poem of *Golpitha*, "Their Everlasting Pity" (Tyanchi sanatani daya),[56] criticizes the politics of compassion. He highlights the dominance of the urban elites to foreground the limitations of their pity. Landlords have hoarded everything; even the sidewalk does not belong to the poor. The poor can't satiate their hunger with mud, either. "They [the elites] don't even sigh while killing us" is his powerful and pithy observation. In this poem, Dhasal defines "us" as humans who stand in opposition to the "they" of the elites, positioned as the other of humans. Though *daya*, or compassion, is an important experiential category evoked by Dalit literature, Dhasal points out the irony of hoarders of wealth expressing compassion. In a poem that is about pity, Dhasal does not discuss any acts of compassion. Instead, he details the exploitation and indifference of the elites toward the urban outcastes. In fact, by qualifying pity with the adjective *sanatani* (orthodox or everlasting), Dhasal foregrounds the formalism and paradoxes of the expressions of compassion. The poem evokes despair and rage at the cycle of injustice obscured by displays of everlasting pity. That cycle needs to be broken.

Dhasal deploys imagery of things rotting and festering and juxtaposes humans with human excrement. This heightens the sense of degradation of the urban poor in the city. For instance, "Ground Down and Secluded People" (Mansa bhadrun)[57] begins with an evocative question: Who has ground down people (humans) and locked them in a paperweight? The reference to objects confined in the glass of a paperweight amplifies the feeling of claustrophobia experienced by urban outcastes. Those who have been ground down are humiliated further by the "shit and sewage" (*gupani*) seeping out of their bodies. This degradation is a spectacle for the elites. They aestheticize it by exhibiting it in art galleries; rotting and festering bodies are objects of display. But the poet is convinced that the degradation will be staunched by those who have been ground down. He deploys the metaphor of castration—for both the person who will castrate and curb the humiliation and also for the ground down, who have been castrated but are capable of rising up against it. The poem ends with the confidence that those witnessing the spectacle of degradation will themselves be eclipsed by the revolution wrought by the ground down.[58] He deploys humans and shit again in "On the Way to a Sufi Shrine" (Dargachya vatevar), in which an orphan—another metaphor he invokes often to depict the lives of urban outcastes—who has grown up on the streets amid human refuse begs for alms on the path leading to the shrine. The orphan barely conceals his rage while begging: "Give me five pennies, take five profanities."[59] The rage does not just simmer but explodes, and excrement plays a part in making the sacred profane. For instance, in "Man, You Must" (Mansane), Dhasal recommends that man destroy everything, including himself, to refashion humanity anew. Man should "tear all the pages of all religious and sacred texts and wipe / Their arses with it when done shitting." In the same poem he counsels man to open

> the manhole of sewers and dump,
> Plato, Einstein, Archimedes, Socrates,
> Marx, Ashoka, Hitler, Camus, Sartre, Kafka,
> Baudelaire, Rimbaud, Ezra Pound, Hopkins, Goethe,
> Dostoevsky, Mayakovsky, Maxim Gorky,
> Edison, Madison, Kalidasa, Tukaram, Vyasa, Shakespeare, Jnaneshvar there,
> And leave them to rot and decompose.

Lest one ascribe man's actions here to mere anti-intellectualism, he also recommends that man execute all religious icons: "Jesus, Prophet Muhammad, Buddha, Vishnu, / And make profane temples, churches, mosques, sculptures, museums." And for good measure man should crush the bones of literary critics and wage "class wars, caste wars, communal wars, party wars, crusades, world wars / And become savage, ferocious, and primitive." This killing rage should not spare kith or kin or neighbors:

> Con your neighbors and kin, smash banks
> Screw the rich . . .
> and bomb hutments and localities of the hungry.[60]

This anarchy would purge the old and produce a new man who would

> Desist from enslaving and robbing people.
> . . . Stop name calling—you are white or black, Brahmin, Kshatriya,
>   Vaishya or Shudra.

Refrain from establishing political parties or property.
... Accomplish dazzling deeds to make the Sun and the Moon seem pale.
Share each morsel of food with others, and compose a hymn
To humanity itself, and man should sing only the song of man.[61]

What is this performance of rage, anarchy, and the emergence of a utopia about? The imagined anarchy is a spectacle—the violence, the profaning of sacred spaces and religious texts, the jettisoning of classics, the
pillage, rape, and murder—intended to capture the imagination of the
readers. The violence is directed at the institutions of the state: the poem
names the police, railway stations, airports; the pillars of Indian society:
caste, class, religion, and the family; the foundations of culture: schools
and classics. These institutions have created man as an obedient subject.
Man in turn relies on them in everyday life. It is this subject—the man—
that Dhasal is coaxing to explode, become insurgent, and destroy the
foundations of state, society, and culture. The raging insurrection is the
route to regain control of his life, body, thoughts, and actions. The purge
heralds a utopia where caste, class, and private property become redundant. This new utopia is tepid, lackadaisical, because Dhasal provides no
space for politics or disagreement. The new man is curiously apolitical.
The insurgent man is now transposed into a content humanity. Perhaps
the dream of an apolitical man, apart from the spectacle of a purge,
accounts for the popularity of *Man, You Must* in the 1970s.

The profaning of the sacrosanct by positing mundane actions in its
vicinity is a theme in other poems too. In the poem "By the Side of the
Crucifix" (Krusacya kanvatila) the poor perform their bodily functions in
the street: "We finished our screwing by the side of the Crucifix." In public
space nothing is sacrosanct; rather, nothing could be sacrosanct, because
the poor inhabit it and use it in ways unintended by the urban planners.
Their use of public space challenges the intent of the state, which is to
restrain the poor. Thus one finds near the crucifix "the empty Home-
guards Maidan present like an enemy ready to thwart us."[62] The presence
of a parade ground for the paramilitary is experienced by the poor as an
antagonist arrayed against them. The poor camp on the streets for the
night: "We're all over the streets spread out long and wide as tar on the
road." Dhasal's poem echoes Bagul's "People on an Open Tract of Land" in
its depiction of urban outcastes having sex and squatting in public spaces.
In "Nimita 15 August," a poem in which Dhasal wonders if Independence
is the name of a donkey, he playfully juxtaposes multiple voices. The tone

of this long poem ranges among playfulness, rage, despair, and hopefulness. One voice belongs to Independence itself, which had turned twenty-
four in 1971. Independence reminds people of the day twenty-four years
ago when they celebrated it with music, dance, and colors, and Mother
India was full of hope for prosperity.[63] Another voice, that of a young
Mahar Dalit child, dampens Independence's ardor. Independence, it says,
is just a three-letter word—*sva-tan-trya*. It has no meaning for a child. The
child attends the Independence Day celebrations out of fear that the
schoolteacher would summon his parents to school if the child were absent.
Compulsion rather than devotion to the nation or an attachment to Independence forces the child to attend its anniversary. The teacher, another
voice in the poem, sings patriotic songs praising the nation and its flag:
"May our beloved tricolor remain victorious and flutter proudly, / Even if
we lose our lives, let us maintain its honor." The child responds in irrever-
ent doggerels and curses: "Mehtaji come home in the evening, / Screw your
mother's nation." There is no heroism or glory in a poem about freedom
and the nation. In fact, there is despondency speckled with rage at freedom's inability to actualize its promise of food, water, clothes, and shelter
for the poor. That is why, at the end of the poem, a Dalit man (Hadaki
Hadvala) implores Independence, on its twenty-fourth anniversary, to
come back for a new beginning.

Dhasal invokes the prostitute frequently in his poems. The prostitute
signifies control over the body, a dominance produced by the possession
and use of a thing, a commodity. It also symbolizes the fetishizing of the
commodity—the bizarre feeling of attraction, lust, fear, and loathing for a
thing. In *Mandakini Patil: My Desired Collage*, Dhasal describes a sixteen-
year-old sex worker, Mandakini Patil.

> Her clothes torn, her thighs ripped open,
> She surrenders herself to pain.
> And a pig, its snout full of blood.[64]

Dhasal highlights the control over Mandakini's body, its abuse, its pain.
He sympathizes with her and other sex workers:

> Never before had I seen a face so humiliated, so lifeless,
> As was yours and many others like you
> Who appear in these cages from so many countries,
> And assume so many different names.[65]

He also acknowledges her ability to stir untapped feelings within him. But this empathy also produces a desire to possess her and be possessed by her.

> I feel your tresses, your clothes, your nails, your breasts,
> They introduce me to something hidden within me, they feel like mine.
>
> . . . Your listless, worn-out face has dazzled me
> The face enters me and possesses me
> It makes me feel torment and lets torment find me
> I scream, a remorseless scream.

The torment and possession introduce him to the light hidden within her, which has familiarized him with her grief and produced a realization about human relationships.

> The paramour: is a sanctified whore
> Her lover: A pimp
> Prostitutes are women with the man's impress
> Men their pimps
> A man woman relationship is like a collage of:
> Prostitution, pimping, or a teeth cleaning twig,
> Spit them out after use and consecrate yourself with the holy water of the
>   Ganges.

The double possession, of and by Mandakini, has produced a bleak and claustrophobic denouement of life inside the brothel. The poet assures her that there is a different world outside the brothel.

> Manda,
> My peahen
> Look out of the window, and a new world is born.

How will Manda apprehend this world that lies outside the social relationships of dominance in which she is a commodity to be used and discarded? How will she override Old Lady Destiny (Niyati), who cages her and grinds her to dust?[66] The poet has an important role to play here. The world outside the cage or the window is his vision. If Manda sees through his eyes, she'll see that

Her eyes emit flames and her touch is revolutionary,
She is sandalwood and the bark of the healing Babhul tree . . .
. . . Her touch will turn stone to platinum.[67]

Manda's new understanding of herself will lead to forgetting her old self. The poet does not reveal whether this new understanding will bring about a radical transformation of the relations in which she was a commodity. He leaves that to the reader's imagination. But this new self, and the leap of imagination that produced it, are assertions of control, first over imagination and then over the body that was consumed and dominated by clients. It is also an attempt to regain some control over space and time. Dhasal, the founder of the Dalit Panthers, through the sex worker, is unmasking the effects of the supremacy of caste, class, and gender over the mind and body of Manda and the urban outcastes: the humiliated, lusterless face, clothes ripped off, thighs smeared in blood, and pain. At the same time, he expresses hope in the ability of the ground down, the Dalits, to dream of an alternate world and forget this world.

The assertion of control over mind, body, and urban space, and its representation in politics and culture is the theme of "When You Pass through Our Lane" (Amchya alitun jatana). The poem addresses the all-knowing and extremely intelligent (*mahajnani*). They could be reformers, bureaucrats, or technocrats, that is, representatives of the state, political representatives of the Dalits, and Marxists. Dhasal questions their legitimacy and their monopoly over representation of the urban outcastes.

These all-knowing people
Roam the alleys
With lit torches
Where mice die of hunger.[68]

The lit torch is a loaded metaphor: it connotes a vision for change but also suggests limited light in a dark, overcrowded lane. Moreover, it signifies limited vision but also captures the legitimacy bestowed on the person holding the lit torch. Dhasal castigates the people holding torches for their limited vision, labeling them narcissistic and ignorant.[69]

They claim to understand,
The darkness of our hovel . . .
. . . those who cannot understand the darkness beneath their arse

Claim to know more than
The kindled [*petlele*] man!

The kindled man connotes not only the enlightened but also the enraged. Dhasal rhetorically snatches credibility away from the self-styled wise person and claims it for the enraged person who sees through the former's limitations: "Today, from every hovel, / We can see the full sun."[70] Dhasal in one broad stroke links the alley, huts, people, and their hunger, and simultaneously questions the legitimacy of the people who represent them. Instead, he posits a self-aware man who can see through the shenanigans of his representatives and asserts control over the mind, body, and space. But how did a poet and activist who projected sovereignty of the outcastes over themselves get his collection of poems published? What relationships of power was he suspended within?

THE POLITICS OF THE FOREWORD

Vijay Tendulkar, an iconic Marathi playwright with progressive leanings, wrote the foreword to *Golpitha*. Narayan Athawale, the publisher, was a journalist whose politics were described as "rightwing Hindu."[71] Why and how would they agree to associate themselves with Dhasal's *Golpitha*? In Dhasal's recounting of the story, both Athawale and Tendulkar were intrigued by the social space of the red-light district and the world of its inhabitants. Dhasal took them on a guided tour of the locality. The writer who asserted control over the representation of *Golpitha* and had ridiculed the insularity of the all-knowing person in "When You Pass through Our Lane," took the famous writer and publisher for a tour of its alleys and cages where sex workers were warehoused. We have Tendulkar's account of the tour.

Dhasal asked Tendulkar to write the foreword to *Golpitha*. They had been briefly acquainted before Dhasal asked him for the preface. Tendulkar was surprised. He had thought of their relationship as a "limited friendship."[72] In his mind, he and Dhasal belonged to different worlds. Their worlds not only involved different spaces in the city with different built forms but also entailed class and caste differences. Tendulkar assumed the Marathi language would transcend these worlds and connect them, even though some of the imagery in Dhasal's poetry and the words he used were unfamiliar.[73] He made a list of words, imagery, and concepts he could not fathom in Dhasal's poetry and asked him to explain them. He became Dhasal's student.[74] He realized that language in itself—even though he was an authority on it—was insufficient to grasp Dhasal's world. Moreover, he sensed diffidence in Dhasal explanations of "filthy and sexual" words.[75] Tendulkar wanted to experience this world. He told Dhasal, "'I want to see your world.' Dhasal smiled and readily agreed."[76]

One day, Dhasal took him on a tour; they roamed around until "two or three" in the morning.[77] Tendulkar's encounter with Golpitha confirmed its difference. He describes it as a "no man's land," beyond the spatial and intellectual limits of Bombay's white-collar, bourgeois world. Sex, sex work, and brothels were the focal point of this no-man's-land. But that is not all, Tendulkar clarifies: Golpitha bustles at night as if it were daytime, hunger abounds, anxiety and death are palpable, humans are devoid of shame and compassion, fetid gutters overflow, diseased youth sleep by these gutters, unemployed, paupers, pickpockets, gangsters and pimps, Sufi shrines and crucifixes populate this world.[78] Golpitha also includes eunuchs, liquor distilleries, smugglers, opium, and photographs of Hindi film stars (Rajesh Khanna). Here everything is commodified: "Even diseased bodies with consumption or leprosy [maharog]" can be purchased for sex. "Sexual acts take place next to bawling children, and prostitutes sing love songs for potential customers."[79] His visit to Golpitha confirmed his notion that it was an all-consuming space with no exit. One cannot escape Golpitha, and if you do, you return. Sympathy, forgiveness, and peace are alien to it.

Tendulkar's encounter with Golpitha reinforced the distance between Dhasal's world and his own. M. N. Wankhede, in recommending social anthropology as a model for Dalit literature, may or may not have had such an encounter in mind, where publisher, interlocutor, and critic are both attracted to and repulsed by the red-light district. Tendulkar's optic resembles the visions of social reformers and sociologists when they visited neighborhoods of the urban poor in the first half of the twentieth century. What captured their attention was not dissimilar to what Tendulkar found fascinating and different about Dhasal's world: fetid gutters and humans coexisting, sex, children, and production and reproduction of the lives of the outcastes in close proximity. Unlike the reformers, though, Tendulkar did not pass moral judgments. Instead, Dhasal's world—its language, his imagery, and his anger—became more legible to him. Dhasal was different, rare, he said. But precisely because he was different and uncommon, he needed to be translated in terms of known forms of poetic expression. Tendulkar compared him to the Marathi poet saint

Tukaram. He discerned Tukaram's influence on the thrilling, passionate, rough and rustic, sharp, and enraged poetry of Dhasal.[80] Dalit writers and intellectuals had explicitly distanced themselves from this genealogy of saintly literature.[81]

Dhasal's smile when Tendulkar expressed the desire to see his world may have been all-knowing. He probably stoked his interlocutor's curiosity enough that it brimmed over into a desire to experience the red-light district. Dilip Chitre narrated a similar story about a collaborative project in the 1990s. Dhasal, Dilip Chitre, and Henning Stegmüller teamed up for a book published in Germany, *Bombay/Mumbai: Images of a Megacity* (Bombay/Mumbai: Bilder einer Mega Stadt). When Dhasal met Stegmüller, he asked the German if he wanted to "see his area. . . . We then went on a guided tour of Kamathipura just when the evening lights were being turned on and the gaudily made-up, scantily dressed prostitutes were displaying themselves in the windows and doors of their dwellings known simply as 'the cages' in local slang."[82] The tour of Golpitha thus led to a publication in Germany. Thus Dhasal the revolutionary poet was himself suspended within webs of power. A generous reading of Dhasal and Tendulkar would emphasize the necessity for the meeting of their worlds in order to appreciate the simultaneous, yet incongruous, worlds of *Outcaste Bombay*. As Dhasal told Dilip Chitre, "I've taken Vijay Tendulkar around this place. I've shown this to Narayan Athavale. I'm showing it to you. I'll show it to anyone that wants to know what life is like here. I grew up here. I have a bond with these people. They are my people—these lumpen; I am one of them. My poetry is about life here."[83]

THE DALIT PANTHERS AND THE INCONGRUITY OF REVOLUTION

In 1972, around the time of the publication of *Golpitha*, Dhasal played an important role in the formation of the Dalit Panthers. Obviously influenced by the Black Panther movement, its organizational structure was inspired by another political formation of the city, the Shiv Sena. The Shiv Sena's "organizational and spatial grid of local units" enabled the party to coordinate spectacular actions across the city.[84] The Dalit Panthers modeled their branches on the Shiv Sena's local units. This helped them register their presence in public space, mobilize people in neighborhoods, and prepare for action. By 1973, they had thirty-two branches in the city, and according to Dhasal, the number rose to one hundred later that year.[85] Some of the units were in tenements of the Bombay Improvement Trust and Bombay Development Department. At one meeting of the Panthers in the Trust tenements in 1972, Raja Dhale recommended a flag for the Panthers with the incongruous image of Lord Buddha carrying a sword in one hand and a lamp in the other. In May 1973, Raja Dhale became the president of the Panthers, and Dhasal was named its defense minister. The Panthers also started a women's wing, albeit in name only.[86] The membership of the Dalit Panthers, even though there was no systematic record, increased significantly in the first year, attracting not just youth from Dalit castes but also the urban poor.

The Dalit Panthers formed action units (*kriti samitis*) to respond to violence against Dalits in the city and villages in the region. J. V. Pawar lists some of the actions of Dalit Panther squads: helping arrest seven people accused of raping a Dalit woman in Bombay's Tardeo slums; attacks on villages such as Pise and Chave in Thane district, where he claimed Panthers had beaten up villagers and even the police, who were accused of violence against Dalits; a visit to Sangamner by Dhasal to investigate rape accusations against a prominent landlord.[87] These spectacular actions were designed to challenge the dominance of other groups and expose the complicity of some members of the state in maintaining that dominance. The other performative aspect of these actions was intended to demonstrate the Panthers' ability to overcome Dalits' fear of dominant groups and in turn strike fear in them. The capacity to overcome one's fear and instead instill fear in dominant groups revealed their aspiration: to demonstrate that the dominance of Dalits in postcolonial India was incomplete.

These actions needed funding. Many Panthers, particularly those who had government jobs, such as J. V. Pawar, spent their own money. But the money also came from politicians affiliated with various factions of the Congress Party. Dhasal recounted one such instance in 1973. India's prime minister, Indira Gandhi, was awarded an honorary doctorate by the University of Pune (then Poona). The Panthers decided to block her path to the university: they mobilized cadres from other units in Maharashtra with funding provided by Sambhaji Kakade of Congress (O), a group that had split from the Congress Party.[88] The Panthers' action units soon became defunct, however, because the Panthers themselves split. The lack of coordination among units, ideological and personal differences among members, and intervention by the state ensured that the movement fragmented by July 1974, with Dhale and Dhasal leading separate factions. Dhale was a proponent of Buddhism and Ambedkar's ideas, while Dhasal was accused of propagating Marxism under the guise of Ambedkarism.[89] Dhasal himself claimed that the Dalit Panthers were not Marxist and expressed disquiet over leftist responses to the question of untouchability.[90] He identified with the lumpen proletariat, which to him was indistinguishable from the name "Dalit."[91] Dhale deemed Buddhism and Ambedkar to be incongruous with Marxism and remonstrated against any synthesis of the two, whereas Dhasal favored this conjugation. Thus Buddha and Marx parted ways in the Dalit Panthers. Just two months before the split and a few months after the demonstration against Indira Gandhi in Pune, on May 1, 1974, Dhasal, the defense minister of the Dalit Panthers, won an award for *Golpitha* from the Maharashtra government. He accepted it.[92]

When Indira Gandhi suspended democracy and declared a national emergency in 1975, Dhasal supported her. He believed that the emergency measures countered American imperialism and the dominance of merchants in India and held that the regime supported workers, peasants, and Dalits.[93] Dhasal had concluded that the revolutionary transformation he wanted could not be accomplished through democratic transformation of society. Significantly, then, a section of the postcolonial Dalit movement that had demanded a democratic society and declared a revolution to actualize it had lost faith in parliamentary politics. Dhasal saw an opening in the suspension of democracy. He published an ode to Indira Gandhi celebrating her as a world historical leader and commended the changes she had brought to the lives of the urban and rural poor, Dalits, and the working class.[94] The emergency, which was unpopular among many sections of society, was lifted in 1977, and in the elections that followed the Congress Party lost at the national level to a coalition of socialist, leftist, and right-wing parties. In Maharashtra, though, the party retained power (albeit divided into factions) because of the hegemonic alliance between dominant Maratha castes in rural areas and their "collaborative alliances with industrial and commercial capital in the cities."[95] The Dalit Panthers splintered further in these years, along with other Dalit political groups. The fragmenting of Dalit political groups, apart from the Panthers, happened along the lines of ideology and caste: Buddha and Ambedkar were pitted against Marx. But interestingly, both the Dhasal and Dhale factions of the Dalit Panthers focused on slums. The Dhasal faction, in a conference in November 1976 attended by three ministers of the regional government, passed a resolution demanding alternate accommodation for those relocated by slum clearance drives, the use of black market proceeds for slum improvement, government protection from slumlords and liquor barons, and provisions for cultural centers, libraries, and study spaces in the slums.[96] The Dhale faction demanded "the resolution of the problems of slumdwellers, along with provisions for co-operative banks, and libraries for Dalits."[97]

Tensions in the Dalit caste cluster also bubbled over. For instance, the Mang and Chambhar Dalits felt that Mahars benefited disproportionately from the affirmative action policies of the state. They sought separate representation, and the state duly obliged. The various factions of Dalit politics sought alliances, recognition, and patronage from the many factions of national and regional politics. Dalit politics in the late 1970s was caught up in the same bind it had been in after Ambedkar's death in 1956: Should Dalits align with the Congress Party, side with those who had opposed it, or forge an alternate and autonomous Dalit politics? As Jayant Lele has pointed out, the state dissipated and then absorbed Dalit movements through patronage and policymaking,[98] preventing Dalits from becoming a counterhegemonic bloc. Annabhau Sathe, the Communist writer who died in the 1960s, was venerated as an icon of the Matang Dalit castes, and the Maharashtra government named a welfare scheme for the Matang castes after him in 1985. Thus, a Communist became a caste icon.

The Dalit literature movement itself splintered into three factions, with Baburao Bagul leading the Dalit Sahitya Parishad, Gangadhar Pantawane leading an Asmita Darsha group, and Bhausaheb Adsul heading a Bauddha Sahitya group. Each sought recognition and separate funding from the Maharashtra government.[99] In 1978, the Maharashtra State Board for Literature and Culture published a study of Dalit literature (*Dalit sahitya: Ek abhyas*) with its president, Lakshmanshastri Joshi, acknowledging that literature and the Dalit movement were intertwined. The editor of the volume, Arjun Dangle, a poet and essayist and one of the founders of the Dalit Panthers, conceded that Dalit literary and social movements had fissured in the 1970s but argued that the literary movement's viewpoint and its attention to questions of caste, class, and untouchability would ensure that it would continue to flourish. Dangle did not mention any women writers in his study of Dalit literature. By the end of the 1970s, Dalit writers like Arun Kamble and Keshav Meshram were teaching in the literature departments of colleges in Bombay city. There were other new avenues of patronage, too: Daya Pawar's autobiography, *Village Servant* (Baluta), and Laxman Mane's *Outsider* (Upara) won Ford Foundation grants. By the mid-1980s Dalit feminists from Bombay formed the Mahila Sansad (Women's Parliament) and a few years later formed a literary forum called Samvadini—Dalit Stree Sahitya Manch. They articulated the importance of their own perspective—distinct from upper-caste feminists and Dalit men—and became embroiled in similar debates over identity politics and solidarity with other movements of the outcastes. These debates positioned caste as central to the constitution and reconceptualization of gender in South Asia and to rethinking the genealogy of feminism itself.

SLUMS AND URBAN PLANNING

Urban planning, housing, and slum clearance saw transformations too. Pressure from social and political movements like the Republican Party of India, the Dalit Panthers, and other political formations made *some* slums durable. Slum dwellers who had photo passes and identity cards either got tenure rights or assurance of resettlement in case of slum demolition.[100] The political demands had an uncanny resonance in policy. But this did not mean that slum clearance disappeared from Bombay. In 1981, the Maharashtra chief minister, A. R. Antulay, ordered Operation Eviction, during which many slum dwellers were deported to suburbs to the north of the city. According to the 1981 census, there were 619 slums in Greater Bombay, up from 144 in 1957.

Operation Eviction followed a shift in housing and slum removal policies. Bombay transitioned from "welfare-oriented urban development solutions to those driven by the market."[101] In 1980 and 1981 a number of committees addressed the issue of slums and housing in the city. These included the S. K. Moghe Committee and the Premanand Awale Committee, both of which submitted reports in 1980. In the same year, a World Bank consultant, Harry W. Richardson, also tendered a study on Bombay city. One important feature of all these plans was the emphasis on market forces as a solution to the problem of slums. The Awale and Moghe Committees recommended providing incentives to the private sector for helping slum dwellers and suggested changes to the law and an increase in the Floor Space Index to enable private developers to build apartments for slum dwellers.[102] The reports met with opposition from within and outside the government, so the Maharashtra government set up another panel: the High-Power Steering Group for Slums and Dilapidated Houses, under the chairmanship of Ajit Kerkar. The Kerkar Committee submitted its report in 1981. It too saw the private sector as having an important role to play in solving the slum question. It connected the proliferation of slums to the shortage of housing in the city. According to the committee, slums abounded in the city because the demand for affordable housing was not matched by the supply of houses.[103] The solution lay in increasing the supply of housing, which in turn would solve the problem of slums. The hidden hand of the market would hasten the slums' demise.

The suggestion to increase housing stock accompanied a proposal to alter the political economy of the city. The committee encouraged the state to shift large-scale labor-intensive industries out of the city and develop the urban area as the financial capital of India. The report emphasized that reducing industrial employment in the city would automatically decrease the influx of new people. For those already living in the slums, the committee proposed a redevelopment plan and envisioned a "standard housing unit": a dwelling measuring at least 180 square feet with a bathing area (*nahni*) inside it. It calculated the cost of each unit to be twenty thousand rupees, based on prices prevalent in 1981. The committee projected that the construction of fifty thousand standard housing units per year over twenty years would meet the shortage of one million housing units in the city.[104] The proposal was that the standard housing unit would semantically and figuratively replace slums, and the change in political economy would reduce overcrowding.[105] In any case, the political economy of the city had been shifting from capital- and labor-intensive large-scale manufacturing industries to chemical and pharmaceutical industries by the 1970s.

The creation of the state of Maharashtra in 1960 augured changes in two fields: urban development and slum policy on the one hand and Dalit literature on the other. Under India's federal system of government, the regional state made important decisions on housing, slums, and industries. The regional state could also ignore policies and schemes recommended by the national government.[106] The state of Maharashtra patronized Marathi literature, including Dalit literature. Dalit literature won recognition in this period, and some Dalit writers, mostly men, won state awards. The social space of slums played a crucial role in urban planning, while the slum as a concept and metaphor was important to Dalit literature. The former wanted to remove them from the city, while Dalit literature and its supporting social movement used the metaphor to signify the fragility of Dalit lives in postcolonial India and to demand tenurial rights or rehabilitation guarantees for slum dwellers. Apart from the slum, another evocative metaphor for Dalit lives was the figure of the sex worker. In Dalit literature, the sex worker was a commodity—used, abused, humiliated, and discarded. How do commodities, ground down by caste, capital, and the state, reclaim their humanity? Dalit writers affiliated with the Dalit Panthers saw a political and social revolution at the global revolutionary conjuncture of the 1960s and 1970s as an antidote to commodification. Revolutionary ardor was enmeshed with literary awards, tenurial rights to slums, and fissuring of Dalit social movements. Factions of the Dalit movement aligned with factions in regional and national politics. And urban planners, who hoped to synchronize Bombay's modernity with global modernity, turned to the market to find solutions for the proliferation of slums. Their prescriptions created more slums.

CONCLUSION

THE SPLINTERING AND CO-OPTATION OF DALIT POLITICS AND
the recognition and fragmentation of Dalit literature were coterminous
with another transformative event in the early 1980s: the Bombay textile
mill strike from 1982 to 1984. Although these disparate processes and events
did not come together because of a grand design—but rather because of
many contingent factors—their convergence shaped the politics of the
urban poor after the 1980s. The textile strike originated as disquiet among
workers over bonus wages and escalated into a significant event. The striking workers believed they were fighting for the future: "Not only for our-
selves but for the coming generation."[1] The mill workers' strike inspired the
city police to also make demands. The police chose India's Independence
Day, August 15, 1982, to express their displeasure. They wore black ribbons
at the flag-hoisting ceremony. The police wanted to unionize and demanded
higher pay and better work conditions.[2] When they were thwarted by the
Maharashtra government, they went on strike for a day on August 18, 1982.
The strike devolved into violence after the striking police, who had halted
trains in the city, fought with those who did not go on strike. When the
striking mill workers joined the fracas on the side of the striking policemen, the National Guard, summoned to the city to maintain order, killed
two mill workers and a policeman at Worli Naka, near the Bombay Development Department tenements.[3] The revolt of the city's police was quelled
through deployment of the Central Armed Police Forces, including the
National Guards, Central Reserve Police Force, and the Border Security
Force. But the workers' strike continued; they were fighting for a new political vision in which their everyday lives would change. Not only would they
have better wages, better bonuses, and better living conditions, but they
also would have better unions to represent their interests and they would
be able to express themselves freely to their employers and their leaders.
The revolt of the police, a force historically used to impose discipline in the
city, seemed like an opening into the future. During the strike, the workers

also received help from peasants: "Thousands of bags of grain would come daily from the . . . districts of Satara, Sangli, and Pune," where the workers had kinship networks.[4]

But by 1984 the strike had collapsed. The mill owners withdrew from the industry, concluding that the value of their real estate—the mill land—was much more than the industry could ever realize. Many had already outsourced their manufacturing to smaller towns near Bombay city like Bhiwandi, Ichalkaranji, and Surat. The new textile policy of 1985 facilitated the sale of mill land, and by end of the 1980s many mills had closed down.[5] The new future that the workers aspired to in 1982, by transforming their present, remained unrealized and instead was superseded by a process through which skyscrapers replaced the mills. Some striking workers left the city permanently, and those who remained sought work in other industries and organized to recover their unpaid wages from mill owners. The deindustrialization of the city, which urban planners had proposed in the 1950s, 1960s, and 1970s, was now becoming a reality. The political failure of the workers' vision and the marginalization of the working class in the city created the conditions for the ascent of right-wing parties like the Shiv Sena in the working-class district. The Shiv Sena deployed ethnic antagonisms based on language (South Indians), caste (Dalits), and religious group (Muslims and Buddhists) to expand its presence in the city. The urban poor sought patronage and a public presence in the city through the Shiv Sena. By the mid-1990s, Namdeo Dhasal supported the Shiv Sena, and the party formed an alliance with the Bharatiya Janata Party, winning elections in 1995 and forming the government in Maharashtra.[6] The fissuring and co-optation of Dalit politics did not mean that Dalits stopped being political. In fact, Dalits became "Ambedkarised by reading and listening about Ambedkar in rallies organized by numerous organizations."[7] Ambedkarization also entailed the installation of statues of Ambedkar and Buddha in Dalit neighborhoods in cities and villages as symbols of recognition and identification.[8] This invited symbolic and physical violence against Dalits. One such act of symbolic violence resulted in the death of ten Dalits in Bombay (by now Mumbai) city. On July 11, 1997, Dalits from the Ramabai Ambedkar Nagar slums in the suburb of Ghatkopar in Mumbai were protesting the desecration of Ambedkar's statue in their neighborhood when police opened fire, killing protestors and bystanders. Violence against Dalits in rural Maharashtra frequently made headlines too. The lynching of Bhaiyyalal Bhotmange's family in September 2006, by a caste Hindu mob in Khairlanji village, was one such event.

In Mumbai city, the slums and the people living there kept increasing. According to the 2011 census, almost 62 percent of the city's population—over nine million people—lived in slums.[9] The state government planned to convert its most populous slum, Dharavi, into a "modern township." From the slums and tenements where Dalit literature had erupted onto the literary scene emerged a new generation of poets in the 2010s. The poets were hip-hop and rap artists who aspired to popularize "their ideologies . . . to bring about change in society."[10] These performers translated hip-hop and rap to invoke life in Mumbai's slums and their desire for a revolution. They identified as Dalits, Muslims, or Christians and spoke about transcending ethnic particularities. They celebrated the juxtaposition of these differences in city slums. Their poetry, like most poetry that espouses revolution, was oriented to the future.

As *Outcaste Bombay* has shown, the slums they depicted and the revolution they invoked had a long history in the city. The built environment of the city and the slum was the spatial expression of capitalism in the city and the intersection of caste and class differences. The number of slums had exploded with industrialization in the city in the late nineteenth and twentieth centuries. Slums warehoused workers for these industries; they were an essential feature of industrial capitalism in the city that kept increasing even after the textile industry disintegrated in the 1980s. At the turn of the twentieth century, the British colonial government and later the Indian postcolonial state, along with the Bombay Municipal Corporation, had hoped that urban planning would stem the proliferation of slums. They built housing and tenements for workers; unfortunately, they were more efficient in demolishing slums than building housing. Grandiose plans of building thousands of tenements at various historical moments never came to fruition. In practice, the plans yielded modest results. Workers hired in Bombay city were recruited through caste and kinship networks. Caste compensated for a lack within capitalism's metabolic system—the ability to recruit and discipline workers through the jobber. Though caste had a different temporality than capital, they intersected in Bombay in this period. South Asian states, including precolonial, colonial, and postcolonial states, augmented the caste system and worked through it to maintain the power of the state. Caste difference fragmented the working class but did not eliminate class politics or class analysis. The urban poor displayed an ability to transcend ethnic differences and revealed a fierce class consciousness at particular historical moments. When the moment passed, they fragmented again.

Dalits migrated to the city to escape caste depredations, famine, and landlessness and to find employment in the city in the nineteenth and twentieth centuries. Migration, they believed, would diminish their subjection to coercive casteism and labor in agrarian settings. In the city, however, they found caste sedimented in class and inscribed in the built environment and language. In other words, caste had adapted to urban settings and played a significant role in the production and reproduction of capital and labor. Their access to work and housing depended on caste, and they found employment mostly in low-paying, stigmatized jobs and housing in slums and tenements. As we have seen, Dalits themselves were divided by class and *jati* differences. Because caste was sedimented in class, it was partially obscured in the discourses of class, like Marathi Marxism, but caste was visible in the conceptual categories and everyday lives of Bombay's Communists. Many Dalits joined the Communist movement in the city and saw it as a vehicle to transcend particularities of caste and embrace the solidarities of class. Some Dalit Communists from the city became founders of Dalit literature in the 1950s, 1960s, and 1970s. They deployed conceptual categories imported from Marxism, like commodification of human relationships, to depict the ravages of caste and class in city slums. But they themselves were part of power relations in Marathi and Dalit literature. They won recognition from the Marathi literati and the state, but the broader ambition of these writers—to bring about a social and political revolution—remained a dream. If the poets and hip-hop artists of today are attentive to these earlier dreams, the conditions that produced them, and the structural and contingent factors that prevented them from being actualized, yet at the same time remain unencumbered by them, maybe they can produce a rupture, a new imaginary, and a new present in which outcaste Bombay lives.

NOTES

INTRODUCTION

1. Risley, *The People of India*, 72; Marriott, *Caste Ranking and Community Structures*.
2. For a synthesis of scholarship that lays out the colonial context and power relationships in early Indian social science, see Uberoi et al., "Introduction." See also Sumit Sarkar's discussion of Risley in Sarkar, *Beyond Nationalist Frames*, 58–60; and Dirks, *Castes of Mind*, 49–52.
3. Ghurye, *Caste and Race in India*, 120.
4. Chhabria, *Making the Modern Slum*, 10.
5. I am borrowing the term "castelessness" from Deshpande, "Caste and Castelessness."
6. On migration and the city in Ambedkar's thought, see Chairez-Garza, "Touching Space."
7. Ambedkar's speech to the Constituent Assembly on November 4, 1948, reprinted in Ambedkar, "On the Draft Constitution," 176.
8. Marx and Engels, *The Communist Manifesto*, 7.
9. As cited in Morris, *The Emergence of an Industrial Labor Force*, 71.
10. I borrow this phrase from Harootunian, *Marx after Marx*, 14.
11. According to Satish Deshpande, caste is invisible to the upper castes, who have converted their traditional caste capital to modern forms of capital. Deshpande, "Caste and Castelessness," 402. See also Bayly, *Caste, Society and Politics in India*, 154–56.
12. Partha Chatterjee, *The Politics of the Governed*, 131–47; Kaviraj, "Filth in the Public Sphere."
13. On illegal spatiality, see Bhan, *In the Public's Interest*, 182.
14. Stein, *Capital City*, 16–17.
15. Government of Bombay, *Gazetteer of Bombay City and Island*, vol. 3; Hazareesingh, *The Colonial City and the Challenge of Modernity*; Kidambi, *The Making of an Indian Metropolis*.
16. Prakash, *Mumbai Fables*; Rao, *House, but No Garden*.
17. Guha, *Beyond Caste*, 2.
18. Klass, *Caste*; Sharma, *Caste*, 7; Guha, *Beyond Caste*, 26.
19. On the role of the colonial state in strengthening caste, see Dirks, *Castes of Mind*.
20. See Bayly, *Caste, Society and Politics in India*; Viswanath, *The Pariah Problem*.
21. I am grateful to S. Anand for pointing out this distinction. See also Mendelsohn and Vicziany, *The Untouchables*, 6.

22. Sharma, *Caste*, 48

23. Cohn, "Notes on the History of the Study of Indian Society and Culture," 142.

24. On labor, see Rupa Viswanath, *The Pariah Problem*. On misrecognition and dispossession of Dalits, see Rawat, *Reconsidering Untouchability*.

25. On caste as the basis of capital accumulation in agrarian settings, see Omvedt, *Dalits and the Democratic Revolution*, 29–31.

26. Dickey, *Living Class in Urban India*, 30–31. See also Singh, Vithayathil, and Pradhan, "Recasting Inequality."

27. O'Hanlon, *Caste, Conflict, and Ideology*, 6.

28. O'Hanlon, *Caste, Conflict, and Ideology*, 6.

29. Deshpande, ed., *Selected Writings of Jotirao Phule*.

30. Omvedt, *Cultural Revolt in a Colonial Society*; Omvedt, *Dalits and the Democratic Revolution*, 97–100.

31. O'Hanlon, *Caste, Conflict, and Ideology*, 8.

32. See Morris, *The Emergence of an Industrial Labor Force in India*, 71.

33. See Y. D. Phadke, "Prastavana," 20.

34. Conlon has provided a wonderful account of the life of Saraswat Brahmins in cities in western and southern India, including Bombay. Conlon, *A Caste in a Changing World*, 114–37; Rao, *House, but No Garden*.

35. Prakash, *Mumbai Fables*, 24.

36. Rao, *House, but No Garden*, 13–19; Roberts, *To Be Cared For*, 82

37. Thompson, *The Making of the English Working Class*, 1966.

38. Chandavarkar, "The Making of the Working Class," 54. Some of the work on labor in Bombay that followed in Thompson's wake includes Newman, *Workers and Union in Bombay*; Lieten, *Colonialism, Class and Nation*; Kooiman, *Bombay Textile Labour*; Chandavarkar, *The Origins of Industrial Capitalism in India*; Chandavarkar, *Imperial Power and Popular Politics*.

39. Chandavarkar, *Imperial Power and Popular Politics*, 7.

40. Chandavarkar, *Imperial Power and Popular Politics*, 8.

41. Some other important and generative histories in this vein that focus on North India include Gooptu, *The Politics of the Urban Poor in Early Twentieth Century India*; Joshi, *Lost Worlds*.

42. Khairmode, *Bhartiya Ghataneche Shilpakar*, 1:59.

43. On the invention of the urban poor as a discursive category by the colonial state, see Gooptu, *The Politics of the Urban Poor*, 6–7.

44. Khairmode, *Bhartiya Ghataneche Shilpkar*, 1:62.

45. I refer here to two intellectual lineages of class, one Marxian, where class is formed through political action, and the other Weberian, where class determines status. Weber, "Classes, Status Groups, Parties."

46. Jeurgensmeyer, *Religion as Social Vision*; Zelliot, *From Untouchable to Dalit*; Omvedt, *Dalits and the Democratic Revolution*; Mendelsohn and Vicziany, *The Untouchables*; Prashad, *Untouchable Freedom*.

47. Rawat and Satyanarayana, "Introduction," 6–8.

48. See Guru, "The Indian Nation in Its Egalitarian Conception."

49. Mohan, *Modernity of Slavery*.

50. Viswanath, "Rethinking Caste and Class"; Viswanath, *The Pariah Problem*; Rawat, *Reconsidering Untouchability*.

51. Menon, *Blindness of Insight*.

52. Guru and Sarrukai, *The Cracked Mirror*.

53. Gopal Guru has recently highlighted Lefebvre as an important thinker and space as an important category for understanding Dalit experiences of untouchability. Guru and Sarukkai, *The Cracked Mirror*, 82–83.

54. There is a rich body of scholarship that highlights the gendering of caste and class: Gupta, *The Gender of Caste*; Chakravarti, *Gendering Caste through a Feminist Lens*; Rao, ed., *Gender and Caste*. On laboring women, see Sen, *Women and Labour in Late Colonial India*; Ray and Qayum, *Cultures of Servitude*; Chatterjee, *A Time for Tea*; Fernandes, *Producing Workers*; Paik, *Dalit Women's Education in Modern India*.

55. On the importance of caste to the production and reproduction of labor, see Natarajan, *The Culturization of Caste*, 130–33.

56. On the question of translation and mistranslation, see Rafael, *Motherless Tongues*, 2016.

57. Rafael, *The Promise of the Foreign*, 14.

58. Chakrabarty, *Provincializing Europe*, 89–91.

59. Sewell, *Logics of History*.

60. Roy, *India in Transition*, 96.

61. On universal solidarity, see Sarkar, *Beyond Nationalist Frames*, 78–79.

62. Chibber, *Postcolonial Theory and the Specter of Capital*.

63. Chakrabarty, *Rethinking Working-Class History*, 225.

64. Chakrabarty, *Rethinking Working-Class History*. See also Chakrabarty, *Provincializing Europe*.

65. Chibber, *Postcolonial Theory and the Specter of Capital*, 233–34.

66. Gidwani's *Capital, Interrupted* studies how the Patels, a landowning caste in western India, harnesses its rural dominance to become a powerful global diaspora in the twentieth century. Chari, *Fraternal Capital*, studies the process where low-caste agrarian peasants of the Gounder caste accumulate capital in urban South India.

67. Harootunian, *Marx after Marx*, 40.

68. Gidwani, *Capital, Interrupted*.

69. Harootunian, *Marx after Marx*; Tomba, *Marx's Temporalities*; Robinson, *Black Marxism*; Nikhil Pal Singh, *Race and America's Long War*.

70. See Bhan, *In the Public's Interest*, 146–87; Weinstein, *The Durable Slum*.

71. Manjapra, *Age of Entanglement*, 6–7.

72. Lenin, *The State and Revolution*, 16–17.

73. Omvedt, *Cultural Revolt in a Colonial Society*, 252.

1. THE HOUSING QUESTION AND CASTE, 1896–1950

1. Dossal, "A Master Plan for the City."

2. Edwardes, *The Rise of Bombay*, 306–12.

3. Dutt, *The Economic History of India in the Victorian Age*, v. For a critique of Dutt, see McAlpin, *Subject to Famine*.

4. Edwardes, *The Rise of Bombay*, 331.

5. According to the 1891 census, the population of the city was 821,764. According to the 1901 census, the population was 776,006. By 1906, the population of the city had risen to 977,822. Government of Bombay, *Gazetteer of Bombay City and Island*, 1:166–67.

6. Engels, *The Housing Question*, 7.

7. Chandavarkar, *Imperial Power and Popular Politics*, 103.

8. Wacha, *Shells from the Sands of Bombay*, 476.

9. Acworth, *History of the Drainage and Sewerage of Bombay*, 7–8.

10. Chandavarkar, "Sewers," in *History, Culture and the Indian City*.

11. Acworth, *History of the Drainage and Sewerage of Bombay*, 34.

12. Lee, "Who Is the True Halalkhore?" "Halalkhor" is a polite term for Bhangis but also denotes Bhangis who converted to Islam.

13. Tam, "Sewerage's Reproduction of Caste," 9.

14. Acworth, *History of the Drainage and Sewerage of Bombay*, 65.

15. Masselos, "Jobs and Jobbery."

16. Masselos, "Jobs and Jobbery," 125.

17. *Labour Gazette*, February 1922, 19.

18. Precolonial Indian states also collected such information. South Asia historians have debated this. The historical anthropologist Nicholas Dirks has highlighted the power of the colonial state in enumerating difference and social hierarchies and has argued that caste evolved into its modern form owing to India's colonial encounter. Sumit Guha and Susan Bayly have criticized Dirks, demonstrating that the precolonial Mughal state in northern India and the Maratha state in western India enumerated groups based on caste even before the advent of the British rule. For example, in Pune, the center of power in western India in the eighteenth century, we come across census reports that list houses belonging to various castes and occupational groups living in every locality (*peth*) of the city. This diminished the claim that caste was a colonial invention. At the very least, the census reports of the precolonial states show that group identities were already being formed in the precolonial period. These precolonial structures of feeling (of caste) survived into the modern age and used the colonial public sphere to assert and amplify their claims.

19. On caste and the India census, see Sundar, "Caste as a Census Category."

20. On this point, see Sumit Guha, *Beyond Caste*; Kanchan Chandra, *Why Ethnic Parties Succeed*.

21. Guha, *Beyond Caste*, 50

22. Public Health Department. Health Officer's Reports, Bombay Municipality [henceforth HORBM], fourth quarter of 1879.

23. HORBM, second quarter of 1896, 4.

24. *Census of India 1901*, vol. 11, part V, 22.

25. Edwardes, *The Rise of Bombay*, 312. The book was reprinted from *Census of India 1901*, vol. 10.

26. Their number rose from 27,000 to 40,000. *Census of India 1901* (Bombay), vol. 11, 53.

27. Orr, *The Need of Co-operation between Neighbours*, 19.

28. Sumit Sarkar has pointed out Risley's awareness of the political value of classification and his political journey after stewarding the 1901 census; Risley played an important role in the partitioning of Bengal in 1905. Sarkar, *Modern Times*, 26–28.

29. Seal, *The Emergence of Indian Nationalism*.

30. Pinto, *The Mayor, the Commissioner and the Metropolitan Administration*, 30–33.

31. Masani, *Evolution of Local Self Government in Bombay*); Michael, *The History of the Municipal Corporation of the City of Bombay*; Pinto, *The Mayor, the Commissioner and the Metropolitan Administration*; Washbrook. "The Rhetoric of Democracy and Development in Late Colonial India," 41.

32. Sarkar, *Modern India*, 20.

33. In the second half of the nineteenth century, social reformers focused on reforming their own castes and communities by advocating widow remarriage. By the end of the century, they looked beyond the boundaries of castes and focused on the urban poor. See Kidambi, *Making of an Indian Metropolis*, 203–5; Susan Bayly, *Caste, Society and Politics*, 180–83.

34. Susan Bayly, *Caste, Society and Politics*, 184.

35. I borrow this phrase from Harootunian, *Marx after Marx*, 14.

36. Chandavarkar, *Origins of Industrial Capitalism in India*, 65–67.

37. Beckert, *Empire of Cotton*, xvi–xvii.

38. Chandavarkar, *Origins of Industrial Capitalism in India*, 67.

39. For details see Krishna, *Overcrowding in Bombay*, 37–38.

40. Banaji, *Theory as History*, 283–91.

41. Banaji, *Theory as History*, 330–31.

42. Charlesworth. *Peasants and Imperial Rule*, 7.

43. I find Banaji's argument more convincing and productive particularly because his account of the proletarianization of the small peasant creates the possibility for the migration of such peasants to the city.

44. Banaji, *Theory as History*, 290–91.

45. Guha, *The Agrarian Economy of the Bombay Deccan*, 2.

46. Chandavarkar, *History, Culture, and the Indian City*, 61–62. Srivastava, in *The Well-being of the Labor Force in Colonial Bombay*, discusses the discourse of childcare and provisions for childbirth for the laboring classes in the city.

47. Mann, "The Mahars of a Deccan Village," 75–76.

48. Morris, *The Emergence of an Industrial Labor Force in India*, 81.

49. Chandavarkar, *History, Culture, and the Indian City*, 76–78.

50. Radha Kumar, "City Lives." See also Conlon, "Industrialization and the Housing Problem in Bombay."

51. *Census of India 1901*, vol. 11, 33. Rajnarayan Chandavarkar (*Origins of Industrial Capitalism*, 27–28) views this important feature of state making, where the government enters localities and seeks compliance, as a feature of the *ryotwari* system of land settlement in India.

52. *Census of India 1901*, vol. 11, part V, 13–14. According to the 1901 definition of a house, there were 30,125 occupied houses and 8,718 unoccupied houses. The census attributed it to the exodus caused by plague. Also see *Census of India 1921*, vol. 9, 87–88.

53. Dwivedi and Mehrotra, *Bombay*, 196–98. In fact, during the national movement in the late 1920s and 1930s, political prisoners were imprisoned in tenements made by the government.

54. Kidambi, *The Making of an Indian Metropolis*.

55. *Act of Parliament Relating to the City of Glasgow Improvement Trust*, 1–2.

56. Sugarman, "Reclaiming Rangoon."

57. Sivaramakrishnan demonstrates in *Modern Forests* how locality is a spatial and cultural entity, and local knowledge helped policymakers, bureaucrats, and intellectuals enter the community of experts. State making encapsulated the process of enumerating, imagining, and representing society and also managing the distinction between state and society.

58. Edwardes, *The Rise of Bombay*, 332.

59. *Census of Bombay City 1901*, vol. 9, 5.

60. For a provocative account of the role of community as the foundation of Indian society and how these concepts became key categories of modernity, see Prakash, "The Colonial Genealogy of Society"; Appadurai, "Numbers in the Colonial Imagination."

61. *Census of India 1921*, vol. 9, part I, 87.

62. *Census of India 1901*, vol. 11, part V, 14.

63. The census attributed it to exodus from the city owing to the plague. But it also gives credence to Conlon's claim that overcrowding was due not to the unavailability of housing but to the shortage of affordable housing.

64. Krishna, *Overcrowding in Bombay*, 7.

65. Hazareesingh, *The Colonial City and the Challenge of Modernity*, 28.

66. Chhabria, *Making the Modern Slum*, 17.

67. The acquisition of land in the city was funded by raising loans at low interest rates. The Trust raised loans at an interest of 4 percent per year over a period of sixty years. According to S. M. Edwardes, by 1908, the Trust had raised Rs 324 lakhs, of which it spent Rs 235 lakhs on buying properties in the city. Government of Bombay, *Gazetteer of Bombay City and Island*, 3:86.

68. Rao, *House, but No Garden*, 17.

69. Government of Bombay, *Gazetteer of Bombay City and Island*, 3:83–85.

70. Krishna, *Overcrowding in Bombay*, 48.

71. Orr, *Social Reform and Slum Reform*, 23.

72. Orr, *Social Reform and Slum Reform*, 23.

73. City of Bombay Improvement Trust, *Administration Report for the Year Ending 31st March 1912*, 108–9 (henceforth cited as COBITAR).

74. Rao, *House, but No Garden*, 41–44.

75. Conlon, *A Caste in a Changing World*, 185.

76. Quoted in Conlon, *A Caste in a Changing World*, 185–86.

77. Conlon, *A Caste in a Changing World*, 188–89.

78. Hazareesingh, *The Colonial City*, 44.

79. Orr, *Need of Co-operation between Neighbours*, 2

80. Indian Industrial Commission, *Minutes of Evidence*, 355.

81. Indian Industrial Commission, *Minutes of Evidence*, 354.

82. Industrial Commission, *Minutes of Evidence*, 354.

83. Industrial Commission, *Minutes of Evidence*, 354.

84. Rao, *House, but No Garden*, 25.

85. "Development Chawls," *Bombay Chronicle*, June 6, 1923, quoted in Desai and Dighe, eds., *Labour Movement in India*, 335–37.

86. "Development Chawls," 336.

87. *Labour Gazette*, quoted in Desai and Dighe, eds., *Labour Movement in India*, 341.

88. Advisory Committee on the Industrial Housing Scheme, *Report of the Special Advisory Committee*, 14 (henceforth cited as ACOIHS).

89. *Servants of India*, June 30, 1921, 255–56.

90. Servants of India Society, *Report of Work and Constitution*, 12–14.

91. *Labour Gazette*, February 1924, 23.

92. Burnett-Hurst, *Labour and Housing*, 81

93. City of Bombay Improvement Trust, *Proceedings of the Improvements Committee and the Board, 1929–30*, 230.

94. City of Bombay Improvement Trust, *Proceedings of the Improvements Committee and the Board, 1929–30*, 394.

95. I am thinking here of the rise of Ambedkar as a political leader, the Mahad movement to demand civil and political rights, and the articulation of these demands in the Bombay Legislative Council.

96. COBITAR, 99.

97. City of Bombay Improvement Trust, *Proceedings of the Improvements Committee and the Board, 1929–30*, 468.

98. ACOIHS, 11.

99. ACOIHS, 11.

100. On the paradox of caste, see Bayly, *Caste, Society and Politics*, 189–90; Rao, *The Caste Question*.

101. Teltumbde, *Mahad: The Making of the First Dalit Revolt*, 107.

102. Quoted in Teltumbde, *Mahad*, 121.

103. Depressed Classes and Aboriginal Tribes Committee, *Report of the Depressed Classes and Aboriginal Tribes Committee of the Bombay Presidency*, 48.

104. He enlisted the members of the Bombay Social Service League for his study. Burnett-Hurst, *Labour and Housing in Bombay*, 123.

105. Shaikh, "Imaging Caste."

106. Burnett-Hurst, *Labour and Housing in Bombay*, 14.

107. Burnett-Hurst, *Labour and Housing in Bombay*, 21.

108. Burnett-Hurst, *Labour and Housing in Bombay*, 20.

109. "Is Picture of Bombay Housing Conditions Overdrawn?," *Times of India*, July 17, 1933.

110. Pradhan, *Untouchable Workers*, 3.

111. Pradhan, *Untouchable Workers*, 4.

112. Pradhan, *Untouchable Workers*, 116.

113. For a discussion of the photographs, see Shaikh, "Imaging Caste."

114. Pradhan, *Untouchable Workers*, 11.

115. Pradhan, *Untouchable Workers*, 13.

116. Pradhan, *Untouchable Workers*, 14.

117. Pradhan, *Untouchable Workers*, 116.

118. Handbill of the Mahar Jati Panchayat Samiti, in Ramesh Shinde's private collection, Mumbai.

119. Pradhan, *Untouchable Workers*, 118.

120. Rent Enquiry Committee, *Report of the Rent Enquiry Committee*, 1:27, 56–57. Some form of rent control was in place during and after World War I but had lapsed in 1928 and remained only on the statute books.

121. I want to thank Jayashree Kamble for suggesting the book. Omvedt, *Building the Ambedkar Revolution*, xvi.

122. Ambedkar, *Scheme of a Social Centre*.

123. "Babasahebancya svapna putisathich" (To fulfill Babasaheb's dream), Loksatta (People's government), July 10, 2016, https://www.loksatta.com/vishesh-news/the-bombay-scheduled-caste-improvement-trust-1265024/.

124. It is important to note that the speech, delivered in Marathi, referred to the Scheduled Castes Federation as the Akhil Bhartiya Dalit Phederation.

125. Jadhav, *Akhil Bhartiya Dalit Phederation*, 7.

126. Jadhav, *Akhil Bhartiya Dalit Phederation*, 6.

127. I refer here to the demand for Pakistan.

128. See Ambedkar's interaction with Beverley Nichols, a British officer, described in Jaffrelot, *Dr Ambedkar and Untouchability*, 81–82.

129. Jadhav, *Akhil Bhartiya Dalit Phederation*, 5–6.

130. Industrial Housing Sub-committee, *Report of the Industrial Housing Sub-committee of the Standing Labour Committee*, 8.

131. Thakurdas, Tata, and Birla, *A Brief Memorandum Outlining a Plan of Economic Development for India*, 10–11.

132. Greater Bombay Scheme Committee, *The Greater Bombay Scheme*, 5 [henceforth cited as GBSC].

133. The report identifies eighty-six slums in wards B, C, D, and E of the city.

134. GBSC, 4–5.

135. GBSC, 8.

136. GBSC, 82.

137. GBSC, 82–84.

138. GBSC, 74.

139. GBSC, 74.

140. Batley, *Bombay Houses and Homes*, 2

141. B. T. Randive, "Rent Sharks of Bombay," *National Front*, July 1938.

142. "Growth of Housing Construction in the Soviet Union," *National Front*, May 22, 1938.

143. "Growth of Housing Construction in the Soviet Union," *National Front*, May 22, 1938.

2. MARXISM, LANGUAGE, AND SOCIAL HIERARCHY, 1920–1950

1. See Dirlik's exposition of the journey from Communism to Marxism in *The Origins of Chinese Communism*. On the importance of jails in the education of Communists in Vietnam, see Zinoman, *The Colonial Bastille*.

2. Manjapra, *M. N. Roy*, 51. However, John Haithcox mentions that Roy engaged with Marx's writings in the New York Public Library in 1916 or 1917 and credited a Soviet emissary in Mexico, Michael Borodin, with breaking down his resistance to Marxism. Roy was one of the founders of the Communist Party of Mexico. Haithcox, *Communism and Nationalism in India*, 7–9.

3. It's not that Marx or socialism was alien to people in India. Two biographies of Karl Marx were published in India in 1912, one by Lala Hardyal, who later founded the Ghadar Party, titled *Karl Marx: A Modern Rishi*, and another, titled *Karl Marx*, in Malayalam, by Ramakrishna Pillai. Joshi and Damodaran, eds., *Marx Comes to India*. Moreover, there were references to socialism, *The Communist Manifesto*, the Paris Commune, and the first Communist International in nineteenth-century India. History Commission, *History of the Communist Movement in India*, 14–18.

4. This group included R. S. Nimbkar, V. D. Sathaye, and R. V. Nadkarni, later joined by S. V. Deshpande and K. N. Joglekar. Sarkar, *Modern India*, 212.

5. Dange, "Gandhi vs Lenin," in *Selected Writings*, vol. 1, 66. More precisely, Dange says, "Capital cares nothing for the length of life of labour power. All that concerns it is simply and solely the maximum of labor power that can be rendered fluent in a working day. . . . Capital extends the labourer's time of production during a given period by shortening his actual life time." Some Communists in Calcutta had read Marx's *Critique of Political Economy*. Chattopadhyay, *An Early Communist*, 95.

6. Dange, *Selected Writings*, 1:44.

7. Dange, *Selected Writings*, 1:130.

8. Dange, *Selected Writings*, 1:96.

9. Dange, *Selected Writings*, 1:59.

10. Dange, "Gandhi vs Lenin," in *Selected Writings*, 1:121.

11. Haithcox, *Communism and Nationalism in India*, 11–13. Roy played an important role in the formulation of the Comintern's policy on national and colonial questions in the 1920s.

12. Government of Bombay [henceforth GOB], Home Department (Spl), Box 63, File 543 (3) 1923, Maharashtra State Archives, Mumbai [henceforth MSA].

13. GOB, Home Department (Spl), Box 63, File 543 (3) 1923, MSA.

14. Lenin, *The State and Revolution*, 34–35, 116–19.

15. See the documents from the first Communist Party of India conference from Kanpur in 1925 in Gupta, ed., *A Documented History of the Communist Movement in India*, 701.

16. Newman, *Workers and Unions in Bombay*, 247.

17. Roy, *India in Transition*, 96.

18. Palme Dutt, *The Problem of India*, 93.

19. Teltumbde, "Introduction," in Ambedkar, *India and Communism*, 31.

20. Omvedt, *Dalits and the Democratic Revolution*, 154.

21. On the point of colonial manipulation of group identities by the colonial state, see Jayal, *Citizenship and Its Discontents*, 21.

22. "Komunijhama va brahmanijhama," *Samata*, Friday P 7, Sept. 21, 1928, Ambedkar Collection, Mumbai.

23. Some of the other Bombay Communists in the chapter are S. V. Ghate, Keshav N. Joglekar, Shapurji Saklatvala, R. S. Nimbkar, and S. S. Mirajkar.

24. For more details of Adhikari's time in Germany, see his interview with Hari Dev Sharma in the Nehru Memorial Library and Museum's oral history project.

25. GOB, Home Department (Spl), Box 63, File 543 (3) 1923, MSA.

26. GOB, Home Department (Spl), Box 63, File 543 (3) 1923, MSA.

27. GOB, Home Department (Spl), Box 63, File 543 (3) 1923, MSA.

28. In the list, T. J. Holmes is referred to as J. J. Holmes. GOB, Home Department (Spl), Box 63, File 543 (3) 1923, MSA.

29. On the effects of the Russian Revolution on Marxian scholarship, see Hobsbawm, "The Fortunes of Marx's and Engels' Writings," 332–33.

30. GOB, Home Department (Spl), Box 63, File 543 (3) 1923, MSA.

31. Yajnik, *Life of Ranchoddas Bhavan Lotvala*, i.

32. Lotwala was not unique among Indian merchants who funded the dissemination of a worldview. Marwari businessmen from eastern and northern India founded the Gita Press in 1926 for the propagation of a Hindu India. Mukul, *Gita Press and the Making of Hindu India*, 2015.

33. Dange, *Selected Writings*, 1:130.

34. Karat, ed., *A World to Win*, 132.

35. Karat, ed., *A World to Win*, 132.

36. GOB, Home Department (Spl), Box 63, File 543 (3) 1923, MSA.

37. The issue dated November 18, 1922, carried the advertisement for these pamphlets. Dange, *Selected Writings*, 1:136.

38. GOB, Home Department (Spl), Box 73, File 543 (43) A 1934, MSA.

39. GOB, Home Department (Spl), Box 73, File 543 (43) A, 1934, MSA.

40. GOB, Home Department (Spl), Box 68, File 543 (18) C, 1938, MSA.

41. See Dange's editorial in the first issue of *The Socialist* titled "Probing at the Root," published on August 5, 1922. Dange, *Selected Writings*, 1:139.

42. Dange, *Selected Writings*, 1:139.

43. Dange, *Selected Writings*, 1:139.

44. See the editorial "All India Socialist Party," dated October 1, 1924, in Dange, *Selected Writings*, 1:399.

45. See his editorial "Paradise Lost," dated August 19, 1922, in Dange, *Selected Writings*, 1:143.

46. Dange, *Selected Writings*, 1:145, emphasis in the original.

47. Dange, *Selected Writings*, 1:145.

48. Dange, *Selected Writings*, 1:146–47.

49. Dange, *Selected Writings*, 1:148.

50. Dange, *Selected Writings*, 1:150. For the preface to the 1888 edition of the *Manifesto* written by Friedrich Engels, see Karat, ed., *A World to Win*, 128.

51. Dange, *Selected Writings*, 1:148. *Guna*: a quality or an attribute of matter or mind that is inherent. *Moksha*: escape from the cycle of birth and rebirth.

52. O'Hanlon, *Caste, Conflict and Ideology*, 141–51.

53. See J. P. Bagerhotta's open letter to M. N Roy in *The Socialist* dated September 24, 1924, in Dange, *Selected Writings*, 1:397. Bagerhotta was the joint secretary of the Communist Party of India when it was formed in 1925, but in 1927 he was expelled from the party for being a "police agent." On this point, see Josh, *The Great Attack*, 23.

54. Kosambi, *An Introduction to the Study of Indian History*, 266.

55. Pollock, *The Language of the Gods in the World of Men*, 12–14.

56. Pollock, "Indian in the Vernacular Millennium."

57. Sumit Guha has noted that vernacular languages did not erase Sanskrit. In fact, in Maharashtra, the Marathi vernacular borrowed from many languages, including Persian and other regional languages. Guha, "Transitions and Translations."

58. History Commission, *History of the Communist Movement in India*, 80.

59. I am hugely indebted to Vicente Rafael's work for this point. See Rafael, *Contracting Colonialism*; Rafael, *The Promise of the Foreign*, 24–25.

60. Naregal, *Language Politics, Elites and the Public Sphere*.

61. O'Hanlon, *Caste, Conflict and Ideology*, 8.

62. Dange, *Selected Writings*, 1:213–15.

63. O'Hanlon, *Caste, Conflict and Ideology*, 131–32.

64. Chandavarkar, *Imperial Power and Popular Politics*, 100.

65. See Adhikari, "Introduction," 21.

66. Quoted in Adhikari, "Introduction," 21.

67. History Commission, *History of the Communist Movement in India*, 113.

68. D. R. Thengdi was the president of the party. S. S. Mirajkar was its secretary. Its executive committee comprised S. V. Ghate, K. N. Joglekar, R. S. Nimbkar, Lalji Pendse, and S. H. Jhabwala.

69. History Commission, *History of the Communist Movement in India*, 116.

70. Newman, *Workers and Unions in Bombay*, 209.

71. Newman, *Workers and Unions in Bombay*, 224.

72. Chandavarkar, *The Origins of Industrial Capitalism in India*, 398.

73. Newman, *Workers and Unions in Bombay*, 170.

74. Newman, *Workers and Unions in Bombay*, 171.

75. Newman, *Workers and Unions in Bombay*, 179.

76. On the importance of stories and fables to history, see Nikulin, *The Concept of History*, 10–11.

77. GOB, Home Department (Spl), Box 68, File 543 (18) C, 1938, MSA.

78. GOB, Home Department (Spl), Box 68, File 543 (18) C, 1938, MSA.

79. GOB, Home Department (Spl), Box 68, File 543 (18) C, 1938, MSA.

80. GOB, Home Department (Spl), Box 68, File 543 (18) C, 1938, MSA.

81. GOB, Home Department (Spl), Box 68, File 543 (18) C, 1938, MSA.

82. GOB, Home Department (Spl), Box 68, File 543 (18) C, 1938, MSA.

83. "Bhaiyya" can be translated literally as "brother," but in this context, it was used derogatorily to refer to mostly poor migrants from North India who spoke Hindi and Urdu and dialects of these languages that marked them as outsiders to the city.

84. GOB, Home Department (Spl), Box 68, File 543 (18) C, 1938, MSA.

85. GOB, Home Department (Spl), Box 68, File 543 (18) A, 1928–29, MSA.

86. Chandavarkar, *Imperial Power and Popular Politics*, 168.

87. Rao and Sen, eds., *Our Doc*, 13.

88. Ahmad, *Communists Challenge Imperialism from the Dock*, vi.

89. On the penchant for underreporting membership of the Communist union, see Newman, *Workers and Unions in Bombay*, 216.

90. Roy was expelled for his alliance with a faction within the Communist Party of Germany which included August Thalheimer and Heinrich Brandler. He was derided by Solomon A. Lozovsky, the Comintern's main link with the Indian Communists, as a "Menshevik." Haithcox, *Communism and Nationalism in India*, 130–32.

91. The Mandal's office was located at the Jariwala Building on Suparibaug Road.

92. They held meetings in Shetye Building Poibavdi and also at the house of J. M. Adhikari (Gangadhar Adhikari's brother) on Turner Road in Bandra. GOB, HD (Spl), File 543 (39) Box 73, 1933, MSA.

93. This meant that the factional disputes were not resolved until 1933, when the Meerut leaders returned from jail. The resolution happened when the Royist faction and Communists joined hands in the general strike of April 1934. The reinvigoration of labor militancy invited a ban on the Communist Part of India in July 1934. GOB, Home Department (Spl), File 543 (39) Box 73, 1933, MSA.

94. For a detailed exposition of the role of *dialogue* among prisoners, see Shaikh, "Translating Marx," 65–73.

95. I acquired a copy of the 1931 translation of *The Communist Manifesto* from the grandson of an activist who had become a Communist and Marxist during this period.

96. Josh, *The Great Attack*, 27.

97. Marx and Engels, *The Communist Manifesto*, 7.

98. Marks and Engels, *Kamyunista Particha Jahirnama*, 123.

99. Marx and Engels, *The Communist Manifesto*, 6.

100. Marks and Engels, *Kamyunista Particha Jahirnama*, 126.

101. I say "probably" because in *The German Ideology*, written in 1845–46, two years before the *Manifesto*, Marx had referenced the caste system in his passages on the conception of history. Marx, "The German Ideology," 165.

102. Ahmad, *Communists Challenge Imperialism from the Dock*, 249.

103. Sardesai, "Prastavik char shabd."

104. Sardesai, "Prastavik char shabd," 2–3

105. Sardesai, "Prastavik char shabd," 3.

106. Lojhavski, *Vasahatitil Deshansathi Treda Uniyan Chalvalicha Onama*, 3.

107. Lojhavski, *Vasahatitil Deshansathi Treda Uniyan Chalvalicha Onama*, 7.

108. Lojhavski, *Vasahatitil Deshansathi Treda Uniyan Chalvalicha Onama*, 14.

109. Lojhavski, *Vasahatitil Deshansathi Treda Uniyan Chalvalicha Onama*, 1.

110. Worley, "To the Left and Back Again," 77.

111. Lojhavski, *Vasahatitil Deshansathi Treda Uniyan Chalvalicha Onama*, 1.

112. *Kamareda Lenina*, 15.

113. "Bahujana Samaj" is a term created by the anti-Brahmin leader Jyotirao Phule in western India in the second half of the nineteenth century.

114. The pamphlet does not specify a writer.

115. *Kamareda Lenina*, 15–16.

116. *Kamareda Lenina*, 16.

117. *Kamareda Lenina*, 16.

118. Marks and Engels, *Kamyunista Particha Jahirnama*, 5.

119. Marx and Engels, *The Communist Manifesto*, 3.

120. *Mawali* (not *mavali*) is an Arabic term used to denote non-Arab Muslims.

121. Destitute and unemployed workers, paupers, and the lumpen proletariat were a step below the working-class *kamgaar varga* on the social ladder.

122. Liedman, *A World to Win*, 305.

123. Karl Marx, *Capital*, 797–98.

124. See Karmwar, "African Diaspora in India"; Harris, *The African Presence in Asia*.

125. See reports of S. S. Mirajkar's speech at the meeting of striking mill workers at Del-isle Road on August 6, 1928. GOB, HD (Spl), File 543 (18) C, Box 68, 1938, MSA.

126. On Marx's assumption about free labor, see van der Linden, *Workers of the World*, 18.

127. I have written about V. B. Kulkarni in an as yet unpublished article.

128. Jagannath Adhikari and R. B. More became close friends. See More, *Kamred Ar. Bi. More*, 171–72.

129. More, *Kamred Ar. Bi. More*, 149.

130. More, *Kamred Ar. Bi. More*, 147.

131. More, *Kamred Ar. Bi. More*, 148–49.

132. Royal Commission on Labour in India, *Report of the Royal Commission*, 42.

133. More, *Kamred Ar. Bi. More*,154.

134. GOB, Home Department (Spl), Box 73-A, File 543 (45), 1934–38, MSA.

135. Pawar, *Asprushyanche Chalis Saval*.

136. GOB, Home Department (Spl), Box 72, File 543 (30), 1934–38, MSA.

137. GOB, Home Department (Spl), Box 72, File 543 (30), 1934–38, MSA.

138. Chandavarkar, *History, Culture, and the Indian City*, 144–45.

139. Sathe, *Marathi rangabhumichya tees ratri*, 2:691.

140. The second edition of *Dhavata Dhota* was published in 1972. See the foreword to the second edition by Mangesh Rajyadhyaksha for the history of its publication. Varerkara, *Dhavata Dhota*, 1–2.

141. Varerkar, *Dhavata Dhota*, 30.

142. Varerkar, *Dhavata Dhota*, 34.

143. Varerkar, *Dhavata Dhota*, 65.

144. Varerkar, *Dhavata Dhota*, 5.

145. See particular chapter 4 of his wonderful dissertation: Kumar, "Learning to Dream." It must also be mentioned that Varerkar's and Kumar's insights subvert historical and archival evidence. For instance, the *Labour Gazette* of April 1922 mentioned the deplorably low standard of literacy among mill workers. "Report of the Industrial Disputes Committee," *Labor Gazette*, April 1922, 26.

146. Sawant, *Majuranchya-samrajyat*, 3.

147. Sawant, *Majuranchya-samrajyat*, 30.

148. Sawant, *Majuranchya-samrajyat*, 25.

149. M. K. Gandhi had held in the Amhedabad textile mill strike of 1917 that the employers and the employed must work toward the good of all, and he believed this was the "traditional Indian way." Tidrick, *Gandhi*, 123.

150. Sawant, *Majuranchya-Samrajyat*, 77.

151. The series in which this novel appears is called the *Char ane kadambari mala*, published by Adarsh Vangmay Prakashan, Pune.

152. Hadap, ed., *Majurachi bayko*, 3–4.

153. Hadap, ed., *Majurachi bayko*, 6.
154. Hadap, ed., *Majurachi bayko*, 12.
155. Hadap, ed., *Majurachi bayko*, 16.
156. Pradhan, *Untouchable Workers of Bombay*, 22.
157. Pradhan, *Untouchable Workers of Bombay*, 12, emphasis added.
158. Hadap, ed., *Majurachi bayko*, 95–96.
159. Nandurbarkar, *Majur-Mahatma*, 15.
160. Nandurbarkar, *Majur-Mahatma*, 14.
161. According to Iyer's *The Mysore Tribes and Castes*, the Kulavadis are Holeyas, who were classified as a depressed class by the 1931 census. In the Konkan region of western India, where Baba Shigvan was from, kulavadis belonged to the kunbi jatis or peasant communities. See Census of India 1931, vol. 9, 42. According to Rosalind O'Hanlon, in the Ratnagiri district of the Konkan region there was separation between Kunbi and Maratha. In Pune district, Kunbi and Maratha were synonymous. In Bombay city, many identified themselves as Maratha Kunbis. O'Hanlon, *Caste, Conflict and Ideology*, 45–47.
162. Varerkar, *Dhavata Dhota*, 66–67.
163. Varerkar, *Dhavata Dhota*, 55.
164. Varerkar, *Dhavata Dhota*, 88.
165. Tea shops became an urban feature and new sites of sociability in the interwar period. Sarkar, *Modern Times*, 305.
166. Newman, *Workers and Unions in Bombay*, 233.
167. Lieten, *Colonialism, Class, and Nation*, 118.
168. Nandurbarkar, *Majur-Mahatma*, 1.
169. Teltumbde, "Introduction: Bridging the Unholy Rift," in Ambedkar, *India and Communism*, 46–47.
170. "Komunijhama va brahmanijhama," *Samata*, Friday P 7, Sept. 21, 1928.
171. Dange, *India from Primitive Communism to Slavery*, xxx.
172. Dange, *India from Primitive Communism to Slavery*, xxvii.
173. Dange, *India from Primitive Communism to Slavery*, 24.
174. Thapar, *The Aryan*, 65–67.
175. Thapar, *The Aryan*, 60.
176. Thapar, *The Aryan*, 69.
177. Dange, *India from Primitive Communism to Slavery*, 26.
178. Dange, *India from Primitive Communism to Slavery*, 26.
179. Dange, *India from Primitive Communism to Slavery*, 47.
180. Dange, *India from Primitive Communism to Slavery*, xvii.

3. URBAN PLANNING AND CULTURAL POLITICS, 1945–1971

1. Overstreet and Windmiller, *Communism in India*, 433–36.
2. The date of the formation of Lal Bavta Kalapathak varies in secondary literature. Baburao Gurav, a biographer of Anna Bhau Sathe, dates it to 1942. Gurav, *Annabhau Sathe*, 38. Bajrang Korde dates it to 1944. Korde, *Anna Bhau Sathe*, 11. I opt for 1944 here, because the troupe was definitely formed by 1944.

3. Sathe, "Mumbaichi lavani," in *Anna Bhau Sathe nivadak vangmay*, 64–65.

4. But despite the progressive inclinations of the realist project in India, scholars like Susie Tharu and K. Lalita ("Introduction") have pointed out that there were significant silences in this project, particularly on the issue of gendered labor *and* the caste question.

5. Korde, *Anna Bhau Sathe*, 6–7.

6. Cholia in fact says that 98 percent of the workers were Mahars. Cholia, *Dock Labourers in Bombay*, 61.

7. This was a year after the Marathi-speaking state of Maharashtra was created by splitting the Bombay Presidency into two states: Gujarat and Maharashtra. In his life as an artiste, Sathe associated with luminaries of the IPTA and considered Hindi film stars like K. A. Abbas, Balraj Sahni, and Raj Kapoor as his friends.

8. By 1965, Sathe was alienated from his friends and associates. According to the playwright Makarand Sathe, Communists and bourgeois Brahmins ignored Sathe after 1965, and the decline of the Communist movement in the city after the split in the CPI in 1964 accentuated his isolation. He died in penury in 1969.

9. Sathe, *Marathi rangabhumichya tees ratri*, 701. The ban on *tamashas* was replete with irony. The government of the Bombay state, headed by B. G. Kher, had ordered *tamasha* troupes to submit scripts of *tamashas* for scrutiny—a steep demand on a form that relied on improvisation and the wit of performers who were often illiterate. The irony of Sathe's contribution of the term *loknatya* was twofold. When the Literature and Culture Department of the Maharashtra state published a collection of Anna Bhau Sathe's works in 1998, his *tamashas* were all categorized as *loknatyas* with no mention of the *tamasha*. The *tamasha* became important, however, when the Marathi-speaking state of Maharashtra was created in 1960. The Maharashtra government, which sought legitimacy as the representative of the Marathi-speaking people, patronized "indigenous" or folk forms of art like the *tamasha* after the formation of the Marathi-speaking state, but only after the *tamasha* had been "sanitized."

10. Sathe, "Shetjiche elecshan," in *Anna Bhau Sathe nivadak vangmay*, 134–35.

11. Sathe, "Shetjiche elecshan," in *Anna Bhau Sathe nivadak vangmay*, 136.

12. Sathe, "Bekaydeshire," in *Anna Bhau Sathe nivadak vangmay*, 148.

13. On this issue of particularities of caste and religion and their relevance to social relationships in working-class neighborhoods, see Chandavarkar, *Imperial Power and Popular Politics*, 1–29.

14. Sathe, "Muka miravanuk," in *Anna Bhau Sathe nivadak vangmay*, 174–75.

15. Sathe, "Muka miravanuk," in *Anna Bhau Sathe nivadak vangmay*, 175.

16. Sathe, "Muka miravanuk," in *Anna Bhau Sathe nivadak vangmay*, 175. As we will see, Worli and Chembur played an important role in the geography of Dalit social movements in the city.

17. The clearance of slums needed a legal architecture. For instance, the Bombay Municipal Corporation amended the Bombay Municipal Corporation Act in 1954 to facilitate slum clearance, and in the 1970s provisions were made under the Maharashtra Slum Areas (Improvement, Clearance and Redevelopment Act) of 1971 and the Maharashtra Slum Improvement Board Act of 1973 to declare an area a slum and demolish it.

18. Sathe, "Muka miravanuk," in *Anna Bhau Sathe nivadak vangmay*, 176.
19. Sathe, "Muka miravanuk," in *Anna Bhau Sathe nivadak vangmay*, 176.
20. Sathe, "Muka miravanuk," in *Anna Bhau Sathe nivadak vangmay*, 177.
21. Sathe, "Muka miravanuk," in *Anna Bhau Sathe nivadak vangmay*, 181.
22. Sathe, "Muka miravanuk," in *Anna Bhau Sathe nivadak vangmay*, 190.
23. Chandavarkar, "From Neighborhood to Nation," 43–44.
24. Sathe, "Muka miravanuk," in *Anna Bhau Sathe nivadak vangmay*, 185.
25. Sathe, "Muka miravanuk," in *Anna Bhau Sathe nivadak vangmay*, 179.
26. Sathe, "Muka miravanuk," in *Anna Bhau Sathe nivadak vangmay*, 182–83.
27. Sathe, "Muka miravanuk," in *Anna Bhau Sathe nivadak vangmay*, 185.
28. Sathe, "Muka miravanuk," in *Anna Bhau Sathe nivadak vangmay*, 185.
29. Sathe, "Muka miravanuk," in *Anna Bhau Sathe nivadak vangmay*, 185.
30. Sathe, "Muka miravanuka," in *Anna Bhau Sathe nivadak vangmay*, 186.
31. Sathe, "Muka miravanuk," in *Anna Bhau Sathe nivadak vangmay*, 189.
32. Chandavarkar, "From Neighbourhood to Nation," 35; Chandavarkar, *The Origins of Industrial Capitalism in India*; Chandavarkar, *Imperial Power and Popular Politics*.
33. Sathe, "Lokmantryancha daura," in *Anna Bhau Sathe nivadak vangmay*, 194.
34. Sathe, "Lokmantryancha daura," in *Anna Bhau Sathe nivadak vangmay*, 195–96.
35. Chakrabarty, *Rethinking Working-Class History*, 1989.
36. Chandavarkar, *Imperial Power and Popular Politics*, 26.
37. Sathe, "Lokmantryancha daura," in *Anna Bhau Sathe nivadak vangmay*, 197.
38. Sathe, "Lokmantryancha daura," in *Anna Bhau Sathe nivadak vangmay*, 202.
39. Sathe, "Lokmantryancha daura," in *Anna Bhau Sathe nivadak vangmay*, 202.
40. Sathe, "Lokmantryancha daura," in *Anna Bhau Sathe nivadak vangmay*, 203–5.
41. Sathe, "Majhi maina gavavar rahili," in *Anna Bhau Sathe nivadak vangmay*, 61.
42. Sathe, "Mumbaichi lavani," in *Anna Bhau Sathe nivadak vangmay*, 64–65, translation mine.
43. Sathe, "Mumbaichi lavani," in *Anna Bhau Sathe nivadak vangmay*, 62.
44. Chandavarkar, "From Neighbourhood to Nation," 48–49.
45. Hansen, *Violence in Urban India*, 42.
46. Harvey. *The Condition of Postmodernity*, 68–69.
47. Prakash, *Mumbai Fables*, 253–54.
48. Shaw, *The Making of Navi Mumbai*, 3.
49. Bombay City and Suburbs Post-War Development Committee, *Preliminary Report*, 284–85 [henceforth BCASPWDC].
50. BCASPWDC, 36.
51. BCASPWDC, 46.
52. BCASPWDC, 3.
53. "Bombay Does Not Want Kurla," *Times of India*, July 19, 1926.
54. "Extending City Limits: City Corporation Debate," *Times of India*, Dec. 17, 1946.
55. Weinstein, *The Durable Slum*, 39–40.
56. Modak and Mayer, *An Outline of the Master Plan for Greater Bombay*, 4.
57. BCASPWDC, 7.
58. BCASPWDC, 7.
59. BCASPWDC, 12–13.

60. BCASPWDC, 9.
61. Modak and Mayer, *An Outline of the Master Plan for Greater Bombay*, 7.
62. Modak and Mayer, *An Outline of the Master Plan for Greater Bombay*, 8.
63. BCASPWDC, 10.
64. Modak and Mayer, *An Outline of the Master Plan for Greater Bombay*, 8–9.
65. Modak and Mayer, *An Outline of the Master Plan for Greater Bombay*, 10.
66. Modak and Mayer, *An Outline of the Master Plan for Greater Bombay*, 13–14.
67. Modak and Mayer, *An Outline of the Master Plan for Greater Bombay*, 13.
68. Modak and Mayer, *An Outline of the Master Plan for Greater Bombay*, 14.
69. Modak and Mayer, *An Outline of the Master Plan for Greater Bombay*, 30.
70. Fernandes, *City Adrift*, 135.
71. Modak and Mayer, *An Outline of the Master Plan for Greater Bombay*, 19.
72. See also Royal Commission on the Distribution of the Industrial Population, *Town and Country Planning*; and BCASPWDC, which recommended that the only way to rectify overcrowding was a "drastic decentralization of the City . . . to reduce the industrial and business concentrations to which these housing areas are related" (10–11).
73. See also *Baburao Shantaram More v. Bombay Housing Board*, https://indiankanoon .org/doc/152211/.
74. See Lakdawala et al., *Work, Wages and Well-Being*, 718–19.
75. I am thinking here of *Babu Barkya Thakur v. the State of Bombay and Others*, https://indiankanoon.org/doc/463201/.
76. See Desai, *Law relating to Slum in Maharashtra*, 424–35.
77. See Guha, *Dominance without Hegemony*; Gidwani, *Capital, Interrupted*, xxi–xxii.
78. See Khilnani, *Idea of India*, 11; Das, "Slum," 207–34.
79. All India Trade Union Congress, *All India Trade Union Congress Report*, 130.
80. GOB, *Report of the Scavengers' Living Conditions Enquiry Committee*, 39–40.
81. GOB, *Report of the Scavengers' Living Conditions Enquiry Committee*, 40.
82. Ranadive, "Eka Aitihasika Sangharsha," *Loksatta*, May 13, 2009.
83. Ranadive, "Eka Aitihasika Sangharsha," *Loksatta*, May 13, 2009.
84. GOB, *Report of the Scavengers' Living Conditions Enquiry Committee*, 96.
85. GOB, *Report of the Scavengers' Living Conditions Enquiry Committee*, 96–97.
86. GOB, *Report of the Scavengers' Living Conditions Enquiry Committee*, 138.
87. GOB, *Report of the Scavengers' Living Conditions Enquiry Committee*, 138.
88. For a wonderful argument about waste as the other of value, see Gidwani and Reddy, "The Afterlives of Waste." See also Gidwani, *Capital*, 22–27.
89. On the point of property and repugnance see Rao, *The Caste Question*, 87.
90. Pawar, *Baluta*, 139.
91. Pawar, *Baluta*, 139.
92. Jadhav, *Untouchables*, 246.
93. Pawar, *Baluta*, 145.
94. Personal interview with Ramesh Haralkar, April 1, 2009.
95. Kakodkar, "Life Gets a Move On from the Stinking Rot."
96. Municipal Corporation of Greater Bombay, *Report on the Development Plan for Greater Bombay*, 87 [henceforth MCOGB].
97. MCOGB, 86.

98. MCOGB, 87.

99. Kundu, *In the Name of the Urban Poor*, 46.

100. The land on which the Dharavi slums stand was acquired by the Bombay Improvement Trust scheme but remained undeveloped owing to the cost of reclamation, whereas the slums in Kamathipura were shaped by their proximity to the industrial areas and docks in the city. MCOGB, 92.

101. MCOGB, 93.

102. MCOGB, 93.

103. MCOGB, 93.

104. Indian Institute of Public Administration, *Problems of Urban Housing*, 35.

105. MCOGB, 93.

106. See Dadasaheb Gaikwad's speech to the fifth session of the RPI. B. K. Gaikwad, Speech by the President of the Republican Party of India, Delhi, 1966, in the Ramesh Shinde Collection, Mumbai.

107. Gaikwad, "Speech by the President of the Republican Party of India," 6.

108. More, *Gharancha Prashna*, 30.

109. More, *Gharancha Prashna*, 30–31.

110. More, *Gharancha Prashna*, 30–31.

111. The colony made use of the Indian federal government's Slum Clearance Plan of 1956 to "clear" slums from South and Central Bombay.

112. YUVA, *Our Home Is a Slum*, 7.

113. YUVA, *Our Home Is a Slum*, 7.

114. YUVA, *Our Home Is a Slum*, 9.

115. YUVA, *Our Home Is a Slum*, 9.

116. The Dalits reject the term "Harijan." It was coined by M. K. Gandhi, and this is one of the reasons for its longevity.

117. Mehta, *The Domestic Servant Class*, 38.

118. Mehta, *The Domestic Servant Class*, 52–54.

119. Mehta, *The Domestic Servant Class*, 140.

120. Mehta, *The Domestic Servant Class*, 44.

121. Morris, *The Emergence of an Industrial Labor Force in India*, 203.

122. Joshi and Joshi, *Surplus Labour and the City*, 51.

123. Breman, *Outcast Labour in Asia*, 2–3.

124. Joshi and Joshi, *Surplus Labour and the City*, 31.

125. YUVA, *Our Home Is a Slum*, 5.

126. MCOGB, xix.

127. MCOGB, 85.

128. MCOGB, xix.

129. Dwivedi and Mehrotra, *Bombay*, 271.

130. MCOGB, 147–49.

131. MCOGB, 88.

132. Dwivedi and Mehrotra, *Bombay*, 271.

133. Dwivedi and Mehrotra, *Bombay*, 271–72.

134. The Bombay Metropolitan Region lies between the Rivers Tansa and Vaitarna and is bounded by the foothills of Sahyadri in the southeastern portion and by the

administrative boundaries of Kalyan and Bhivandi *tehsils* in the northeastern portion. On the west it is bounded by the Arabian Sea. The Patalganga in the south and
the Tansa in the north form the limits of the region. Metropolitan Regional Planning Board, *Strategy for Bombay Metropolitan Region: A Summary of Volumes I and
II of the Report of the Draft Regional Plan 1970–1991* (Bombay: Bombay Metropolitan
Regional Planning Board, 1970), 5–6 [henceforth MRPB].

135. MRPB, 5.
136. MRPB, 28.
137. MRPB, 28.
138. MRPB, 28.

4. REVOLUTIONARY LINEAGES OF DALIT LITERATURE, 1950–1972

1. Shaw, *The Making of Navi Mumbai*, 91.
2. Shaw, *The Making of Navi Mumbai*, 93.
3. Shaw, *The Making of Navi Mumbai*, 191.
4. Shaw, *The Making of Navi Mumbai*, 261.
5. Kundu, *In the Name of the Urban Poor*, 159.
6. Weinstein, *The Durable Slum*, 63–63.
7. Weinstein, *The Durable Slum*.
8. The region is a spatial unit that spans subnational and multinational formations
   and is produced by political, institutional, and cultural processes. Sivaramakrishnan and Agarwal, "Regional Modernities in Stories and Practices of Development,"
   14.
9. Committee on Untouchability, Economic and Educational Development of the
   Scheduled Castes and L. Elayaperumal, *Report of the Committee on Untouchability*.
10. Dhasal, *Dalit Panther*, 51.
11. Dhasal, "Nimita 15 August," in *Golpitha*, 72.
12. Sathe, "Mumbaicha girnikamgar," in *Anna Bhau Sathe nivadak vangmay*, 44.
13. S. D., "Children of God Turn Panthers."
14. Dangle, *Dalit vidroh*, 36–38.
15. Interview with J. V. Pawar, April 7, 2009.
16. Dhasal, *Dalit Panther*, 343.
17. Dhasal, *Dalit Panther*, 321.
18. Moon and Pawar, *Amhihi Itihas Ghadavla*, 96–97.
19. Chitre, *An Anthology of Marathi Poetry*, 1–3. See also Dharwadker, *The Future of the
    Past*.
20. Nerlekar, *Bombay Modern*, 21.
21. Tharu and Satyanarayana, "Dalit Writing," 11. The authors consider the annihila-
    tion of caste and the embrace of a caste-based identity as a dialectic.
22. Tharu and Satyanarayana, "Dalit Writing," 9–10.
23. See Wankhede, "Dalit Sahityachya Prerana," 59–67.
24. Wankhede et al., "Maharashtratil Aaj Udayache Samskrutik Sangharsh ani Vang-
    mayin Samasya," 61.
25. Gokhale, *From Concession to Confrontation*.

26. Lefebvre, *Introduction to Modernity*, 1–2.

27. Kharat, *Dalit Vangmay*, 6.

28. Dangle, "Nivedana," 1–43.

29. Suma Chitnis, *Literacy and Education Enrolment*, 54.

30. Sathe, "Hi prthvi dalitancya talahatavar tarleli ahe," 87–90.

31. Bagul, *Dalita Sahitya*, 19–20.

32. Bagul, *Jevha mi jat chorali hoti*, 44.

33. Bagul, "Dalit Sahitya Mhanje Sudavadyance Sahitya Nahi" (Dalit literature is not literature of revenge seekers), in *Dalit Sahitya*, 237.

34. Bagul, *Dalit Sahitya*, 21.

35. Bagul, *Dalit Sahitya*, 18.

36. He says that Dalit signifies revolution, it stands in for a revolution. Bagul, *Dalit Sahitya*, 20.

37. Bagul, *Dalit Sahitya*, 19.

38. De Certeau, *The Practice of Everyday Life*, 117.

39. Bagul, *Dalit Sahitya*, 15.

40. Bagul, *Dalit Sahitya*, 15.

41. Bagul, *Dalit Sahitya*, 19.

42. Bagul, *Dalit Sahitya*, 19.

43. Zelliot, *From Untouchable to Dalit*; Ganguly, *Caste, Colonialism and Counter Modernity*, 178.

44. Beltz, *Mahar, Buddhist, and Dalit*, 15–17.

45. Zelliot, *From Untouchable to Dalit*, 259.

46. Zelliot, *From Untouchable to Dalit*, 259.

47. Zelliot, *From Untouchable to Dalit*, 259.

48. Jadhav, *Untouchables*, 214.

49. Jadhav, *Untouchables*, 214.

50. Jadhav, *Untouchables*, 216.

51. Jadhav, *Untouchables*, 215.

52. Jadhav, *Untouchables*, 217.

53. Jadhav, *Untouchables*, 226.

54. Moon and Pawar, *Amhihi Itihasa Ghadavala*, 117.

55. See Bagul's foreword to Arun Kamble's collection of poems in Bagul, *Dalit Sahitya*, 153.

56. Wankhede, *Dalitance vidrohi vanngmay*, 2.

57. Wankhede, *Dalitance vidrohi vanngmay*, 3.

58. Wankhede, *Dalitance vidrohi vanngmay*, 4.

59. Wankhede, "Dalitanon vidrohi vangmay liha," 1–5.

60. Wankhede, "Dalitanon vidrohi vangmay liha,"5.

61. Wankhede, "Dalitanon vidrohi vangmay liha,"5.

62. The other founder of *Asmitadarsh* was Dr. Gangadhar Pantawane.

63. Welfare of the Dalit castes in the five-year plans drafted by the Bombay state included promises of building hostels for Dalit students and housing for conservancy staff in the city, as well as plans to support co-operative societies of the backward castes.

64. See Wankhede, "Bhumika."

NOTES TO CHAPTER 5   199

65. Wankhede et al., "Maharashtratil Aaj Udayache Samskrutik Sangharsh ani Vang-mayin Samasya."

66. Wankhede et al., "Maharashtratil Aaj Udayache Samskrutik Sangharsh ani Vang-mayin Samasya," 59.

67. Wankhede et al., "Maharashtratil Aaj Udayache Samskrutik Sangharsh ani Vang-mayin Samasya," 57.

68. For an excellent analysis of the global 1960s, see Connery, "The End of the Sixties."

69. Chitre, "Introduction," 28.

70. Murugkar, *Dalit Panther Movement of Maharashtra*, 49.

71. Dangle, *Dalit vidroh*, 92.

72. As quoted in S. D., "Children of God Turn Panthers," 1398.

73. Connery, "The End of the Sixties," 188.

74. Dangle, "Nivedan," 20.

75. Dangle, "Nivedan," 19–20.

76. Dangle, "Nivedan," 21.

77. Deshpande, "Fashioning a Postcolonial Discipline."

78. Deshpande, "Fashioning a Postcolonial Discipline."

79. Wankhede et al., "Maharashtratil Aaj Udayache Samskrutik Sangharsh ani Vang-mayin Samasya," 47–64.

80. Anand and Rademacher, "Housing in the Urban Age," 1752. Also Chatterjee, *The Politics of the Governed.*

81. Weinstein, *The Durable Slum*, 64.

82. Kundu, *In the Name of the Urban Poor*, 159.

83. Murugkar, *Dalit Panther Movement of Maharashtra*, 138.

5. SLUMS, SEX, AND THE FIELD OF POWER, 1960–1984

Translations in this chapter are my own.

1. Phadke, *Politics and Language*, 2

2. Hansen, *Violence in Urban India*, 41.

3. For an account that lays out the role of caste and class in the SMS, see Lele, "Caste, Class, and Dominance," 165–69; Phadke, *Politics and Language*, 44–45; Hansen, *Violence in Urban India*, 42–43.

4. Phadke, *Politics and Language*, 256.

5. Phadke, *Politics and Language*, 41; Rao, *The Caste Question*, 185–86.

6. Bagul, "Svagat," in *Jevha mi jat chorali hoti*, 133.

7. Rajadhyaksha, *Maharashtra State Board for Literature and Culture*, 1–3.

8. Rajadhyaksha, *Maharashtra State Board for Literature and Culture*, 1.

9. Times of India, "Marathi Encyclopedia Gets Poor Response," *Times of India*, Jan. 2, 1984; Rajadhyaksha, *Maharashtra State Board for Literature and Culture*, 8.

10. See Wankhede, "Bhumika," 7.

11. See Joshi, "Don Shabd."

12. Shripad Mate, a non-Dalit writer, had published *Upekshitanche antarang* in 1941.

13. Kirvale, *Samagra lekhak*, 23.

14. This is Krishna Kirvale's list. Kirvale, *Samagra lekhak*, 26.

15. Kirvale, *Samagra lekhak*, 19.
16. Moon and Pawar, *Amhihi itihas ghadavla*, 96–103.
17. Jaaware, "Eating, and Eating with, the Dalit."
18. Manto, *Bombay Stories*.
19. Wankhede, "Bandachya yashasvitesathi atmashodh avashyak" (It's important to do some soul searching for a successful rebellion), in *Dalit Sahitya*, 68–69.
20. Bagul, *Dalit Sahitya*, 200–201.
21. Bagul, *Dalit Sahitya*, 205.
22. Bagul, "Gund," in *Jevha mi jat chorali hoti*, 30.
23. Bagul, *Dalit Sahitya*, 6–10
24. Bagul, *Dalit Sahitya*, 205.
25. Bagul, *Jevha mi jat chorali hoti*, 136.
26. Bagul uses the term *Gangeta dumbanara*, or splashing about in the river Ganga, 118.
27. Bagul, *Jevha mi jat chorali hoti*, 110–11.
28. See Anjaria, *The Slow Boil*, 40.
29. Bagul, "Spardha," in *Jevha mi jat chorali hoti*, 93.
30. Bagul, "Svagat," in *Jevha mi jat chorali hoti*, 152.
31. On the importance of violence to maintaining the social boundaries of caste, see Mendelsohn and Vicziany, *The Untouchables*; Menon, *The Blindness of Insight*; and Rao, *The Caste Question*.
32. Sewell, *Logics of History*, 146.
33. Bagul, "Svagat," in *Jevha mi jat chorali hoti*, 148.
34. Bagul, "Svagat," in *Jevha mi jat chorali hoti*, 148.
35. Bagul, "Svagat," in *Jevha mi jat chorali hoti*, 148.
36. Bagul, "Svagat," in *Jevha mi jat chorali hoti*, 141.
37. Bagul, "Svagat," in *Jevha mi jat chorali hoti*, 141.
38. Bagul, "Svagat," in *Jevha mi jat chorali hoti*, 151.
39. Bagul, "Saktamajuri" (Hard labor), in *Maran swast hot ahe*, 15.
40. Bagul, "Mavali," in *Maran swast hot ahe*, 78
41. The Maratha caste is higher than Dalits in the caste hierarchy and was a mostly agrarian caste of landholders even as the size of their landholding varied.
42. Butchering was an occupation available to outcasts, either Muslims or untouchables.
43. Therefore, Bagul considers Dalit Sahitya to be the literature of humans. He wants his readers to consider what happens with the loss of humanity.
44. Bagul, "Dalit Sahitya mhanje sudvadyancha sahitya nahi," 223.
45. See Wankhede, "Bhumika," 4.
46. See Marx, *Theses on Feuerbach*, 143–45.
47. Bagul, *Dalit Sahitya*, 244.
48. Bagul, *Dalit Sahitya*, 245.
49. Bagul, *Dalit Sahitya*, 246.
50. See J. V. Pawar, "Dalit Pantharchi Sthapna . . . ," in *Dalit Panther*, ed. Dhasal, 29–30.
51. Dhasal, *Dalit Panther*, 32.
52. See Pawar, "Dalit Pantharchi Sthapna . . . ," in *Dalit Panther*, ed. Dhasal, 33–36.
53. Khairmode, *Bhartiya Ghataneche Shilpakar*, 2:61.

54. Chitre, "Poetry of the Scum of the Earth," in Dhasal, *Namdeo Dhasal*, 22.

55. Chitre, "Introduction," 23.

56. Dhasal, *Golpitha*, 1. Chitre translated *sanatani* as "orthodox." This is an apt translation too. I prefer "everlasting" because it accentuates the difficulty of moving beyond pity.

57. Dhasal, *Golpitha*, 2.

58. Chitre has translated the poem as "Who Has Sheared and Enclosed People in a Glass Paperweight?," in Dhasal, *Namdeo Dhasal*, 54. I have referred to the published translation but have generally relied on my translation for analysis.

59. Dhasal, *Golpitha*, 31.

60. Dhasal, *Golpitha*, 30–32.

61. Dhasal, *Golpitha*, 32.

62. Dhasal, "By the Side of the Crucifix," in *Namdeo Dhasal*, 52.

63. Dhasal, *Golpitha*, 73.

64. Dhasal, *Golpitha*, 56.

65. Dhasal, *Golpitha*, 57.

66. Dhasal, *Golpitha*, 59.

67. Dhasal, *Golpitha*, 60.

68. Dhasal, *Golpitha*, 7.

69. He says, "Jyaana aaplya gandikhalalaca andhara kalata nahin" (Those who cannot understand the darkness underneath their arse). Dhasal, *Golpitha*, 7.

70. Dhasal, *Golpitha*, 7.

71. Chitre, "Namdeo's Mumbai," 160.

72. Tendulkar, "Prastavana," 5.

73. Tendulkar, "Prastavana," 5–6.

74. Tendulkar, "Prastavana," 6.

75. Tendulkar, "Prastavana," 7.

76. Tendulkar, "Prastavana," 7

77. Tendulkar, "Prastavana," 7.

78. Tendulkar, "Prastavana," 8.

79. Tendulkar, "Prastavana," 8–9.

80. Tendulkar, "Prastavana," 11.

81. In fact, another saint poet, Chokhamela, was seen as an Uncle Tom by many Dalit writers. See Gokhale, "The Evolution of a Counter Ideology," 262.

82. Dilip Chitre, "Poetry of the Scum of the Earth," in Dhasal, *Namdeo Dhasal*, 18.

83. Chitre, "Namdeo's Mumbai," 162.

84. Hansen, *Violence in Urban India*, 48.

85. Dhasal, *Dalit Panther*, 61

86. Dhasal, *Dalit Panther*, 62

87. Pawar, *Mumbaichya tarunancha shauryacha alekha*, 3–5.

88. Dhasal, *Dalit Panther*, 95.

89. Dhasal, *Dalit Panther*, 67.

90. Dhasal, "Namdeo on Namdeo," in *Dalit Panther*, 167–68.

91. Chitre, "Poetry of the Scum of the Earth," in Dhasal, *Namdeo Dhasal*, 19–20.

92. Dhasal, *Dalit Panther*, 66.

93. Dhasal, *Dalit Panther*, 176.

94. Dhasal, *Amchya itihasatila ek apariharya patra, priyadarshini.*

95. Lele, "Caste, Class, and Dominance," 191.

96. Murugkar, *Dalit Panther Movement of Maharashtra*, 161.

97. Murugkar, *Dalit Panther Movement of Maharashtra*, 163.

98. Lele, "Caste, Class, and Dominance,"204.

99. Gokhale, "The Evolution of a Counter Ideology," 269.

100. Burra, "Towards a Pro-Poor Framework for Slum Upgrading in Mumbai, India," 70.

101. YUVA, *Our Home Is a Slum*, iv.

102. High Power Steering Group for Slums and Dilapidated Housing, *Report of the High Power Steering Group for Slums and Dilapidated Houses* (henceforth HPSGFSADH).

103. HPSGFSADH, 33.

104. HPSGFSADH, 48.

105. HPSGFSADH, 33.

106. Burra, "Towards a Pro-Poor Framework for Slum Upgrading in Mumbai, India," 68.

CONCLUSION

1. Babu, *Death of an Industrial City*, 1.

2. "Four Are Killed in Bombay Riots Set Off by Rebellion of Policemen," *New York Times*, August 19, 1982.

3. "Four Are Killed in Bombay Riots."

4. Chandavarkar, "From Neighbourhood to Nation," 67.

5. D'Monte, *Ripping the Fabric*, 4.

6. Ranjit Hoskote, "Their Journey from Ambedkar to Thackeray," *The Hindu*, March 29, 2004.

7. Waghmore, *Civility against Caste*, 36.

8. On symbolic violence as the continued stigmatization of Dalits, see Rao, *The Caste Question*, 25.

9. Bhavika Jain, "62% of Mumbai Lives in Slums," *Hindustan Times*, October 17, 2010.

10. Anvita Singh, "Bombay 70 Review: Meet Naved Shaikh, the Original 'Gully Boy,'" *Indian Express*, February 11, 2019.

BIBLIOGRAPHY

ARCHIVES AND PRIVATE COLLECTIONS

British Library, India Office Records

Government of Bombay, Political Department Proceedings 1900–1945

Government of Bombay, Public and Judicial Department 1900–1945

Maharashtra State Archives, Mumbai

Government of Bombay, Home Department (Political) 1896–1940

Government of Bombay, Home Department (Special Proceedings) 1900–1938

Government of Bombay, Political and Services Department 1930–35

Government of Bombay, Public Works Department 1860–1921

Ramesh Shinde Collection, Mumbai

GOVERNMENT PUBLICATIONS

Act of Parliament Relating to the City of Glasgow Improvement Trust. Glasgow: Robert Maclehose, 1894.

Advisory Committee on the Industrial Housing Scheme. *Report of the Special Advisory Committee on the Industrial Housing Scheme.* Bombay: Government Central Press, 1927. [Cited as ACOIHS]

Bombay City and Suburbs Post-War Development Committee. Preliminary Report of the Development of Suburbs and Town Planning Panel. Bombay: Government Central Press, 1946. [Cited as BCASPWDC]

Census of India, 1901. Vol. 11. Bombay, 1901.

Census of India 1911. Vol. 8. Bombay, 1912.

Census of India 1921. Vol. 9. Bombay, 1922.

Census of India 1931. Vol. 8. Bombay, 1933.

Census of India 1931. Vol. 9. Bombay, 1933.

City of Bombay Improvement Trust. *Administration Report for the Year Ending 31ˢᵗ March 1912.* Bombay: Times Press, 1912. [Cited as COBITAR]

———. *Proceedings of the Improvements Committee and the Board, 1929–30.* Bombay: Karnataka Printing, n.d.

Committee on Untouchability, Economic and Educational Development of the Scheduled Castes and L. Elayaperumal. *Report of the Committee on Untouchability,*

Economic and Educational Development of the Scheduled Castes and Connected Document. New Delhi: Department of Social Welfare, 1969.

Depressed Classes and Aboriginal Tribes Committee. *Report of the Depressed Classes and Aboriginal Tribes Committee of the Bombay Presidency.* Bombay: Government Central Press, 1930.

Government of Bombay. *Gazetteer of Bombay City and Island.* 3 vols. Bombay: Times Press, 1910.

———. *Report of the Scavengers' Living Conditions Enquiry Committee State of Bombay.* Bombay: Government Printing, Publications and Stationery, 1958.

Greater Bombay Scheme Committee. *The Greater Bombay Scheme: Report of the Housing Panel.* Bombay: Municipal Printing Press, 1946. [Cited as GBSC]

High Power Steering Group for Slums and Dilapidated Housing. *Report of the High Power Steering Group for Slums and Dilapidated Houses: Appointed by the Government of Maharashtra.* Bombay: High Power Steering Group, 1981. [Cited as HPSGFSADH]

Indian Industrial Commission. *Minutes of Evidence 1916–1918: Volume IV, Bombay.* Calcutta: Superintendent Government Printing, 1918.

Industrial Housing Sub-Committee, Government of India. *Report of the Industrial Housing Sub-Committee of the Standing Labour Committee.* Delhi: Indian Press, 1946.

Metropolitan Regional Planning Board. *Strategy for Bombay Metropolitan Region: A Summary of Volumes I and II of the Report of the Draft Regional Plan 1970–1991.* Bombay: Bombay Metropolitan Regional Planning Board, 1970. [Cited as MRPB]

Modak, N. V., and A. Mayer. *An Outline of the Master Plan for Greater Bombay.* Bombay: Bombay Municipal Printing Press, 1948.

Municipal Corporation of Greater Bombay. *Report on the Development Plan for Greater Bombay.* Bombay: Government Central Press, 1964. [Cited as MCOGB]

Public Health Department. Health Officer's Reports, Bombay Municipality, 1879–1930. British Library, Oriental Collections. [Cited as HORBM]

Rajadhyaksha, D. Y. *Maharashtra State Board for Literature and Culture: Objectives, Programmes, Progress.* Bombay: Government of Maharashtra, 1976.

Rent Enquiry Committee. *Report of the Rent Inquiry Committee.* 2 vols. Bombay: Government Central Press, 1939.

Royal Commission on Labour in India. *Report of the Royal Commission on Labour in India.* London, 1931.

Royal Commission on the Distribution of the Industrial Population. *Town and Country Planning as Portrayed in the Reports of the Barlow Commission and the Scott and Uthwatt Committees.* London: Staples and Staples, 1943.

COURT CASES

Baburao Shantaram More v. Bombay Housing Board. https://indiankanoon.org/doc /152211. Accessed September 28, 2017.

Babu Barkya Thakur v. the State of Bombay and Others. https://indiankanoon.org/doc /463201. Accessed October 6, 2017.

INTERVIEWS

Adhikari, Gangadhar. Interviewed by Hari Dev Sharma on March 1, 1977. Nehru Memorial Museum and Library Oral History Project.

Dangle, Arjun. May 13, 2009, Mumbai.

Dhasal, Namdeo. May 15, 2009, Mumbai.

Haralkar, Ramesh. April 1, 2009, Mumbai.

Pawar, J. V. March 25 and April 7, 2009, Mumbai.

NEWSPAPERS AND PERIODICALS

Asmita (Marathi)
Bombay Chronicle
The Hindu
Hindustan Times
Indian Express
Labour Gazette (Bombay), *1921–1940*
Loksatta (Marathi)
National Front
New York Times
Outlook India
Samata (Marathi)
Servants of India
Times of India

SECONDARY SOURCES

Achalkhamb, Rustum. *Tamasha lokrangbhumi: Sankalpna, swarup, ani prayogikta.* Pune: Sugava Prakashan, 2006.

Acworth, Harry. *History of the Drainage and Sewerage of Bombay.* London: William Clowes and Son, 1896.

Adhikari, Gangadhar, ed. *Documents of the History of the Communist Party of India,* vol. 3A, *1926.* New Delhi: People's Publishing House, 1978.

——, ed. *Documents of the History of the Communist Party of India,* vol. 3B, *1927.* New Delhi: People's Publishing House, 1979.

——. "Introduction." In *Documents of the History of the Communist Party of India,* vol. 3A, *1926,* edited by Gangadhar Adhikari. New Delhi: People's Publishing House, 1978.

Ahmad, Muzaffar. *Communists Challenge Imperialism from the Dock.* Calcutta: National Book Agency, 1967.

All India Trade Union Congress. *All India Trade Union Congress Report: Twenty-Third Session, Bombay, 1949.* Bombay: AITUC, 1949.

Ambedkar, B. R. *India and Communism.* New Delhi: Leftword Books, 2017.

——. "On the Draft Constitution." In *Thus Spoke Ambedkar,* vol. 1, *A Stake in the Nation,* edited by Bhagwan Das. New Delhi: Navayana, 2010.

——. *Scheme of a Social Centre for the Depressed Classes to Be Started in Bombay.* India Office Records.

Anand, Nikhil, and Anne Rademacher. "Housing in the Urban Age: Inequality and Aspiration in Mumbai." *Antipode* 43 (2011): 1748–72.

Anjaria, Jonathan Shapiro. *The Slow Boil: Street Food, Rights, and Public Space in Mumbai.* Stanford, CA: Stanford University Press, 2016.

Appadurai, Arjun. "Numbers in the Colonial Imagination." In *Orientalism and the Postcolonial Predicament: Perspectives from South Asia,* edited by Peter Van Der Veer and Carol Beckenridge. Philadelphia: University of Pennsylvania Press, 1993.

Arnold, David. "The Self and the Cell: Indian Prison Narratives as Life Histories." In *Telling Lives in India, Biography, Autobiography, Life History,* edited by David Arnold and S. Blackburn. New Delhi: Permanent Black, 2004.

Babu, Hemant. *Death of an Industrial City: Testimonies of Life around the Bombay Textile Strike of 1982.* Noida: V. V. Giri National Labor Institute, 2002.

Bagul, Baburao. *Dalit Sahitya: Aajche krantivijnana.* Nashik: Disha Prakashana, 2004.

———. "Dalit Sahitya mhanje sudvadyancha sahitya nahi." In *Dalit Sahitya: Ek abhyas,* edited by Arjun Dangle. Mumbai: Maharashtra Rajya Sahitya-Samskriti Mandala, 1978.

———. *Jevha mi jat chorali hoti* (When I concealed my caste). Mumbai: Abhinava Prakasana, 1976.

———. *Maran swast hot ahe* (Death is becoming cheap). Mumbai: Lokvangmay Griha, 2008.

———. *Suda.* Mumbai: Abhinav Prakashan, 1970.

Banaji, Jairus. *Theory as History: Essays on Modes of Production and Exploitation.* Chicago: Haymarket Books, 2011.

Basu, Jyoti, et al., eds. *Documents of the Communist Movement in India,* vol. 3, *1929–1938.* Calcutta: National Book Agency, 1997.

Batley, Claude. *Bombay Houses and Homes.* Bombay: National Information and Publications, 1949.

Bayly, Susan. *Caste, Society and Politics in India from the Eighteenth Century to the Modern Age.* Cambridge: Cambridge University Press, 1999.

Beckert, Sven. *Empire of Cotton: A Global History.* New York: Alfred A. Knopf, 2015.

Beltz, Johannes. *Mahar, Buddhist, and Dalit: Religious Conversion and Socio-Political Emancipation.* New Delhi: Manohar: 2005.

Benjamin, Walter. *Illuminations: Essays and Reflections.* New York: Schocken Books, 1969.

Bhan, Gautam. *In the Public's Interest: Evictions, Citizenship, and Inequality in Contemporary Delhi.* Athens: University of Georgia Press, 2016.

Breman, Jan. *Outcast Labour in Asia: Circulation and Informalization of the Workforce at the Bottom of the Economy.* New Delhi: Oxford University Press, 2010.

Burnett-Hurst, A. R. *Labour and Housing in Bombay: A Study in the Economic Conditions of the Wage Earning Classes in Bombay.* London: P. S. King, 1925.

Burra, Sundar. "Towards a Pro-Poor Framework for Slum Upgrading in Mumbai, India." *Environment and Urbanization* 17 (2005): 67–88.

de Certeau, Michel. *The Practice of Everyday Life.* Berkeley: University of California Press, 1988.

Chairez-Garza, J. F. "Touching Space: Ambedkar on the Spatial Features of Untouchability." *Contemporary South Asia* 22 (2014): 37–50.

Chakrabarty, Dipesh. *Provincializing Europe: Postcolonial Thought and Historical Difference*. Princeton, NJ: Princeton University Press, 2000.

———. *Rethinking Working-Class History: Bengal 1890–1940*. Princeton, NJ: Princeton University Press, 1989.

Chakravarti, Uma. *Gendering Caste through a Feminist Lens*. Calcutta: Stree, 2009.

Chandavarkar, Rajnarayan. "From Neighborhood to Nation: The Rise and Fall of the Left in Bombay's Girangaon in the Twentieth Century." In *One Hundred Years, One Hundred Voices: The Millworkers of Girangaon: An Oral History*, edited by Meena Menon and Neera Adarkar. Calcutta: Seagull Books, 2004.

———. *History, Culture, and the Indian City: Essays*. Cambridge: Cambridge University Press, 2009.

———. *Imperial Power and Popular Politics: Class, Resistance, and the State in India c. 1850–1950*. Cambridge: Cambridge University Press, 1998.

———. "The Making of the Working Class: E. P. Thompson and Indian History." In *Mapping Subaltern Studies and the Postcolonial*, edited by Vinayak Chaturvedi. London: Verso Books, 2000.

———. *The Origins of Industrial Capitalism in India: Business Strategies and the Working Classes in Bombay, 1900–1940*. Cambridge: Cambridge University Press, 1994.

Chandra, Kanchan. *Why Ethnic Parties Succeed: Patronage and Ethnic Headcounts in India*. Cambridge: Cambridge University Press, 2004.

Chari, Sharad. *Fraternal Capital: Peasant Workers, Self-Made Men, and Globalization in Provincial India*. Stanford, CA: Stanford University Press, 2004.

Charlesworth, Neil. *Peasants and Imperial Rule: Agriculture and Agrarian Society in the Bombay Presidency 1850–1935*. Cambridge: Cambridge University Press, 1985.

Chatterjee, Partha. *The Politics of the Governed: Reflections on Popular Politics in Most of the World*. New York: Columbia University Press, 2004.

Chatterjee, Piya. *A Time for Tea: Women, Labor, and Post/Colonial Politics on an Indian Plantation*. Durham, NC: Duke University Press, 2001.

Chattopadhyay, Suchetana. *An Early Communist: Muzaffar Ahmad in Calcutta 1913–1929*. New Delhi: Tulika Books, 2012.

Chhabria, Sheetal. *Making the Modern Slum: The Power of Capital in Colonial Bombay*. Seattle: University of Washington Press, 2019.

Chibber, Vivek. *Postcolonial Theory and the Specter of Capital*. London: Verso, 2013.

Chitnis, Suma. *Literacy and Education Enrolment among the Scheduled Castes of Maharashtra*. Bombay: Tata Institute of Social Sciences, 1974.

Chitre, Dilip, ed. *An Anthology of Marathi Poetry, 1945–65*. Bombay: Nirmal Sadanand Publishers, 1967.

———. "Introduction." In Namdeo Dhasal, *Namdeo Dhasal: Poet of the Underworld, Poems 1972–2006*. Chennai: Navayana, 2007.

———. "Namdeo's Mumbai." In Namdeo Dhasal, *Namdeo Dhasal: Poet of the Underworld, Poems 1972–2006*. Chennai: Navayana, 2007.

Cholia, Rasiklal P. *Dock Labourers in Bombay*. Bombay: Longmans, Green, 1941.

Cohn, Bernard. "Notes on the History of the Study of Indian Society and Culture."
In *The Bernard Cohn Omnibus*, 136–71. New Delhi: Oxford University Press, 2004.

Conlon, Frank. *A Caste in a Changing World: The Chitrapur Saraswat Brahmans
1700–1935.* Berkeley: University of California Press, 1971.

———. "Industrialization and the Housing Problem in Bombay, 1850–1940." In
Changing South Asia, vol. 4, *Economy and Society*, edited by Kenneth Ballhatchet
and David Taylor. London: School of Oriental and African Studies, 1984.

Connery, Christopher. "The End of the Sixties." *Boundary 2* 36 (2009): 183–210.

Dange, Shripad Amrit. *India from Primitive Communism to Slavery: A Marxist Study of
Ancient History in Outline.* New Delhi: People's Publishing House, 1955.

———. *Selected Writings.* Vol. 1. Bombay: Lok Vangmaya Griha, 1974.

———. *Selected Writings.* Vol. 2. Bombay: Lok Vangmaya Griha, 1977.

Dangle, Arjun. *Dalit vidroh* (Dalit revolt). Mumbai: Lokavangmaya Gruha, 2007.

———. "Nivedana." In *Dalit Sahitya: Ek abhyas*, edited by Arjun Dangle. Mumbai:
Maharashtra Rajya Sahitya-Samskriti Mandala, 1978.

Das, P. K. "Slum: The Continuing Struggle for Housing." In *Bombay and Mumbai: The
City in Transition*, edited by Sujata Patel and J. Masselos. New Delhi: Oxford
University Press, 2007.

Desai, A. R., and S. Dighe, eds. *Labour Movement in India, 1923–1927.* Delhi: Pragati
Publications, 2004.

Desai, Shruti A. *Law relating to Slum in Maharashtra.* Mumbai: Snow White Publication, 2009.

Deshpande, G. P., ed. *Selected Writings of Jotirao Phule.* Delhi: LeftWord Books, 2010.

Deshpande, Satish. "Caste and Castelessness: Towards a Biography of the General
Category." In *The Problem of Caste*, edited by Satish Deshpande. Hyderabad: Orient
BlackSwan, 2015.

———. "Fashioning a Postcolonial Discipline: M. N. Srinivas and Indian Sociology." In
Anthropology in the East: Founders of Indian Sociology and Anthropology, edited by
Patricia Uberoi, N. Sundar, and S. Deshpande. New Delhi: Permanent Black, 2012.

Dharwadker, Vinay. *The Future of the Past: Modernity, Modern Poetry, and the
Transformation of Two Indian Traditions.* 2 vols. Chicago: University of Chicago,
1989.

Dhasal, Namdeo. *Amchya itihasatila ek apariharya patra, Priyadarshini* (An inevitable
part of our history, Priyadarshini). Mumbai: Dalit Panther Prakashan, 1976.

———. *Dalit Panther: Ek sangharsh* (Dalit panther: A struggle). Mumbai: Bhashya
Prakashan, 2014.

———. *Golpitha.* Pune: Nilakantha Prakashan, 1975.

———. *Namdeo Dhasal: Poet of the Underworld.* Translated by Dilip Chitre. Chennai:
Navayana, 2007.

Dickey, Sara. *Living Class in Urban India.* Ranikhet: Permanent Black, 2016.

Dirks, Nicholas. *Castes of Mind: Colonialism and the Making of Modern India.* Delhi:
Permanent Black, 2003.

Dirlik, Arif. *The Origins of Chinese Communism.* New York: Oxford University Press,
1989.

D'Monte, Darryl. *Ripping the Fabric: The Decline of Mumbai and Its Mills*. New Delhi: Oxford University Press, 2002.

Dossal, Mariam. *Imperial Designs and Indian Realities: The Planning of Bombay City*. Delhi: Oxford University Press, 1991.

———. "A Master Plan for the City: Looking at the Past." *Economic and Political Weekly* 40 (2005): 3897–3900.

———. *Theatre of Conflict, City of Hopes: Mumbai, 1660 to Present Times*. New Delhi: Oxford University Press, 2010.

Dutt, Romesh. *The Economic History of India in the Victorian Age, 1837–1900*. Delhi: Ministry of Information and Broadcasting, 1960.

Dwivedi, Sharda, and Rahul Mehrotra. *Bombay: The Cities Within*. Bombay: India Book House, 1995.

Edwardes, S. M. *The Rise of Bombay: A Retrospect*. Bombay: Times of India Press, 1902.

Engels, Friedrich. *The Housing Question*. New York: International Publishers, 1935.

Fernandes, Leela. *Producing Workers: The Politics of Gender, Class, and Culture in the Calcutta Jute Mills*. Philadelphia: University of Pennsylvania Press, 1997.

Fernandes, Naresh. *City Adrift: A Short Biography of Bombay*. Aleph: New Delhi, 2013.

Ganguly, Debjani. *Caste, Colonialism and Counter Modernity: Notes on Postcolonial Hermeneutics of Caste*. London: Routledge, 2005.

Ghurye, G. S. *Caste and Race in India*. Bombay: Popular Prakashan, 2008.

Gidwani, Vinay. *Capital, Interrupted: Agrarian Development and the Politics of Work in India*. Minneapolis: University of Minnesota Press, 2008.

Gidwani, Vinay, and Rajyashree N. Reddy. "The Afterlives of Waste: Notes from India for a Minor History of Capitalist Surplus." *Antipode* 43, no. 5 (2011): 1625–58. doi: 10.1111/j.1467-8330.2011.00902.

Gokhale, Jayashree. "The Evolution of a Counter Ideology: Dalit Consciousness in Maharashtra." In *Dominance and State Power in Modern India: Decline of a Social Order*, vol. 2, edited by Francine R. Frankel and M. S. A. Rao. Delhi: Oxford University Press, 1990.

———. *From Concession to Confrontation: The Politics of an Indian Untouchable Community*. Bombay: Popular Prakashan, 1993.

Gooptu, Nandini. *The Politics of the Urban Poor in Early Twentieth Century India*. Cambridge: Cambridge University Press, 2001.

Guha, Ranajit. *Dominance without Hegemony: History and Power in Colonial India*. Cambridge, MA: Harvard University Press, 1997.

Guha, Sumit. *The Agrarian Economy of the Bombay Deccan, 1818–1941*. Delhi: Oxford University Press, 1985.

———. *Beyond Caste: Identity and Power in South Asia Past and Present*. Ranikhet: Permanent Black, 2016.

———. "Transitions and Translations: Regional Power and Vernacular Identity in the Dakhan, 1500–1800." *Comparative Studies of South Asia, Africa, and the Middle East* 24 (2004): 23–31.

Gupta, Charu. *The Gender of Caste: Representing Dalits in Print*. Ranikhet: Permanent Black, 2016.

Gupta, Sobhanlal Dutt, ed. *A Documented History of the Communist Movement in India 1923–1925*. New Delhi: Sunrise Publications, 2007.

Gurav, Baburao. *Annabhau Sathe: Samajvichar ani Sahityavivechan*. Mumbai: Lokvangmaya Gruha, 1999.

Guru, Gopal. "The Indian Nation in Its Egalitarian Conception." In *Dalit Studies*, edited by Ramnarayan Rawat and K. Satyanarayan. Durham, NC: Duke University Press, 2016.

Guru, Gopal, and Sundar Sarrukai. *The Cracked Mirror: An Indian Debate on Experience and Theory*. New Delhi: Oxford University Press, 2013.

Hadap, Vitthal Vaman, ed. *Majurachi bayko* (The worker's wife). Pune: Adarsh Vangmay Prakashan, 1933.

Haithcox. John P. *Communism and Nationalism in India: M. N. Roy and Comintern Policy 1920–1939*. Princeton, NJ: Princeton University Press, 1971.

Hansen, Thomas Blom. *Violence in Urban India: Identity Politics, Mumbai, and the Postcolonial City*. Delhi: Permanent Black, 2002.

Harootunian, Harry. *Marx after Marx: History and Time in the Expansion of Capitalism*. New York: Columbia University Press, 2015.

Harris, Joseph. *The African Presence in Asia: The Consequences of the East African Slave Trade*. Evanston, IL: Northwestern University Press, 1971.

Harvey, David. *The Condition of Postmodernity: An Enquiry into the Origins of Cultural Change*. Cambridge: Blackwell Publishers, 1995.

Hazareesingh, Sandip. *The Colonial City and the Challenge of Modernity: Urban Hegemonies and Civic Contestations in Bombay City, 1900–1925*. Hyderabad: Orient Longman, 2007.

History Commission of the Central Committee of the Communist Party of India (Marxist). *History of the Communist Movement in India*, vol. 1, *The Formative Years, 1920–1933*. New Delhi: CPI (M) Publications, 2005.

Hobsbawm, Eric J. "The Fortunes of Marx's and Engels' Writings in Hobsbawm." In *The History of Marxism*, vol. 1, *Marxism in Marx's Day*, edited by Eric Hobsbawm. Bloomington: Indiana University Press, 1982.

Indian Institute of Public Administration. *Problems of Urban Housing*. Bombay: Popular Book Depot, 1960.

Iyer, L. K. A. *The Mysore Tribes and Castes*. 5 vols. Mysore: Mysore University, 1928–36.

Jaaware, Aniket. "Eating, and Eating with, the Dalit: A Reconsideration Touching upon Marathi Poetry." In *Indian Poetry: Modernism and After*, edited by K. Satchidanandan, 262–93. New Delhi: Sahitya Academy, 2001.

Jadhav, G. M. *Akhil bhartiya dalit phederation adhiveshan teesre: Svagatadhyaksache bhashan*. Mumbai: Bharat Bhushan Printing Press, 1945.

Jadhav, Narandra. *Untouchables: My Family's Triumphant Journey out of the Caste System in Modern India*. New York: Scribner, 2005.

Jaffrelot, Christophe. *Dr Ambedkar and Untouchability: Analysing and Fighting Caste*. Delhi: Permanent Black, 2005.

Jayal, Niraja Gopal. *Citizenship and Its Discontents: An Indian History*. Ranikhet: Permanent Black, 2013.

Jeurgensmeyer, Mark. *Religion as Social Vision: The Movement against Untouchability in Twentieth-Century Punjab.* Berkeley: University of California Press, 1982.

Josh, Sohan Singh. *The Great Attack: Meerut Conspiracy Case.* New Delhi: People's Publishing House, 1979.

Joshi, Chitra. *Lost Worlds: Indian Labour and Its Forgotten Histories.* London: Anthem Press, 2005.

Joshi, Heather, and Vijay Joshi. *Surplus Labour and the City: A Study of Bombay.* Delhi: Oxford University Press, 1976.

Joshi, Lakshmanshastri. "Don shabd (Two words)." In *Dalit Sahitya: Ek abhyas,* edited by Arjun Dangle. Pune: Sugava Prakashan, 1998.

Joshi, P. C., and K. Damodaran, eds. *Marx Comes to India: Earliest Biographies of Karl Marx.* Delhi: Manhohar Book Service, 1975

Kaiwar, Vasant. "The Colonial State, Capital, and Peasantry in Bombay Presidency." *Modern Asian Studies* 28 (1994): 793–832.

Kakodkar, Priyanka. "Life Gets a Move On from the Stinking Rot." *Outlook,* March 10, 2003. https://www.outlookindia.com/magazine/story/life-gets-a-move-on-from-the -stinking-rot-of-social-garbage/219317.

Kamred Lenin. Mumbai: Kamgara Vangmaya Prasaraka Mandala, 1933.

Karat, Prakash, ed. *A World to Win: Essays on the Communist Manifesto.* New Delhi: LeftWord Books, 1999.

Karmwar, Manish. "African Diaspora in India." *Diaspora Studies* 3 (2010): 69–91, doi: 10.1080/09739572.2010.10597342.

Kaviraj, Sudipta. "Filth in the Public Sphere: Concepts and Practices about Space in Calcutta." *Public Culture* 10 (1997): 83–113.

Khairmode, Changdev Bhavanrao. *Bhartiya ghataneche shilpakar: Dr Bhimrao Ramaji Ambedkar Charitra* (The architect of India's constitution: Dr. Bhimrao Ramji Ambedkar biography). 12 vols. Pune: Sugava Prakashan, 2002.

Kharat, Shankararav. *Dalita vangmay: Prerana va pravriti.* Pune: Inamadar Bandhu Prakashan, 1978.

Khilnani, Sunil. *The Idea of India.* New York: Farrar, Strauss, Giroux, 1999.

Kidambi, Prashant. *The Making of an Indian Metropolis: Colonial Governance and Public Culture in Bombay, 1890–1920.* Aldershot: Ashgate, 2007.

Kirvale, Krishna. *Samagra lekhak: Baburao Bagul.* Pune: Pratima Prakashan, 2002.

Klass, Morton. *Caste: The Emergence of the South Asia Social System.* Philadelphia: Institute for the Study of Social Issues, 1980.

Kooiman, Dick. *Bombay Textile Labour: Managers, Trade Unionists, and Officials, 1918–1939.* New Delhi: Manohar Publications, 1989.

Korde, Bajrang. *Anna Bhau Sathe.* New Delhi: Sahitya Akademi, 1999.

Kosambi, D. D. *An Introduction to the Study of Indian History.* Bombay: Popular Book Depot, 1956.

Krishna, Bhalchandra. *Overcrowding in Bombay and the Problem of Housing the Poor and Working Classes.* Bombay: Times Press, 1904.

Kulkarni, V. *Vedya mana talamalasi: Atmacaritra.* Pune: Sri Vidya Prakasana, 1989.

Kumar, Arun. "Learning to Dream: Education, Aspiration, and Working Lives in Colonial India, 1880s–1940s." PhD diss., University of Goettingen, 2017.

Kumar, Radha. "City Lives: Workers' Housing and Rent in Bombay, 1911–1947." *Economic and Political Weekly* 22, no. 30 (1987): 47–56.

Kundu, Amitabh. *In the Name of the Urban Poor: Access to Basic Amenities.* New Delhi: Sage, 1993.

Lakdawala, D. T., V. N. Kothari, J. C. Sandesara, and P. A. Nair. *Work, Wages and Well-Being in an Indian Metropolis: Economic Survey of Bombay City.* Bombay: Bombay University Press, 1963.

Lee, Joel. "Who Is the True Halalkhore? Genealogy and Ethics in Dalit Muslim Oral Traditions." *Contributions to Indian Sociology* 52, no. 1 (2018): 1–27.

Lefebvre, Henri. *Introduction to Modernity: Twelve Preludes, September 1959–May 1961.* London: Verso, 2011.

Lele, Jayant. "Caste, Class, and Dominance: Political Mobilization in Maharashtra." In *Dominance and State Power in Modern India: Decline of a Social Order,* vol. 2, edited by Francine R. Frankel and M. S. A. Rao. Delhi: Oxford University Press, 1990.

Lenin, V. I. *The State and Revolution.* London: Penguin, 1992.

Liedman, Sven-Eric. *A World to Win: The Life and Works of Karl Marx.* London: Verso, 2018.

Lieten, Georges. *Colonialism, Class and Nation: The Confrontation in Bombay around 1930.* Calcutta: K. P. Bagchi, 1984.

Lojhavski, Aleksandra. *Vasahatitil Deshansathi Treda Uniyan Chalvalicha Onama.* Mumbai: Kamgar Vanmaya Prasaraka Mandala, 1932.

Madden, David, and Peter Marcuse. *In Defense of Housing.* London: Verso, 2016.

Manjapra. Kris. *Age of Entanglement: German and Indian Intellectuals across Empire.* Cambridge, MA: Harvard University Press, 2014.

———. *M. N. Roy: Marxism and Colonial Cosmopolitanism.* New Delhi: Routledge, 2010.

Mann, Harold H. "The Mahars of a Deccan Village." In *The Social Context of Agriculture,* edited by Daniel Thorner. Bombay: Vora, 1967.

Manto, Saadat Hasan. *Bombay Stories,* Translated by Matt Reeck and Aftab Ahmad. New York: Vintage Books, 2012.

Marks, Karl, and Phredrik Engels. *Kamyunista Particha jahirnama.* Mumbai: Kamgar Vangmaya Prasaraka Mandala, 1931.

Marriott, McKim. *Caste Ranking and Community Structures in Five Regions of India and Pakistan.* Poona: Deccan College Postgraduate and Research Institute, 1965.

Marx, Karl. *Capital: A Critique of Political Economy.* Vol. 1. New York: Penguin, 1990.

———. *The German Ideology.* In *The Marx-Engels Reader,* 2d ed., edited by Robert C Tucker. New York: W. W. Norton, 1978.

———. *Theses on Feuerbach.* In *The Marx-Engels Reader,* 2d ed., edited by Robert C Tucker. New York: W. W. Norton, 1978.

Marx, Karl, and Friedrich Engels. *The Communist Manifesto.* Oxford: Oxford University Press, 1998.

Masani, R. P. *Evolution of Local Self Government in Bombay.* London: Milford, 1929.

Masselos, Jim. "Jobs and Jobbery: The Sweeper in Bombay under the Raj." *Indian Economic and Social History Review* 19 (1982): 101–39.

McAlpin, Michelle. *Subject to Famine: Food Crisis and Economic Change in Western India, 1860–1920.* Princeton, NJ: Princeton University Press, 1983.

Mehta, Aban. *The Domestic Servant Class*. Bombay: Popular Book Store, 1960.

Mendelsohn, Oliver, and Marika Vicziany. *The Untouchables: Subordination, Poverty, and the State in Modern India*. Cambridge: Cambridge University Press, 2000.

Menon, Dilip M. *The Blindness of Insight: Essays on Caste in Modern India*. New Delhi: Navayana, 2006.

———. *Caste, Nationalism, and Communism in South India, Malabar 1900–1948*. Cambridge: Cambridge University Press, 1994.

Michael, L. H. *The History of the Municipal Corporation of the City of Bombay*. Bombay: Union Press, 1902.

Mohan, P. Sanal. *Modernity of Slavery: Struggles against Caste Inequality in Colonial Kerala*. New Delhi: Oxford University Press, 2015.

Moon, Meenakshi, and Urmila Pawar. *Amhihi itihas ghadavla: Ambedkari chalvalit striyancha sahbhag* (We created history too: Women in the Ambedkarite movement). Pune: Sugava Prakashan, 2000.

More, Satyendra. *Gharancha prashna*. Pune: Magova Prakashan, 1981.

———. *Kamred Ar. Bi. More: Dalit Va Kamyunist Chalvalicha Sashakt Duva* (Comrade R. B. More: A link between the Dalit and Communist movements). Mumbai: Paryay Prakashan, 2003.

Morris, Morris D. *The Emergence of an Industrial Labor Force in India: A Study of the Bombay Cotton Mills, 1854–1947*. Bombay: Oxford University Press, 1965.

Mukul, Akshaya. *Gita Press and the Making of Hindu India*. Noida: HarperCollins Publishers India, 2015.

Murugkar, Lata. *Dalit Panther Movement of Maharashtra: A Sociological Appraisal*. Bombay: Popular Prakashan, 1981.

Nandurbarkar, D. L. *Majur-mahatma: Shri S. H. Jhabwala hyancha jivan vrutant* (Worker–great soul: The life story of S. H. Jhabwala). Mumbai: D. L. Nandurbarkar, 1929.

Naregal, Veena. *Language Politics, Elites and the Public Sphere: Western India under Colonialism*. New Delhi: Permanent Black, 2001.

Natarajan, Balmurli. *The Culturization of Caste: Identity and Inequality in a Multicultural Age*. Abingdon: Routledge, 2015.

Nerlekar, Anjali. *Bombay Modern: Arun Kolhatkar and Bilingual Literary Culture*. Evanston, IL: Northwestern University Press, 2016.

Newman, Richard. *Workers and Unions in Bombay, 1918–1929: A Study of Organizations in the Cotton Textile Industry*. Canberra: Australian National University, 1981.

Nikulin, Dmitri. *The Concept of History*. London: Bloomsbury, 2017.

O'Hanlon, Rosalind. *Caste, Conflict and Ideology: Mahatma Jotirao Phule and Low Caste Protest in Nineteenth Century Western India*. Cambridge: Cambridge University Press, 1985.

Omvedt, Gail. *Building the Ambedkar Revolution: Sambhaji Tukaram Gaikwad and the Kokan Dalits*. Mumbai: Bhashya Prakashan, 2011.

———. *Cultural Revolt in a Colonial Society: The Non-Brahman Movement in Western India*. Bombay: Scientific Socialist Education Trust, 1976.

———. *Dalits and the Democratic Revolution: Dr. Ambedkar and the Dalit Movement in Colonial India*. New Delhi: Sage Publications, 1994.

Orr, J. P. *The Need of Co-operation between Neighbours in the Development of Building Estates Part II: Established Slums*. Bombay: Premier Art Printing Works, 1915.

———. *Social Reform and Slum Reform: Part II, Bombay Past and Present*. British Library.

Overstreet, Gene, and Marshall Windmiller. *Communism in India*. Berkeley: University of California Press, 1960.

Paik, Shailaja. *Dalit Women's Education in Modern India: Double Discrimination*. New York: Routledge, 2014.

Palme Dutt, Rajani. *The Problem of India*. New York: International Publishers, 1943.

Pawar, Daya. *Baluta* (Village servant). Translated by Jerry Pinto. New Delhi: Speaking Tiger, 2015.

Pawar, Govind Pandurang. *Asprushyanche chalis saval*. Mumbai: Anand Ramchandra Sonavane, 1932.

Pawar, J. V. *Ambedkarottar Ambedkari Chalwal*. 2 vols. Mumbai: Asmita Communication, 2006.

———. *Mumbaichya tarunancha shauryacha alekha*. Mumbai: Bhai Sangare, 1974.

Phadke, Y. D. *Politics and Language*. Bombay: Himalaya Publishing House, 1979.

———. "Prastavana" (Foreword). In Manohar Kadam, *Bhartiya kamgar chalvaliche janak Narayan Meghaji Lokhande* (The father of the India labor movement Narayan Meghaji Lokhande). Mumbai: Akshar Prakashan, 2002.

Pinto, David A. *The Mayor, the Commissioner and the Metropolitan Administration*. New Delhi: Vikas Publishing, 1995.

Pollock, Sheldon. "Indian in the Vernacular Millennium: Literary Culture and Polity, 1000–1500." *Daedalus* 127 (1998): 41–74.

———. *The Language of the Gods in the World of Men: Sanskrit, Culture, and Power in Premodern India*. New Delhi: Permanent Black, 2011.

Pradhan, G. R. *Untouchable Workers of Bombay City*. Bombay: Karnatak Publishing House, 1938.

Prakash, Gyan. "The Colonial Genealogy of Society: Community and Political Modernity in India." In *The Social in Question: New Bearings in History and the Social Sciences*, edited by Patrick Joyce. London: Routledge, 2002.

———. *Emergency Chronicles: Indira Gandhi and Democracy's Turning Point*. Princeton, NJ: Princeton University Press, 2019.

———. *Mumbai Fables: A History of an Enchanted City*. Princeton, NJ: Princeton University Press, 2010.

Prashad, Vijay. *Untouchable Freedom: A Social History of a Dalit Community*. New Delhi: Oxford University Press, 2001.

Rafael, Vicente L. *Contracting Colonialism: Translation and Christian Conversion in Tagalog Society under Early Spanish Rule*. Ithaca, NY: Cornell University Press, 1988.

———. *Motherless Tongues: The Insurgency of Language amid Wars of Translation*. Durham, NC: Duke University Press, 2016.

———. *The Promise of the Foreign: Nationalism and the Technics of Translation in the Spanish Philippines*. Durham, NC: Duke University Press, 2005.

Rao, Anupama. *The Caste Question: Dalits and the Politics of Modern India*. Berkeley: University of California Press, 2009.

————, ed. *Gender and Caste*. New Delhi: Kali, 2003.

Rao, M. B., and Mohit Sen, eds. *Our Doc: Tributes to Comrade Gangadhar Adhikari on His Seventieth Birthday*. New Delhi: Communist Party of India, 1968.

Rao, Nikhil. *House, but No Garden: Apartment Living in Bombay's Suburbs, 1898–1964*. Minneapolis: University of Minnesota Press, 2013.

Rawat, Ramnarayan. *Reconsidering Untouchability: Chamars and Dalit History in North India*. Bloomington: Indiana University Press, 2011.

Rawat, Ramnarayan, and K. Satyanarayana. "Introduction: Dalit Studies; New Perspectives on Indian History and Society." In *Dalit Studies*, edited by Ramnarayan Rawat and K. Satyanarayan, 1–30. Durham, NC: Duke University Press, 2016.

Ray, Raka, and Seemin Qayum. *Cultures of Servitude: Modernity, Domesticity and Class in India*. Palo Alto, CA: Stanford University Press, 2009.

Risley, Sir Herbert H. *The People of India*. Calcutta: Thacker, Spink, 1915.

Roberts, Nathaniel. *To Be Cared For: The Power of Conversion and Foreignness of Belonging in an Indian Slum*. New Delhi: Navayana, 2016.

Robinson, Cedric. *Black Marxism: The Making of the Black Radical Tradition*. Chapel Hill: University of North Carolina Press, 2000.

Roy, Manabendra Nath. *India in Transition*. Bombay: Nachiketa Publications, 1971.

Sardesai, S. G. "Prastavik char shabd." In Karl Marks, *Mol-majuri va bhandval* (Wage labor and capital). Translated by R. M. Jambhekar. Mumbai: Marksist Vangmay Pracharak Mandal, 1932.

Sarkar, Sumit. *Beyond Nationalist Frames: Relocating Postmodernism, Hindutva, History*. Delhi: Permanent Black, 2002.

————. *Modern India, 1885–1947*. Chennai: Macmillan India Press, 2008.

————. *Modern Times: India 1880s–1950s, Environment, Economy, Culture*. Ranikhet: Permanent Black, 2014.

Sathe, Anna Bhau. *Anna Bhau Sathe nivadak vangmay*. Edited by Arjun Dangle. Mumbai: Maharashtra Rajya Sahitya ani Sanskriti Mandala, 1998.

————. "Hi prthvi Dalitancya talahatavar tarleli ahe (The earth is balanced on the palm of Dalits)." In *Shatkatil Dalit vichar* (Dalit ideas of the century), edited by Sharanku-mar Limbale. Pune: Dilipraja Prakashan, 2001.

Sathe, Makarand. *Marathi rangabhumichya tees ratri: Eka samajik-rajkiya itihas* (Thirty nights of Marathi theater: A social political history). 3 vols. Mumbai: Popular Prakashan, 2011.

Sawant, P. S. *Majuranchya-samrajyat*. Mumbai: Manohar Mitra Mandal, 1935.

S. D. "Children of God Turn Panthers." *Economic and Political Weekly* 8, nos. 31–33 (1973): 1398.

Seal, Anil. *The Emergence of Indian Nationalism: Competition and Collaboration in the Later Nineteenth Century*. London: Cambridge University Press, 1968.

Sen, Samita. *Women and Labour in Late Colonial India: The Bengal Jute Industry*. Cambridge: Cambridge University Press, 1999.

Servants of India Society. *The Servants of India Society: Report of Work and Constitution (June 1923–May 1926)*. Bombay: Bombay Vaibhav Press, 1926.

Sewell, William H., Jr. *Logics of History: Social Theory and Social Transformation*. Chicago: University of Chicago Press, 2005.

Shaikh, Juned. "Imaging Caste: Photography, the Housing Question, and the Making of Sociology in Colonial Bombay, 1900–1939." *South Asia: Journal of South Asia Studies* 37, no. 3 (2014): 491–514.

———. "Photography, the Housing Question and the Making of Sociology in Colonial Bombay, 1900–1939." *South Asia: Journal of South Asia Studies* 37, no. 3 (2014): 491–514.

———. "Translating Marx: Mavali, Dalit and the Making of Mumbai's Working Class, 1928–1935." *Economic and Political Weekly* 46, no. 31 (July 2011): 65–73.

Sharma, Ursula. *Caste*. New Delhi: Viva Books, 2005.

Shaw, Annapurana. *The Making of Navi Mumbai*. Hyderabad: Orient Longman, 2004.

Singh, Gayatri, Trina Vithayathil, and Kanhu Charan Pradhan. "Recasting Inequality: Residential Segregation by Caste Overtime in Urban India." *Environment and Urbanization* 31, no. 2 (2019): 615–34. DOI: 10.1177/0956247818812330.

Singh, Nikhil Pal. *Race and America's Long War*. Oakland: University of California Press, 2017.

Sivaramakrishnan, K. *Modern Forests: Statemaking and Environmental Change in Colonial Eastern India*. Stanford, CA: Stanford University Press, 1999.

Sivaramakrishnan, K., and Arun Agarwal. "Regional Modernities in Stories and Practices of Development." In *Regional Modernities: The Cultural Politics of Development in India*, edited by K Sivaramakrishnan and Arun Agarwal. Stanford, CA: Stanford University Press, 2003.

Srivastava, Priyanka. *The Wellbeing of the Labor Force in Colonial Bombay: Discourses and Practices*. Cham: Palgrave McMillan, 2018.

Stein, Samuel. *Capital City: Gentrification and the Real Estate State*. London: Verso, 2019.

Sugarman, Michael. " Reclaiming Rangoon: (Post-)imperial Urbanism and Poverty, 1920–1962." *Modern Asian Studies* 52, no. 6 (2018): 1856–87.

Sundar, Nandini. "Caste as a Census Category: Implications for Sociology." *Current Sociology* 48, no. 3 (July 2000): 111–26.

Tam, Stephanie. "Sewerage's Reproduction of Caste: The Politics of Corpology in Ahmedabad, India." *Radical History Review* 116 (Spring 2013): 5–30.

Teltumbde, Anand. *Mahad: The Making of the First Dalit Revolt*. Delhi: Aakar, 2016.

Tendulkar, Vijay. "Prastavana" (Foreword). In Namdeo Dhasal, *Golpitha*. Pune: Nilakantha Prakasana, 1975.

Thakurdas, Sir Purshottamdas, J. R. D. Tata, and G. D. Birla. *A Brief Memorandum Outlining a Plan of Economic Development for India*. Harmondsworth: Penguin Books, 1944.

Thapar, Romila. *The Aryan: Recasting Constructs*. Gurgaon: Three Essays Collective, 2008.

Tharu, Susie, and K. Lalita. "Introduction." In *Women Writing in India: 600 BC to the Present*, vol. 1, *600 BC to the Early Twentieth Century*, edited by Susie Tharu and K. Lalita. New York: Feminist Press, 1991.

Tharu, Susie J., and K. Satyanarayana. "Dalit Writing: An Introduction." In *The Exercise of Freedom: An Introduction to Dalit Writing*, edited by K. Satyanarayana and Susie Tharu. New Delhi: Navayana, 2013.

——. *No Alphabet in Sight: New Dalit Writing from South India.* New Delhi: Penguin Books, 2011.

Thompson, E. P. *The Making of the English Working Class.* New York: Vintage Books, 1966.

Tidrick, Kathryn. *Gandhi: A Political and Spiritual Life.* London: Verso, 2013.

Tomba, Massimiliano. *Marx's Temporalities.* Chicago: Haymarket Books, 2013.

Uberoi, Patricia, Satish Deshpande, and Nandini Sundar. "Introduction: The Professionalization of Indian Anthropology and Sociology—People, Places, and Institutions." In *Anthropology in the East: Founders of Indian Sociology and Anthropology,* edited by Patricia Uberoi, Satish Deshpande, and Nandini Sundar. Ranikhet: Permanent Black, 2010.

van der Linden, Marcel. *Workers of the World: Essays toward a Global Labor History.* Leiden: Brill, 2008.

Varerkara, Mama. *Dhavata Dhota.* Mumbai: Abhinav Prakasana, 1972.

Viswanath, Rupa. *The Pariah Problem: Caste, Religion, and the Social in Modern India.* Navayana: New Delhi, 2015.

——. "Rethinking Caste and Class: 'Labour,' the 'Depressed Classes' and the Politics of Distinction, Madras, 1918–1924." *International Review of Social History* 59 (2014): 1–37.

Wacha, Sir D. E. *Shells from the Sands of Bombay: Being My Recollections and Reminiscences, 1860–1875.* Bombay: K. T. Anklesaria, 1920.

Waghmore, Suryakant. *Civility against Caste: Dalit Politics and Citizenship in Western India.* New Delhi: Sage Publications India, 2013.

Wankhede, M. N. "Bhumika" (Foreword). In Baburav Bagula, *Suda.* Mumbai: Abhinav Prakashan: 1970.

——. "Dalit Sahityacya Prerana." In *Dalitance Vidrohi Vangmaya,* edited by Vamanrao Nimbalkar and Yashwant Manohar. Nagapur: Prabodhan Prakashan, 1981.

——. "Dalitanon Vidrohi Vangmaya Liha." In *Dalitance Vidrohi Vangmaya,* edited by Vamanrao Nimbalkar and Yashwant Manohar. Nagapur: Prabodhan Prakashan, 1981.

Wankhede, M. N, V. L. Kulkarni, R. G. Jadhav, M. P. Rege, and M. B. Chitnis. "Maharashtratil Aaj Udayache Samskrutik Sangharsh ani Vangmayin Samasya." In *Dalit Sahitya: Ek abhyas,* edited by Arjun Dangle. Pune: Sugava Prakashan, 1998.

Washbrook, David. "The Rhetoric of Democracy and Development in Late Colonial India." In *Nationalism, Democracy, and Development: State and Politics in India,* edited by Sugata Bose and Ayesha Jalal. New Delhi: Oxford University Press, 2001.

Weber, Max. "Classes, Status Groups, Parties." In *Max Weber: Selection in Translation,* edited by W. G. Runciman, translated by E. Matthew. Cambridge: Cambridge University Press, 1978.

Weinstein, Lisa. *The Durable Slum: Dharavi and the Right to Stay Put in Globalizing Mumbai.* Minneapolis: University of Minnesota Press, 2014.

Worley, Matthew. "To the Left and Back Again: The Communist Party of Great Britain in the Third Period." In *In Search of a Revolution: International Communist Parties in the Third Period,* edited by Matthew Worley. London: I. B. Tauris, 2004.

Yajnik, Indulal. *Life of Ranchoddas Bhavan Lotvala*. Bombay: Libertarian Book House, 1952.

YUVA. *Our Home Is a Slum: An Exploration of a Community and Local Government Collaboration in a Tenants' Struggle to Establish Legal Residency in Janata Squatters Colony, Mumbai, India*. Geneva: United Nations Research Institute for Social Development, 1999.

Zelliot, Eleanor. *From Untouchable to Dalit: Essays on the Ambedkar Movement*. Delhi: Manohar, 1992.

Zinoman, Peter. *The Colonial Bastille: A History of Imprisonment in Vietnam 1862–1940*. Berkeley: University of California Press, 2001.

INDEX

GLOBAL
SOUTH
ASIA

Padma Kaimal
K. Sivaramakrishnan
Anand A. Yang
SERIES EDITORS

GLOBAL SOUTH ASIA takes an interdisciplinary approach to the humanities and social sciences in its exploration of how South Asia, through its global influence, is and has been shaping the world.